BLOOD SECRETS

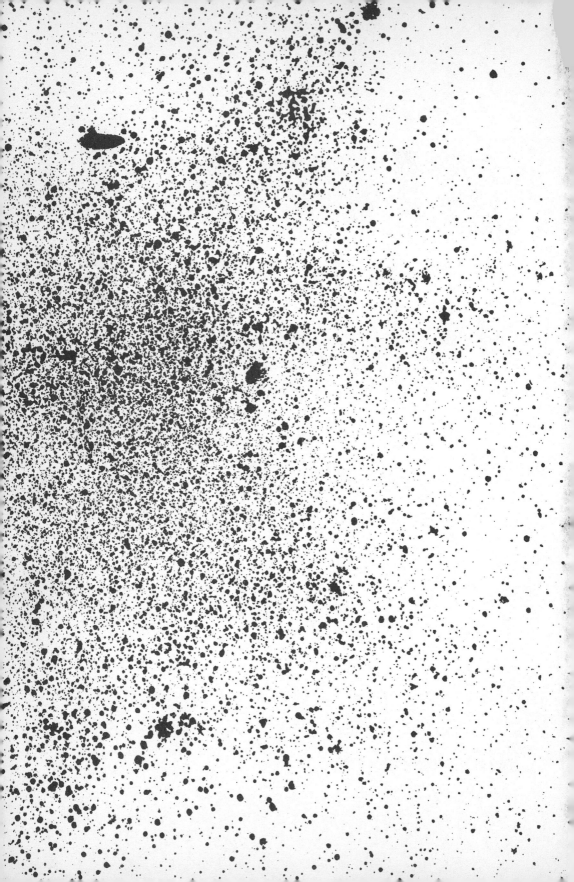

BLOOD SECRETS

Chronicles of a Crime Scene Reconstructionist

ROD ENGLERT

with Kathy Passero

Foreword by Ann Rule

THOMAS DUNNE BOOKS

St. Martin's Press 📖 New York

THOMAS DUNNE BOOKS.
An imprint of St. Martin's Press.

BLOOD SECRETS. Copyright © 2010 by Rod Englert with Kathy Passero. Foreword copyright © 2010 by Ann Rule. All rights reserved. Printed in the United States of America. For information, address St. Martin's Press, 175 Fifth Avenue, New York, N.Y. 10010.

www.thomasdunnebooks.com
www.stmartins.com

Book design by Phil Mazzone

Blood spatter illustrations in chapter 5 by Rosie Welch

Library of Congress Cataloging-in-Publication Data

Englert, Rod.
    Blood secrets : chronicles of a crime scene reconstructionist / Rod Englert with Kathy Passero ; foreword by Ann Rule.—1st ed.
        p. cm.
    Includes bibliographical references and index.
    ISBN 978-0-312-56400-1
    1. Bloodstains. 2. Blood. 3. Forensic hematology. 4. Evidence, Expert.
    5. Criminal investigation. 6. Evidence, Criminal. I. Passero, Kathy. II. Title.
    HV8077.5.B56E54 2010
    363.25'62—dc22

                                                                    2009040294

First Edition: April 2010

10   9   8   7   6   5   4   3   2   1

Author's Note: Where indicated with an asterisk (*), pseudonyms have been used.

Editor's Note: In the world of professional crime solving, the proper terminology is "bloodspatter." However, for the purposes of readability in this book, the term has been broken into two separate words and appears throughout the text as "blood spatter."

For the victims

Contents

Foreword

SEVERAL YEARS AGO, I was invited to Aspen, Colorado, to present a seminar on serial killers to the Colorado Association of Sex Crimes Investigators. After driving from Denver, we arrived late in Aspen— too late to order room service or to find an open restaurant. I looked forward to a hearty breakfast, something you can usually count on at a law enforcement convention.

The next morning arrived and I was hungrier than ever. As I walked into the large room where speakers would lecture, one whole side was taken up by tables covered with spotless white tablecloths, tables laden with heated silver serving dishes. The menu was replete with eggs, bacon, sausage, ham, hash browns, grits, pancakes, waffles, and fruit. One could not ask for a more appealing breakfast.

Alas, my good friend Rod Englert was slated as the first speaker of the day. I knew what that meant. Rod had decorated the other three walls of the room with his unique style. Life-size photos of recently and not so recently departed suicide and murder victims were everywhere I looked. In between, there were white sheets of paper with red splotches, sprays, droplets, and streaks. I thought I saw some jars with red fluid in them, but I didn't look closely enough to determine what it was.

As the author of more than thirty books on actual murders and some fourteen hundred magazine articles, I have learned much from Rod about solving homicides with the "code" that is inherent in the life fluid of human beings. He has taught me and thousands of others about low-, medium-, and high-velocity blood spatter—enough so I can usually tell from photographs or viewing crime scenes whether a club or a bullet or a "transfer" left a particular pattern in scarlet.

Even so, as much as I admire his brilliance, I cannot eat and look at Rod Englert's photos and charts at the same time. Several dozen detectives from all over Colorado and adjoining states, and a sprinkling of FBI special agents, filled their plates to overflowing and chewed away undeterred, listening avidly to his explanation of how the victims on the walls died.

Not me. My empty stomach could barely manage black coffee and ice water. Despite my queasiness, I learned a great deal at that "breakfast seminar." After thirty years of researching often grisly crimes, I suppose I should be inured to the shock of what violence can do to the human body. But I'm not.

Rod Englert is an uncommonly kind man, but he has transcended his own distress and sorrow at man's (or woman's) inhumanity to man to offer remarkable insights into what the dead can tell us, even after they can no longer speak.

Blood Secrets is a fascinating book on many levels. It is autobiographical, showing the fulfillment of a small Texas boy's dreams to be a police officer through his rookie years, his close calls, his mistakes—which he admits freely—to his years as a homicide detective and now to his career as one of the foremost experts in the world on the silent stories written in blood.

Most of us involved in the circle of forensic science experts know one another, even though we come from many different regions. We are a motley crew, a fraternity who studies the blackest side of human nature and manages to find justice for victims of crime and the truth for their survivors. In our group are forensic anthropologists (identification by the derivation of bone structure), forensic odontologists (identification by teeth), medical examiners, psychological profilers, fingerprint experts, fiber and hair experts, DNA experts, tool mark experts, ballistic experts, forensic entomologists (bug experts), forensic geologists (soil and stone identification), forensic botanists, and all manner of skilled criminalists who now solve baffling crimes in ways no one ever imagined even a few decades ago.

I often think that anyone contemplating the commission of a crime would be frightened away if they knew how much evidence they leave behind them—all unaware.

Still, contrary to most laymen's belief, there *is* such a thing as a perfect murder, thousands of them. And an eyewitness is *not* necessarily the best way for a prosecutor to win a case. A jury benefits most by being able to see, feel, smell, and examine physical evidence. And it takes skilled forensic experts like Rod Englert to winnow out the truth.

When I first met Rod in the 1970s, he had recently become a homicide detective with the Multnomah County Sheriff's Office in Portland,

Oregon. About a dozen and a half detectives and a CSI team were crowded into an upper floor of a rather dingy building, their desks just far enough apart so they could move the chairs back and get up from time to time.

Along with his partner, Joe Woods, Rod Englert was solving a number of bizarre and difficult murder cases. At the time, I was a "stringer" covering the Northwest for *True Detective* magazine and her six sister fact-detective magazines.

I made $200 an article and $12.50 for every photograph I sent in to accompany the text. I was raising four children on my own after their father died at forty-three, and the Multnomah County detectives were as nice to me as Seattle investigators were and agreed to let me interview them about cases that had been adjudicated—either in a trial or through a confession. They knew that my career, somewhat rare for a female, was supporting my family. Rod, Joe, Blackie Yazzolino, Stu Wells, Bob Walliker, Bobby Graham, Neil McCarthy, John Kerslake, and Lieutenant Jim Purcell had an enviable record of convictions.

In *Blood Secrets*, Rod Englert recalls many of the cases he participated in closing successfully in the greater Portland area. I recognize a lot of them, and they are as fascinating as they were back in the seventies when we first met. The sheriff's homicide unit in Multnomah County was one of my regular stops. While I was researching murder cases, I was learning. And while Rod was solving those cases, he was learning about the mysteries that could be solved with the blood of victims. And, sometimes, by the blood of killers.

In my first three published books, there were aspects that Rod Englert had handled. It was chance, probably, but he had his investigational fingers in multiple pies—or, more accurately, any number of homicidal mysteries. Sometimes I teased him, saying he would probably appear in every book I ever wrote. In the end, of course, I began to write about cases all over America, and Rod's expertise in blood spatter identification made him in demand thousands of miles away from my killers' stalking areas.

Now, when we run into each other, it is at one training seminar or another. In Aspen, the hotel where he and I spoke on our particular subjects was in the shadow of the Wildwood Inn, where one of Ted Bundy's victims—Caryn Campbell—had vanished two decades before. I can't recall how many conferences there have been, but there have been many, and I look forward to seeing Rod and his wife, Penny, to catch up.

Usually, we get an honorarium and travel expenses, and on occasion, Rod and I meet up to speak for nothing at all to high school students who aspire to become members of law enforcement. Rod has always had time to work with youth groups.

Gradually, Rod Englert's name began to appear at the top of the list of blood spatter experts in America. At first, it was surprising to watch television news shows and see Rod testifying at high-profile trials. Within a few years, it became commonplace. Until I read the galleys of *Blood Secrets,* I really didn't know how many celebrity trials Rod was part of. He gives the reader an insider's peek at what went on behind the scenes of a number of these investigations and trials.

I always encouraged Rod to write a book. He worked with author Kathy Passero, whose seamless style meshes perfectly with the subject, and the team has produced a worthy book, unique and captivating.

One would think that after spending more than half my life writing about homicide cases, I wouldn't enjoy reading a book on bodies, murder, and blood. But I did. This book is instructional for both detectives and crime aficionados. I thought I was well versed in the meaning of blood trails and marks, but I learned at least three things in this book about blood that I didn't know before.

Blood Secrets is much more than a textbook for homicide investigators; it is an absorbing story of the journey of a barefoot boy who picked cotton in Texas to his discovery of a forensic science that is partly art, partly science, and partly gut instinct.

I highly recommend this book!

—ANN RULE

Ann Rule is a former Seattle police officer and the author of thirty *New York Times* Bestsellers on true crime cases—from *The Stranger Beside Me* to her newest, *But I Trusted You.*

BLOOD SECRETS

1

Early Days

THE FOG WAS ALREADY getting thick before I reached the station for roll call at eleven-thirty P.M. It meant the roads would be dangerous, so I drove slowly and kept an eye peeled for the inevitable drunks behind the wheel at that hour. I was coming down with the flu, and the dampness hanging in the air didn't help. It blanketed everything with a clammy mist more typical of Seattle than Southern California.

I'd been a uniformed officer on patrol for almost two years in Downey, a bedroom community of Los Angeles, and though I was hardly a seasoned veteran, I no longer considered myself a pup. That night would prove how wrong I was. It would also change the course of my future.

No sooner had I arrived than I got pulled out of roll call to respond to a suspicious circumstances complaint: A woman suspected there might be a dead body at an apartment building in south Downey, the seedy side of the town's main street and unofficial dividing line. The guys who were going off duty at midnight could have responded themselves—technically the call came in on their shift—but a dead body takes hours of work to process, so they'd left this one for me.

The woman who'd made the call was waiting for me when I pulled into the parking lot. This was 1964, and in those days in Downey we worked solo, so I was by myself.

"He's up there," she said tersely, pointing to a dingy stairway and then retreating. It was obvious she wanted to stay as far away as possible.

As I made my way up to the second floor, the entire place seemed eerily quiet. Aside from the shabby stairs creaking under my footsteps, I heard nothing—no voices, no movements, no blaring TV sets sounded from behind the closed doors lining the hallway. Soon I found the room number the woman had given me and cautiously pushed the door open.

The apartment beyond was pitch-black and stuffy. Without stepping inside, I switched on my flashlight to get a better sense of the surroundings and saw a single room furnished with little more than a bed and dresser. As I moved the beam over the walls, the procedure I'd learned in the police academy ran through my mind: Disturb as little as possible of the crime scene, don't turn on lights because touching a switch might destroy potential evidence or blow you sky-high if there's a gas leak. And that's when I saw it.

Blood was everywhere—spattered over the walls, pooled on the floor, soaking into the sheets of the bed, smeared on the dresser and a small vacuum cleaner standing next to it. Lying in the middle of all this, half on the bed and half off, was the body of an emaciated, balding middle-aged man clad only in boxer shorts. Like everything around him, he was covered in blood.

My mind cast frantically through a catalog of possible scenarios. What could cause a body to lose all that blood? A hatchet? A machete? An ax? The man must have been murdered—and put up quite a fight, judging from the bloody handprints all over the walls.

I switched off my flashlight, closed the door, and hurried back down to my patrol car to alert the detectives. "Murder victim," I announced confidently over my radio. "Looks like he's been assaulted with an ax."

I waited until the detectives and medical examiner arrived, then left the scene. The rest of my shift passed uneventfully, and I headed home from work in the morning still fighting off the flu, but congratulating myself on a solid night's police work.

It wasn't until a few days later that I noticed the telltale grins breaking across the faces of my fellow officers whenever I walked into the room.

"What's so funny?" I demanded.

"Your murder victim," one of the detectives said, barely able to stifle his laughter. "Turns out the guy didn't have a scratch on him."

"*What?*"

"Nobody touched him."

I stared at him in disbelief. How could that be possible? The man was soaked in blood. The whole room looked like the set from a second-rate slasher film.

"But, how . . . ," I began, baffled.

"Ulcers," he said.

I shook my head, still confused.

"Bleeding ulcers. One of them must have ruptured, and he was throwing up all over the room," the detective said. "It made quite a mess, as you saw."

Snorts of laughter erupted around me.

"So much for your ax-wielding madman," the detective said, chuckling.

Stupid, stupid, stupid move, I chastised myself. Why had I been so quick to announce my theory about an ax murder over the air?

Even after I learned that it had taken the detectives themselves some time to realize my "murder victim" had bled to death all by himself—most likely as a result of alcoholism—I cringed when I thought about the jokes floating around the police station with me as the punch line. The incident became infamously known among my colleagues as the Vomit Case.

Never again, I told myself. I resolved then and there to learn all I could about blood patterns in crime scenes and to make that the last time I drew such a misguided conclusion.

A Life in Blood

I've devoted much of my life and career since that night in south Downey to studying blood patterns. After the Vomit Case, I read what few textbooks there were, though the field was in its infancy then and—as I would eventually discover through investigating thousands of crime scenes—much of what you could find in print was erroneous. Early sources, for example, claimed the higher the height from which you drop blood, the bigger the spatter produced. I remember reading and memorizing that point. In truth, blood spatter reaches terminal velocity at a height of about fifteen feet. That means the droplets look different when blood hits the ground from, say, a height of one inch as opposed to a height of four feet. But there's virtually no difference between the spatter you'd see if you dropped blood from thirty feet or a thousand feet. You'd get the same-size drops. What creates varying patterns is the texture and porosity of the material the blood hits, the angle at which it hits, and the surface it's dropped from. I'll show you how these factors work in the chapters to come.

Crime scene reconstruction has become my passion—particularly when it comes to interpreting telltale clues left in the bloodshed that often accompanies a homicide—and I've developed an amount of expertise in it. I've been called in to consult on hundreds of crime scenes, including high-profile cases like Robert Blake's, O. J. Simpson's, and Bob Crane's. I've taught courses to help cops catch criminals using blood pattern analysis everywhere from rural Indiana to Scotland Yard to Bogotá. No matter how much knowledge I accumulate, I still learn something new from every case.

I've been doing this work for decades—since long before series like *CSI* made the average American an armchair forensics pro. One of the questions I get asked a lot these days is, "Do the TV shows get it right?" Sometimes. More often, they get it wrong. But then at times so do the experts . . . at least initially. This isn't Sherlock Holmes, where cracking the case is elementary if you do the deductive reasoning. It's real life, which means it's often messy and usually muddled, but invariably fascinating.

I didn't expect to set out on a career path so filled with blood. But, looking back, maybe I should have. As a typical small-town southern kid growing up in the days of *Leave It to Beaver* and *The Andy Griffith Show*, I was fascinated by everything related to law enforcement—even when I ended up on the wrong side of it.

Cotton Fields and Cherry Bombs

I grew up in Wall, Texas. The town center was so tiny, you'd miss it if you sneezed while you were driving through—just a school, a post office, a few cotton gins, and a handful of stores, most of which are now abandoned. To me, it was home and I loved it. But to most people, it was nothing more than miles and miles of sprawling cotton farms like the one where I was raised.

Everybody picked cotton when I was a kid. School gave us a week off in the fall because so many of us had to help pick cotton on our families' farms. I remember the scrape the sacks made as they dragged behind me through the fields and the sting of bleeding hands when I tried to pick the sharp-edged bolls without gloves. We went to school barefoot when the weather was warm in those days, and the land was so flat that gazing out the classroom window, I could see my family's farmhouse four miles away.

Every year seasonal workers showed up at our door, many of them African-American and Hispanic, to help pick our cotton. The one I remember best was Earl Lee Cook. As kids, we called him "Early" Cook. Early was among the most polite men I've ever met, but he stuttered so badly that getting a sentence out looked like pure torture.

If my little brother, Mickey, and I were ever tempted to make fun of Early, my father set us straight. Dad treated everyone with respect and dignity, and he made sure we did the same.

That attitude was somewhat unusual in Texas in the 1950s. There were a lot of people who took the opposite view, especially when it came to the workers on their farms. Whenever rumors started buzzing around that the immigration authorities were moving in—and they often did—more than one local farmer suddenly found an excuse not to get around to paying his workers. The "wetbacks" will soon be gone, they figured. If their wages run a little short, so what? What can they do about it? Why not save a little cash at someone else's expense?

My dad did the reverse. He made a point to pay every Mexican worker as soon as he got wind of the rumors, before immigration swooped in.

I learned a lot from my father. He taught us to treat people with compassion but never condescension. Those lessons have served me well throughout my life and my career as a police officer and a crime scene investigator.

The other person who taught me a lot was my cousin Ralph. He was six years older than me, and he was my idol. When Ralph became a baseball fanatic and set his sights on making it as a professional ballplayer, so did I. I filled my room with baseball paraphernalia and my head with dreams of pitching under the bright lights of the major leagues. Then when Ralph blew out his arm while training for the Cleveland Indians and joined the air force, I announced my plans to enlist, too. I was crushed when the National Guard broke the news that I'd have to wait to sign up until I got out of high school.

There I was, stuck on the farm hunting rabbits and raising pigs for 4-H ribbons, while Ralph headed off on grand adventures I could only imagine. The year he left, I turned twelve—old enough in Texas back then to get my driver's license, which I did. By the time I was fourteen, I was experienced enough behind the wheel to land a job driving a dump truck for the county whenever I wasn't in school, helping my dad out with the farm animals, or hauling grain with our 1946 Ford pickup.

But there was a drought around that time, and like many farm families in the area, ours ended up heavily in debt. I remember my mom and dad sitting at the kitchen table, faces taut and worried, discussing the enormous amount we owed—$10,000, which sounded like all the money in the world to me back then—and racking their brains for a way we could scrape together enough to pay it back. There was a lot of talk among the men of Wall about building an irrigation system and digging canals. Rather than wait for that plan to come to fruition and save the day, Dad got a second job driving cars for Goodyear on a high-speed track in the countryside nearby, testing their tires to see if they'd pass muster on the highway. They tested all kinds of tires there; I used to like to stand inside the colossal wheel wells of the tires used on mining equipment—massive tires fit for a giant's wagon. To be closer to Dad's second job, we moved twelve miles down the road, from Wall to the outskirts of San Angelo. Dad still drove back to Wall every day to tend the farm, and we often went with him.

With a population of seventy-five thousand, San Angelo seemed like a major city compared with Wall. On my first day as a junior at Lakeview High School, I remember thinking that I'd have a huge graduating class—forty kids—compared with Wall's sixteen, augmented now and again by an occasional migrant worker's child. We'd been driving to San Angelo to go to church all my life, so I already knew a few of my Lakeview classmates from youth group, including Jim Newsom, who would become my best pal and a lifelong friend. Still, everything seemed new and exciting. One day shortly after we arrived, a short, skinny boy named Martin Mosely showed up in the school parking lot and popped open the trunk of his car to reveal a bulging feed sack.

I joined a cluster of my classmates peering down curiously at it.

"Whatcha got in there?" someone asked.

Martin grinned and plunged a catcher's stick deep inside the bag, then drew out a long, shiny black object.

"Get that thing away from me!" cried the boy standing closest to him, stepping backward hurriedly and bumping into the people behind him.

"Rattlesnakes!" Martin announced proudly, opening the bag to reveal at least fifteen hissing reptiles coiled in the bottom of the dusty bag.

"What do you do with them?"

"Make belts out of 'em and sell 'em," he explained, describing how he drove to the outskirts of town and combed the hillsides for rattlers' dens. When he found one, he gassed the snakes inside to make them woozy and nonaggressive, then used the catcher's stick to scoop them into a bag. Later he would skin them, turning their hides into belts and their heads into buckles. The rattlers he used as embellishments for western hats.

Like everything else in San Angelo, football was different. I had played six-man football in Wall, but here at Lakeview they had a full team. This being Texas, every self-respecting male student wanted to be a part of it, so I tried out and ended up playing halfback. My dad spent all day farming, then headed straight to the track to drive until ten P.M. on weeknights, which meant that he never made it to my games. He didn't say anything to me about them, not even when I made a touchdown, but Mom assured me that he listened to every one on the radio while he worked.

When I wasn't playing football or baseball, running track, or studying, I was helping on the farm. On Sundays, mornings started with mass at the local Catholic church with my dad and ended with services and youth group at the local Protestant church with my mom.

Still, I managed to find time to get bored and cause trouble as a teenager. Our whole community was German-Catholic, which meant beer drinking was part of everyday life for us. Even my grandparents drank it. Nobody looked askance at a seventeen-year-old with a glass of beer. But getting caught sneaking cigarettes—which I did—got you a tongue-lashing and worse.

One dry and dusty summer day after my junior year, I hit upon a memorable way to liven things up in town for my friends and me. I convinced them it would be a bright idea to toss a cherry bomb into a little bar at the edge of town, a place notorious as a watering hole for the local drunks. I rounded up some friends—three girls and two guys—to pile into my pal Nelson Word's 1952 Mercury. The plan was for Nelson to pull up near the bar's front entrance and keep the Mercury running while I hopped out, yanked open the door, and chucked the firecracker inside.

The bar was housed in a narrow building about ten feet wide—long and low and dark—and when the cherry bomb exploded, it let off an eardrum-shattering *bang!* It literally shook the rafters.

As the sounds of panicked shouts and screams rose from inside the bar, we doubled over laughing uproariously—failing to notice that the bar's owner was standing nearby openmouthed, staring at us and still clutching the bulging trash bags he'd been emptying into bins in the parking lot. Nelson, our getaway driver, hit the gas and off we sped as the enraged owner raced to his pickup truck.

No sooner had we rounded the corner on our getaway than the engine gave a raspy mechanical cough and died. Nelson was trying desperately to restart it when the pickup roared past us and screeched to a halt inches from our fender, penning us in. The owner of the bar jumped out, slammed his door, and stalked over. By the look on his face, he hadn't found the cherry bomb nearly as hilarious as we had.

He marched us back to the street in front of the bar, where things were still in an uproar thanks to the cluster of staggering, slurring patrons who had stumbled out, all convinced someone had fired a gun and all hotly debating exactly what had gone down.

"I'm tellin' ya, Mary shot John!"

"Naw, you're way off. It was John who shot Mary!"

Ignoring them, the owner ordered us to wait while he called the cops.

The next thing we knew, we were en route to the local police station. As we pulled to a stop in front of the civic auditorium, which housed police headquarters in its basement, I thought wistfully back to the last time I'd been here. That afternoon I'd been elbowing my way to the front of a crowd of mesmerized San Angelo residents standing on the sidewalk, gaping at a young Elvis Presley as he stepped out of a gleaming pink Cadillac. He flashed his trademark whiplash grin, then headed inside to warm up for a concert he was giving that night, leaving the air filled with lively chatter.

Today the place was a stark contrast—silent and somber. You could hear a pin drop as we marched down the steps, past the dispatcher and the drunk tank, all of us trembling silently at the thought of what our parents would do when they found out we'd been hauled in by the cops. I was calculating just how mad my dad was likely to be and how badly I'd be punished when the scene in front of me snatched those worries completely out of my head.

I was standing in the middle of one of the most fascinating places I'd ever seen. Every wall was lined with posters and pictures, many bearing faces of menacing-looking criminals glaring defiantly at the camera over descriptions of their crimes. I squinted to read the details. Rumpled drunks peered curiously out at us from between the bars of their holding cells. All around us, officers were busy at work on important-looking jobs, hunched over their desks, filing reports, jotting down notes as they listened to callers. A sign indicated that the detectives' bureau lay just down the hall, out of sight. While my friends hung their heads and waited morosely, I stared around wide-eyed, taking everything in. So what if I was on the wrong side of it all? This place was amazing.

On the way home, as my dad reprimanded me for my stupidity, I nodded silently, only half hearing, still mesmerized by the police station.

Murder in the Junkyard

Another incident from a different summer would also shape my future, though I didn't know it at the time. It began with football.

We were all football crazy when I was a teenager, and knowing I would want to go out for the team in San Angelo, I set out to find a job that would help me bulk up the summer we moved. Thanks to a friend of my dad's, I got work at the Acme Iron & Metal Company junkyard. It was an enormous, rambling place with acres and acres of smashed cars in towering stacks and mounds of scrap metal as tall as buildings. The work was hot, filthy, and backbreaking. Day after day I lugged huge chunks of greasy, broken-down chassis, rolled heavy barrels, and cleaned insulation off copper. By the time I headed home, my arms were always black and coated in flecks of broken glass.

The guy in charge of the junkyard was called Red, and the men he hired were a rough crowd. When someone didn't show up for work, odds were pretty good that he had landed in jail. Their talk was as colorful as it was cuss-laden, and listening to their stories made me feel as if I had landed in the middle of a crew of pirates. I was the only kid working there, but they all treated me fairly and decently. One of my favorite co-workers was a big, rowdy African-American guy named George.* He was jovial, loudmouthed, foulmouthed, and tough as nails.

One day I showed up to work to find several members of the San Angelo Police Department surrounding an old beater of a pickup parked on the truck scales near the junkyard's entrance. I walked over to Joe,* one of my co-workers, who was ripping usable parts out of a rusted sedan, acting as if he hadn't even noticed the cluster of cops nearby.

"What happened over there?" I asked him.

Joe glanced in the direction I was pointing and wiped sweat off his forehead with the back of his hand. "George and the guy drivin' that pickup got in a fight," he told me. "George shot him." He said it so casually, you would have thought things like that happened at work every day.

"*Shot* him?" I gasped. "Is he dead?"

"I reckon he is. He got shot in the head, close up." Joe said the authorities had carted off both George and the dead man less than an hour ago. When I had pestered him with all the questions I thought he could tolerate without losing his temper, I forced myself to get down to work. The slam of doors and the sound of an engine starting a short while later told me the police were leaving.

I tried to concentrate on the copper I was cleaning, but I couldn't resist glancing over at that abandoned pickup every few minutes. Back in those days, nobody put yellow tape around the crime scene—at least not for a crime like this one. No lab coat–clad team of forensic technicians was prepping to comb the vehicle with an armload of fancy equipment. No gaping onlookers or nightly news crews were buzzing around. No tow truck showed up to haul it away. It just sat there like the rest of the battered, rusted cars and trucks that littered the Acme junkyard.

I kept thinking about the pickup, wondering what it looked like inside. Finally, I dropped what I was doing and went to get a closer look. I walked cautiously over and edged up close enough to see into the empty driver's seat with its open windows. Blood, blackish red and dried by that time, was smeared all over the seat back on the driver's side.

A strange feeling came over me as I stood there gawking at it, unable to move away. Somebody had been shot in there. Somebody had died sitting right in that spot, less than a foot away from where I was standing. I felt horrified. But at the same time, I was utterly mesmerized. Dozens of questions started bubbling up in my mind. Who was the murdered man? Where did he come from? What was his story?

Did he and George know each other? What did he say to George to provoke him? Did the argument start over the price of scrap metal? What kind of gun did George use? How close was he when he pulled the trigger? I wanted to know everything about the murder.

I thought about that blood for a long time. Even today, I get the same feeling in my bones when I'm working a challenging case. I'm still just as fascinated, just as relentlessly intent on finding out every how and why of the crime.

Law and Disorder

One spring a few years later, my father and I were back in Wall helping my uncle Alois tend his garden when Dad asked, "So, have you heard from Ralph lately?"

My uncle took a break from his digging. "He's out of the air force now," he told us. "He just became an officer in the San Angelo Police Department."

Ralph, my role model, was a cop? While my dad and my uncle discussed Ralph's new job, scenes from my brief brush with the law rolled through my mind—posters of escaped felons, drunks in holding tanks, ringing phones, important-looking people hurrying around doing important-looking work.

Forget baseball. Forget the military. I went home that evening, my head filled with images of myself in uniform catching bad guys and keeping the streets safe for ordinary citizens. A new career goal was fast taking shape in my mind. I wanted to be a cop.

Ralph soon discovered my fascination with his job and offered me a ride-along. After that, I became a frequent passenger while he was on duty.

One summer night when I was about eighteen, I was riding through town with Ralph in his patrol car when a call came in that two suspects had been apprehended outside a local beer warehouse. He turned the car around and we headed to the address immediately.

By the time we arrived, several other officers were already on the scene, surrounding a pair of men who were lying facedown on the ground in cuffs near a converted Quonset hut. One was shirtless and had been locked in thumbcuffs, a contraption I'd never seen before.

I felt like a spellbound kid watching an action flick. Here were two real, live bad guys—burglars who had broken into the cavernous metal dome and were obviously planning to steal the cases and kegs inside it. Their empty pickup truck was parked nearby, ready to be loaded up with beer. Fortunately, the good guys had arrived in the nick of time to nab them, just as in any cops-and-robbers drama.

Ralph was starting to ask what had happened when the rumble of tires on gravel interrupted him. We turned and spied the unmistakable Studebaker Lark of local police chief Melvin James pulling up.

The door swung open and out stepped James, clad as always in his trademark western hat and string tie.

Without waiting for his officers to fill him in on the details, he strode up to the shirtless man on the ground and looked down at him disdainfully. Then he drew back his heel and kicked the man in the face.

No one said a word.

James kicked him again. Then again. He kept kicking him until blood was pouring out of the man's nose and mouth onto the ground around him. Finally, he wedged his boot under one bloodied shoulder and flipped the man onto his back. The suspect lay there, helpless, blinking up through the blood.

James brought his boot down onto the man's neck, and I braced myself for the crunch of breaking bones. Instead, he spoke in a low, menacing voice.

"You will never come back to this town again. *Ever.* Understand me?"

I stood rooted to my patch of dirt, transfixed, until I felt a sudden yank on my arm.

"We're outta here," Ralph whispered.

He wheeled me around and marched me forcibly away from the cluster of men, with me twisting my head over my shoulder the whole time to see what would happen next. He shoved me into the passenger's seat and slammed the door, then stalked around to the driver's side and revved the engine.

He didn't speak until we were several blocks away from the bloody scene. When he did, he was every bit as furious and every bit as menacing as James, but for a very different reason.

"Rod, what you just saw back there is wrong," he told me. "That's not how all cops act. It's not how any cop should act. You should never treat another human being that way, no matter what he's done or what you think he might have done."

I never forgot what James did or what Ralph told me. I promised myself that when I became a cop, I would never do that and never let it happen on my watch. And I never did. I've made it a point to treat people with decency, always.

I'd been on the force in Los Angeles for a few years when I heard through the grapevine that Melvin James had finally gotten his just deserts, though there were people in San Angelo who would have argued that he deserved even worse.

One night, he took a seventeen-year-old African-American kid he had arrested behind the San Angelo Police Department, beat him senseless, then shot him three times. Remarkably, the teenager survived. James claimed it was self-defense; the kid claimed it was attempted murder. Whatever the truth, the incident made the Feds suspicious enough to investigate James. After taking a closer look at his policing methods—which more than one source claimed included using electric cattle prods on suspects to extract confessions—the authorities charged him with assault with intent to commit murder.

Until Melvin James's downfall, cops had to watch their backs and bite their tongues in San Angelo. Everyone knew the chief was mean and he was dirty and he had an iron grip on the careers of his officers. The man could make your future or he could destroy it.

During the trial, some of them spoke out at last. One of James's own officers testified that he'd watched the chief pistol-whip the black kid and kick him in the head. James copped a plea deal and received a $1,000 fine, which San Angelo residents who were still devoted to their chief raised funds to cover. He also assured the city commission that he would never seek office again—a promise he promptly forgot. Just two years later, James ran as a write-in candidate for what would have been his sixth term as police chief. Fortunately, he lost.

Cracking the Code of Bloodshed

Those early experiences were instrumental in my decision to become a cop and eventually a crime scene reconstructionist and blood pattern analyst. In the years since I left Texas, I have investigated thousands of murders, testified in almost four hundred court cases, and given nearly six hundred lectures about the telltale evidence to be found in blood smeared on walls, pooled on floors, soaked into sheets, and spattered on clothing. To me, blood is a road map—a route that leads to the truth after a murder has been committed. It reveals what really happened before investigators reached the scene and began the painstaking process of piecing a broken puzzle back together. It tells what the victim can't and the killer won't.

Of course, I don't get it right every time. In nearly five decades of police work, I have investigated plenty of homicides that I couldn't solve. Many of them are still classified as open cases. I recently became part of a team assembled by forward-thinking Multnomah County sheriff Robert Skipper to reexamine such cold cases in Oregon in the hopes that new technology may shed light on these long-dormant mysteries.

Lately it seems that nearly every time I turn on my television I see a *CSI* spin-off or a report on the latest DNA evidence details from yet another high-profile criminal trial. America has developed a pop culture obsession with crime, where everyone is an armchair sleuth. To those of us who do this work professionally, the inaccuracies on TV crime dramas are sometimes so ludicrous that they make us chuckle. At other times they make us groan or genuinely worry. But with so many Americans curious about crime scenes, it's time someone who has actually been there—countless times—took them behind the yellow tape for the uncensored inside story. I've sifted through thousands of pages of case notes that fill my lab in Oregon and handpicked the most compelling, curious, and chilling crimes to share with you. As you'll see, they're filled with just as many gripping twists, turns, and red herrings as a prime-time crime drama. What sets them apart? They're all true-life stories. Every one. All the close calls and the clever crooks you'll read about in these pages, all the ones we got and the ones who got away with it, sprang not from a screenwriter's overactive imagination, but from life. They were—and in some cases still are—out there.

From Rookie to Undercover Ace

By THE TIME WE graduated from high school in 1960, many of my childhood friends were getting ready to take over their families' farms, stepping into their fathers' long-familiar roles. Dad hoped I would do the same, but my heart was elsewhere. I was determined to become a cop. I was also eager to go to college. When my uncle Wes and aunt Louise Chamless offered to let me live with them rent-free in Los Angeles if I attended school there, I seized the chance.

In the fall of 1961, I packed up my Chevy and drove straight to Southern California, stopping just long enough to refuel. As soon as I had settled in there, I headed down to the police station—a wide-eyed, eager nineteen-year-old—and asked for an application. "Sorry, kid," the desk sergeant told me. Nineteen, I learned, was two years too young to become a cop.

Disappointed but with no other choice, I channeled my energy into studying instead. I spent the next two years at East Los Angeles Junior College, where I earned my associate degree in 1964. Then, with the help of a Johnson administration grant, I enrolled at Cal State at Los Angeles, majoring in police science and administration. Veteran cops from police departments in the area would show up regularly to guest lecture and serve as adjunct professors, and I would listen spellbound to their tales of thwarted robberies and special investigations, hoping one day to be working cases like those myself.

As soon as I turned twenty-one, I applied at the LAPD's Parker Center—named after the force's chief at the time, William H. Parker, a no-nonsense former war hero beloved in those days for his integrity and for purging the force of corruption. After completing the paperwork, I had to take a medical exam at a local hospital. I had worn contacts for years, so I wasn't surprised to find myself struggling to read the minuscule letters lining the bottom of the eye chart. I was stunned, however, when three months later an official rejection letter arrived because of it. Twenty-twenty vision, it turned out, was a prerequisite for joining the LAPD.

After years of anticipation, my dream was about to fall apart. Resolved not to let that happen, I started applying at all the other police stations within driving distance. A few months later—in early 1963—a letter showed up from the Downey Police Department, just south of L.A., congratulating me on my acceptance to the force and telling me where to report to begin training. I was elated, but still smarting over my rejection from what I deemed the big leagues of the LAPD itself. At least I would get to attend the Los Angeles Police Academy for training, I told myself. I'd get to become a cop.

Looking back, I realize Downey turned out to be the best career move I could have made. L.A.'s department was so huge and sprawling that I would have spent years edging my way up the ranks. Downey was small—small enough for an eager, energetic young cop to work every assignment. I volunteered for all of them, even offbeat ones like presentations at PTA meetings in the evenings, where I taught parents how to recognize narcotics and how to know when their kids were revealing signs of drug use. That public-speaking experience would prove invaluable training ground when I started lecturing on blood pattern analysis decades later.

Basic Training

The next three months of my life involved little more than abject misery and crushing exhaustion. Toiling through the sweltering rows of cotton plants under the Texas sun was grueling, but the Los Angeles Police Academy had it beat for sheer physical punishment.

I knew I was in trouble when the muscle-bound ex-marine standing next to me collapsed during training. His knees buckled, and down for the count he went. The academy training officers spat on us, humiliated us, called us every foul name in the book. The Los Angeles Police Academy is in Elysian Park, right by Dodger Stadium, and we ran around the field so many times, I lost count. I might have found the experience awe-inspiring in those deep summer days of my childhood, when I was back in Texas idling away hours dreaming of becoming a professional baseball player. But the reality was starkly devoid of romance. There were no cheering throngs urging us on as we barreled through the heat until our legs trembled and our calves balled up into stabbing cramps. The officers running the program did everything they could to break us psychologically and physically. Along the way, they pounded us into shape—just the intense physical and mental conditioning we needed to prepare for what we would soon face on the streets of Southern California.

I started at the academy with five other new Downey recruits—Frank Riesenhuber, Mike Hadley, Bart Kirk, Bob Bradfield, and Larry Olson. We all stuck it out, went through orientation together, and forged the kind of lasting, loyal camaraderie that comes only through sharing one of life's defining experiences.

We never knew when the officers in charge would march solemnly into the police academy classroom at Elysian Park and turn to face a hundred of us new recruits standing at attention, silent and terrified. One of them would belt out a recruit's last name, followed by the words we all dreaded.

"Johnson," they would yell, "get your books!"

That would be the last you would see of the guy. Head hanging, he would fall out of the ranks, gather his belongings, and slink away, publicly disgraced, weeded out for reasons usually unknown. Sometimes they just perceived a character flaw that convinced them the man in question wouldn't cut it on the force.

The classroom work was just as brutal as the physical training—they drilled us on search and seizure, arrest procedure, investigation technique, use of deadly force, radio communication, and every other angle of law enforcement. Then came firearms training, weapons care, marksmanship, defensive driving, pursuit driving, and safe vehicle handling. On and on it went.

I slogged through and eventually got both my wishes: I became a cop, and I got my bachelor's degree in fall 1968. L.A.'s own Chief Parker, in full dress uniform, shook my hand and congratulated me at the commencement ceremony as my own new chief, Ivan Robinson of Downey, handed me my badge.

By this time, I had also married my first wife, Carolyn, whom I met at a wedding I attended with my aunt and uncle. I was twenty-one when we married; she was twenty-five. It sounds young now, but it seemed ordinary then. I was proud to be married, proud to be a full-fledged adult. But nothing made me prouder than being a police officer. I kept my navy blue uniform with its vivid orange patches pressed and my black shoes polished to a glow (a much easier task now that I'd left the academy and nobody was spitting on them). Even my keys hung flat and precise on my gun belt, with one slipped between the three layers of leather to hold them in place, the others dangling below in easy reach.

Graveyard Shift

I started out working the graveyard shift—the postmidnight hours that the guys with more pull and experience are eager to avoid. For the first few weeks, an older officer rode along with me so that if anything he deemed me too green to handle came up, he could jump in.

Finally, my first night working solo as a uniformed patrolman arrived. Christmas Eve. I checked all my gear, checked my shotgun, then reported officially that I was on duty. We termed it "clearing for calls" or "ten-eight."

This is gonna be great, I thought as I pulled out of the station parking lot. *I'm finally a cop.*

Two hours passed uneventfully. Then just after two A.M., a call came crackling across the radio.

"We've got a multiple-car accident on I-Five, the Santa Ana Freeway, near Florence Avenue."

I responded and reached the scene on the darkened highway minutes after the crash. As my headlights cut through the darkness, what I saw made me feel numb and short of breath, as if all the oxygen had suddenly been sucked out of the car. Sprawled out along the still and deserted road was the bloodiest mess I had ever seen.

Cars were overturned, and random scraps of metal were scattered as if a bomb had exploded. Beyond the cars, I could make out the shape of a motorcycle lying on its side. There were bodies in every direction. My mind and my heart started sprinting at what felt like a hundred miles an hour, as if they were trying to outstrip each other. I called for backup, working hard to keep my voice steady. Then I leapt out of the car.

What to do first? Save lives. I ran to the nearest body. A man I guessed to be in his late twenties was sprawled flat on his back on the concrete, white and still, eyes fixed on nothing. One look and a quick pulse check told me he was dead.

I hurried on. More limp and crumpled bodies lay motionless at strange angles. No one was breathing. Hadn't anybody survived this thing? I glanced around frantically, looking for someone to save, and caught sight of a pair of boots a lane and a half away. Something about them looked familiar, and I felt my stomach lurch. The motor-cyclist had skidded across nearly two lanes of pavement and ended up wedged under a chain-link fence that served as the divider in the center of the freeway. As I drew closer, I saw that the man's body was on my side of the fence, but his head and neck were on the other side. Standing over him confirmed my fear. I was looking down at a Cali-fornia Highway Patrol cop in uniform. Over my shoulder I heard a car stop, and a concerned passerby appeared out of the darkness, rushing up to offer assistance.

"Can I do anything to help, Officer?"

The man's question shook me out of my paralysis. I told him to grab the fence and yank it upward as hard as he could to lift it off the cop's neck. Meanwhile, I crouched down and gently eased the injured man toward me, trying not to look at the blood everywhere, not to think about what it meant: There was too much of it. We were too late. As I leaned over the fallen officer, a strong, sharp aroma of alcohol pierced my nostrils. It didn't take brilliant detective work to deduce what had happened here.

The officer had been out partying, celebrating Christmas Eve, probably at the end of his shift. He had knocked back one too many eggnogs, maybe with friends from work, and headed home on his bike. In his hurry, he had tried to slip between two cars, passing them on the white stripe.

But I didn't care that this man had had too much to drink. I didn't care that he had used questionable judgment. As a cop—even a new recruit—when you see someone in uniform wounded, you feel an instant bond. You think, That could be me. That could be one of my friends on the force. That could be a member of my family. By the looks of it, the guy wasn't much older than me. What if this officer had a new wife at home waiting for him, too? What if he had little kids? It was Christmas Eve, for God's sake. What kind of Christmas would his family have now?

I knelt beside him and slipped my hand behind his head to give him mouth-to-mouth resuscitation. Where his skull should have felt solid, it felt as soft as an overripe melon. It seemed to settle between my fingers like a floppy, half-full water balloon. I wrestled down a rising tide of nausea and a nagging internal whisper that this was a losing battle. Instead I focused only on the CPR motions. Five compressions to the chest . . . one rescue breath . . . five compressions . . . one breath. Every time I pushed on his chest, I was pushing on his nameplate. It read, "DeWitt."

I'm going to save him, I told myself fiercely. I was so intent on it that I didn't realize backup had arrived until a sergeant reached around to my gunbelt and took my keys. "Don't worry about your car," he said. "We've got it. Just get in the ambulance with him."

All the way to Lynnwood Community Hospital, I sat next to this colleague I had never met, staring at him, willing him to revive, trying not to remember the horrible softness of his head, trying not to look at his blood covering my hands, caked around my fingernails. Officer DeWitt was pronounced DOA, like the rest of the victims of that accident, and I went home for Christmas Day with my family.

I got an official commendation for my efforts. I clipped the article about the accident out of the local newspaper and tucked it in a drawer. I had done all I could, I assured myself. Still, I couldn't stop that gruesome reel from replaying in my mind. Every time I closed my eyes, the bloodstains and the rag-doll bodies on the freeway reappeared. I had nightmares and woke up in cold sweats. To a casual outsider, I looked as if I were holding it together. I was still doing my job. But I was losing it. Maybe I wasn't cut out for police work after all. Doubt, remorse, and thoughts of turning in the badge that had meant everything to me at graduation were creeping up and threatening to overwhelm me every day.

All of that came spilling out during my review when Vance Reynolds, the sergeant evaluating my performance, asked a simple question.

"So, how've things been going?"

"Pretty well," I began heartily.

Reynolds didn't answer.

I hesitated. Then I started again. "Actually, not so well. I've been thinking about quitting."

He looked at me impassively. "Hmm," he said. "Why?"

Out poured the countless night terrors: *I'm kneeling on the highway in the dark, realizing the cop is dead, only to have the corpse's bloodied hands reach up suddenly and close viselike on my arms. I'm racing in slow motion to a body trapped under a fence, bending close and seeing . . . not the real victim's face, but the faces of cops I know, friends in the department, my brother Mickey, my cousin Ralph, sometimes my own face.*

I felt embarrassed telling Reynolds all this. Frankly, it was anti-thetical to the strong, unflappable macho persona we all strove for, the stoicism we vehemently believed was a prerequisite for being a great cop. But it was cathartic. Sitting in that chair venting all the anguish, guilt, and fear I had pent up was necessary in some way.

Reynolds didn't say anything. He didn't pat me on the back or re-assure me or tell me brusquely to snap out of it. He listened. When I walked out of the evaluation, I knew I would be okay. I wouldn't forget it, but I would be able to file that case away mentally with the many others I was accumulating and go on with my work.

Still, of all the bloodshed I've seen in the years since, that bloody Christmas Eve wreck on I-5 still ranks as one of the most disturbing scenes in my memory.

Not long ago, I was asked by decorated former LAPD detective and District Attorney investigator Buck Henry, now among the top crime scene reconstructionists in the business, to examine blood evi-dence for a case that brought back all those memories.

It was Friday afternoon in Oceanside, California, when Tony Zep-petella, a twenty-seven-year-old police officer, pulled a car over for a routine traffic stop in the crowded parking lot of the Navy Federal Credit Union at Avenida de la Playa and College Boulevard. Behind the wheel of the car he stopped was Adrian Camacho, a criminal alien who had been deported from the United States for his lengthy record of drug and weapons convictions. Camacho had already spent much of his adult life in prison, and rather than risk going back, he opened fire on Zeppetella in front of more than a dozen witnesses and then fled in the officer's police cruiser.

It was my job to re-create precisely what happened at the Navy Fed-eral Credit Union that afternoon based on the blood spatter. Camacho fired the first shot with a loaded semiautomatic lying beside him on the seat as Zeppetella stood at the driver's-side window. When the impact knocked Zeppetella to the ground, Camacho leapt out and kept shooting until he ran out of bullets. He then pistol-whipped Zeppetella. Next he grabbed the wounded officer's gun and emptied it into the dying man's back as he struggled in vain to crawl to shelter—thirteen shots in all. The entire incident unfolded in less than two minutes.

The blood evidence bore out what the witnesses saw: This was a vicious, senseless murder, committed without a fragment of mercy or human compassion. It earned Camacho—whose blood test revealed that he was hopped up on a blend of heroin, methamphetamine, and Paxil when the shooting occurred—a spot on death row.

As a consultant, I cannot get emotionally involved in my cases. Detached impartiality is crucial for accurate assessment and analysis. But I will confess that when I examined Officer Zeppetella's blood-soaked notebook and found a photograph of his wife and baby son tucked inside it, I felt as if I were once again standing on the Santa Ana Freeway in the damp and chilly night air, in the first hours of that Christmas morning forty years ago.

This could have been me on countless occasions. This could have been my blood spattered all over a parking lot, all over my notebook, all over a photograph of my children, then left for someone else to analyze. It could have been the blood of any of the cops I've known over the years—men simply trying to do their jobs, trying to keep the streets safe from murderers and drug dealers, and pulling over the wrong car on the wrong Friday afternoon.

The $8.00 Incident

The I-5 accident was one of two memorable events in my life that took place on a California freeway. The second would provide the catalyst for the worst moments of my entire career, a potentially ruinous crisis that snuck up and blindsided me. And it all started with an incident that seemed downright trivial.

I was on patrol late one night with a ride-along—a young radio operator with dreams of becoming a cop, just as I'd had in my own days riding with Ralph back in San Angelo—when a call came in: "Possible drunk driver southbound on Paramount Boulevard."

"I'm on it," I told the dispatcher.

I soon found the car in question and tailed him as he turned east onto Imperial Highway. Then I switched on my lights and pulled the driver over.

"Could you step out of the car, please, sir?" I asked him.

These were the days before Breathalyzers, so I did a sobriety test by making him stand with his feet together, then apart, walk in a straight line, and so on. It was obvious the guy was not quite drunk. He wasn't belligerent, either. He just stood there calmly watching while I searched his car. I found a pinch of marijuana—enough to dump out, but not enough to justify arresting him.

I had no choice but to fill out a field interrogation report (a three-by-five paper we called an "FI card" that showed I had stopped someone but hadn't found cause to bring him in) and to send him on his way.

I watched him drive off and didn't give him another thought.

Six months later, we had just finished a big drug raid on La Reina Avenue and booked forty people when my lieutenant, Jim Shade, pulled me aside.

"There's been a complaint against you," he said, handing me a piece of paper. He seemed almost casual about it, but as I scanned the page, I shook my head in disbelief.

It was signed by a man named Green, who said he was writing on behalf of his friend Robert Thornton to complain that I had pulled Thornton over six months earlier on Imperial Highway and stolen $8.00 from his pocket while I was patting him down.

The next day, I found myself summoned to Chief Ivan Robinson's office. He threw me a rueful glance as I walked in.

"Officer Englert," he said, "have a seat."

As I sat down, he swiveled his chair around so that his back was toward me. From the wall behind his desk, he carefully removed a plaque that bore the Law Enforcement Code of Ethics. He began to read aloud from it.

"As a Law Enforcement Officer, my fundamental duty is to serve mankind; to safeguard lives and property; to protect the innocent against deception, the weak against oppression or intimidation . . ."

I was scared to death. How could this be happening? I had been on the department only two years. I had wrestled with some serious demons after I-5, but I had conquered them and I had been scrupulously ethical every day on this job, my dream job.

"Honest in thought and deed in both my personal and official life, I will be exemplary in obeying the laws of the land and the regulations of my department . . . ," he went on, reading the words slowly.

He finished and swiveled around to face me across his desk, eyebrows raised quizzically.

"I didn't do it," I told him. "Why would I steal eight dollars?"

"Yeah, Jim Shade said the same thing," Robinson told me. "He's sure you're innocent. He offered you up for a polygraph. So I guess we'll find out. Won't we?"

My heart sank. I had always had great respect for Chief Robinson. During my first few weeks on the force he had sat all his newly minted officers, including my five pals from the police academy and myself, down as a group to share some simple words of wisdom with us.

"Gentlemen," he told us, "never lower yourself to the level of the people you are dealing with."

Now that was exactly what Robinson thought I had done. The chief of police, my commanding officer, was convinced that I had betrayed the public trust and disgraced my department by lowering myself to the level of a thief, a pickpocket. If he doubted me, I wasn't sure how much it mattered that I was innocent.

The next morning, as Deputy Chief L. D. Morgan drove me to the sheriff's office in downtown L.A., I was still petrified and baffled about why anyone would make up such a bizarre story about me. When we arrived Morgan introduced me to Bob Murphy,* the officer who would administer my polygraph.

Murphy shot me a skeptical, appraising glance, then ordered me to sit. He soon made it clear he didn't feel any kinship with me as a fellow officer. Nor did he subscribe to the old notion of being innocent until proven guilty in cases like mine.

"You know what a field mouse is?" he barked at me. "Are you gonna be a man or a field mouse and not tell the truth?"

"I don't know what you're talking about," I told him honestly, just as I had told Chief Robinson back at the station. "I've never done anything like that. Why would I jeopardize my entire career for a lousy eight dollars?"

But he was bent on hearing a confession. As the minutes dragged by, he grew more aggressive and frustrated with me for refusing to crumble.

At last he leaned back in his chair and growled, "All right, you're done." He ordered me to stay put while he talked with Morgan, who, unbeknownst to me, had watched the whole conversation through a two-way mirror.

"Well, Englert," Morgan said, "you didn't do so well."

I failed? How could I have failed a lie detector test when I told the truth?

We rode back to Downey in silence. When we got there, Morgan said, "You go home and think about this tonight. We'll talk to the chief tomorrow."

It was the most miserable night of my life.

"It's over. My whole career is over," I told my wife. "All that education went down the tubes."

"It'll be okay," she said, though she didn't have much luck convincing me. "You told the truth. That's what matters."

"Not if you fail the polygraph," I replied.

The next day, Chief Robinson asked if I had anything to tell him.

"Just what I told you before. I didn't do it."

Later that day, I found myself being chauffeured by Morgan to yet another polygraph. I was bracing for more hostility, but instead we went to an apartment in Glendale. The man who opened the door greeted Morgan like an old friend. It turned out that's just what he was: a retired former colleague who ran a polygraph operation out of his home.

Like the setting, the approach contrasted starkly with my first ordeal. This time no one badgered me—Morgan's pal just took me into a separate room, where he asked me questions about Thornton and the infamous $8.00.

When he finished he said, "Only you know whether you're telling the truth or not."

"That's not exactly giving me a clean bill of health," I replied.

He smiled and shrugged.

He spoke to Morgan in private, then we said good-bye and got back in the car. By this time it was almost midnight, but instead of returning to the station, Morgan drove straight to Chief Robinson's house and told me to wait in the car. My heart pounding, I watched from the passenger seat as Morgan knocked on the front door and stood waiting. At last, Robinson answered. He leaned in the door frame, wearing pajamas and a bleary-eyed look. Our arrival had obviously woken him up. I could see Morgan talking—and Robinson nodding occasionally—but I couldn't hear a word of the conversation I knew would determine my fate.

At last, Robinson closed the door and Morgan climbed back in the car. "Well," he said simply, "it's over."

What was over? The investigation? My career? I glanced at him apprehensively.

He left me in suspense for a few more minutes before telling me that I had passed polygraph number two and that Robinson had decided to drop the issue. After that night, they both acted as if it had never happened. Case closed.

More than a year passed before I got an unexpected call to testify in superior court about a field interrogation report card I had filled out on one Robert Thornton. I soon learned that Thornton was on trial for raping six women in Los Angeles County and for using the unique and horrible MO of shoving rocks into their vaginas after his attacks.

I stepped into the courtroom and there he sat—the man who had almost demolished my career. I barely recognized him behind the pair of Coke-bottle glasses he was wearing.

As soon as I took the witness stand, pieces of the story started to click into place: I had pulled Thornton over when he was fleeing one of his crime scenes. He had been remarkably composed for a man who had just committed a brutal rape. But why would a guy with such a sinister secret to hide write to the chief of police? Why call attention to himself?

I soon found out.

"Officer Englert, when you're on duty, it's not unusual for you to stop three or four people a night. Is that correct?" the prosecutor asked.

"Yes, sir," I answered.

"Mr. Thornton did nothing significant. You didn't even arrest him. Why would you remember him so well from an event that occurred more than two years ago?"

The tension on Thornton's face was evident. It turned out that his entire case hinged on one of the little boxes I had checked on the FI card.

Thornton fit the description all the victims gave of their attacker, except for one crucial point: The man who had raped them hadn't worn glasses. The defense attorney claimed his client was innocent because he was almost legally blind without corrective lenses.

On my FI card, I had noted "no glasses."

"Mr. Thornton has stated under oath that his poor vision requires him to wear glasses at all times," the DA continued.

"Well," I replied, and I looked directly at the jury as I spoke, "I know that when I stopped him he wasn't wearing glasses. And he was driving at the time."

Thornton was convicted on all counts. Case closed.

So that's why I had been put through hell. Thornton wanted to discredit me—to get me out of the way so I wouldn't be able to testify and blow his disguise if he ever got caught. I had just been in the wrong place, wrong time.

Chief Robinson never apologized when he learned the truth. He just shrugged. "It made you a stronger person," he said.

I never forgot it. Even when every instinct tells me a suspect is guilty, I reserve judgment until all doubt is removed, because I know how it feels to have everyone in the room be convinced you committed a crime when you're innocent. And though I've submitted plenty

of defendants to polygraph tests because I know that a skilled operator can coax a confession out of a guilty man by convincing him that
the machine has already revealed the truth, I never rely solely on the
results of a lie detector test.

Nine Ninety-Nine!

It didn't take me long to discover that for a cop, the unexpected was
inevitable. It was always waiting just around the corner, behind the
door, or at the end of the blind alley. And it always seemed to happen
in the dead of night.

At around three A.M. on one particular night, I was patrolling a
notoriously rough part of Downey known as the Boot. The neighborhood, which lay just inside the city limits, was infamous for drugs, prostitutes, and worse. And the hub of the action was a sprawling complex
with a hotel, nightclub, and restaurant known collectively as Tahitian
Village. Word at the time was that organized crime ran the operation.

I get hunches about trouble, and that night mine led me into the
narrow alley that emptied out in back of the nightclub. I drove through
it, past the trash bins and into a nearly empty parking lot hidden behind the bar. Sure enough, I spied a car parked at a peculiar angle,
straddling two spaces. Something about it didn't look right. I got out
and edged closer.

A man sat slumped over the steering wheel, eyes closed, mouth
agape. Asleep? Maybe. Dead? Possibly. Drunk or on drugs? Probably.

I knocked on the window.

At once, he jerked upright, looked around wildly, and spied me.
His eyes narrowed and his face lit up with a sort of murderous inten-
sity. I had only a second to register his bizarre expression before he
flung open the door and launched himself at me. He was enormous,

a head taller than me, and out of his mind with rage. Like a kick-boxer in overdrive, he flew at me, punching, kicking, biting, throt-tling, and grabbing for my gun in the holster.

Before I knew it, I was in a fight for my life, swinging and ducking as fast as I could to keep this lunatic from knocking me senseless and then killing me with my own bullets.

As yet another sharp right flew out of nowhere and caught me be-low the eye, I thought ruefully of my baton, lying uselessly on the front seat of my patrol car. I ducked a blow and landed one on his jaw. But this guy wasn't going down. He just kept coming back for more, as if the only thing that would satisfy him was to murder me.

We didn't carry radios in those days, so all I could do was keep fighting and try to steer the brawl back toward my car in the hope that I could get close enough to grab the radio and call for backup.

The stranger caught me around the neck and started to drag me across the parking lot, choking me until stars popped in front of my eyes. I twisted loose and dove for the car. Luckily, I had left the door open.

My hands slipping frantically over the radio, I pressed the button and shouted, "Car seven. Nine ninety-nine. Repeat, nine ninety-nine!"

When an officer called a nine ninety-nine, all hell broke loose. It was the police version of SOS or 911. Mayday. No matter what else you were doing on duty, you abandoned it and raced to the officer's aid. (The verbal shorthand for "Emergency! Officer needs assistance!" varies by city and state. Some departments have scrapped codes alto-gether in favor of plain English to simplify things. However, the most common police call for help is "code zero," which we used in Oregon.)

I barely got the words out before a pair of massive bleeding knuckles reached in and yanked me upward, hoisting me out of the car. The stranger flung himself on me, trying to force me down to the pavement, his hands still scrabbling at my holster. I hit him as hard as I could, sending him reeling backward, then grabbed my gun.

I had done everything I could think of not to kill this guy, but I was in trouble. I was exhausted, and he was not only bigger than me, but full of the hyperenergetic, superwired kinetic strength people get when their systems are loaded with drugs. What the hell was wrong with him? Why was he bent on killing a complete stranger and a cop, no less? All I did was tap on the window to see if he was okay. I wasn't going to shoot him, but I had to end it. Soon. So I pulled out the .38 Smith & Wesson with the six-inch barrel that I had bought myself when I became a cop and cracked him hard across the head with its hefty barrel several times. (Cops had to buy their own guns in Downey in those days.) He let go of me instantly and crumpled to the pavement with a thump. I jumped on him and got him handcuffed.

By this time, our brawl had made enough of a racket to alert the crowd inside the bar. A straggle of onlookers had drifted out the back door and everyone was standing in a semicircle staring down at me, panting and bleeding as the surging adrenaline that had sent my heart into a furious gallop finally subsided. I dragged a shaking hand across my forehead to wipe away the sweat. That's when I heard the sound of sirens in the distance. Relief coursed through me. Help was on the way. It's hard to describe what that sound means to a cop in trouble. It's like the cavalry storming in.

I didn't even realize I had dropped my .38 until a stranger in the crowd silently handed it back to me. It had been one hell of a fight. Blood was all over the parking lot, and I had been lucky—very lucky—to come out on top.

My opponent, the mysterious Mike Tyson of the back alley, ended up in the hospital with twenty-five stitches. But the way I saw it, I was lucky to be alive and so was he. Things could have ended a lot worse. Nonetheless, I found myself in court over the incident. And of all the courtrooms I didn't want to land in, this one topped the list. It belonged to Leon Emerson, a hard-nosed judge whose courtroom I had been in before and who seemed to dislike me intensely.

I walked in, and there sat the psycho from the parking lot, ready for his arraignment, clad in a business suit but sporting a massive, turbanlike bandage on his head. As bad luck would have it, he turned out to be a VIP with North American Aviation.

"I was completely out of it. Really drunk," he testified. "I swear I thought I was back in Vietnam. I just went nuts."

Emerson didn't buy a word of it. It didn't matter that the man was trying to apologize, pleading mea culpa. He was a high-ranking executive, a big shot with a big corporation, and he had suffered what looked like some serious police brutality from the judge's viewpoint. Emerson didn't seem to care that the man had been drunk out of his mind and had attacked a public servant. He made his opinion clear with a slew of snide remarks aimed at me from the bench.

I sat there, black and blue and boiling, biting my swollen lip, as he prattled on, Monday-morning quarterbacking in his robes. What did Emerson know about it? He wasn't the one lying on his back in a parking lot in the middle of the night getting the crap kicked out of him and thinking he was about to die. I was out there trying to do my job. I didn't have any other avenues. I could have been killed. The guy was insane. He was trying to get my gun.

I kept my anger in check, but when I got back to the station, I wrote a memo to the chief of police defending myself and complaining about Emerson's comments. The result wasn't exactly what I had hoped for: The chief wrote his own complaint to the judge, saying that he supported my actions. But he still ordered the whole department to go to baton-training school. Worse, thanks to me and my boxing match behind Tahitian Village, we had to carry our batons in rings on our belts at all times from then on, which made walking, running, driving, and even sitting down at your desk awkward and cumbersome.

"Thanks a lot, man," my colleagues grumbled. They were as ticked at me as I was at Judge Emerson.

A Nose for Narcotics

Licking my wounds, I went back to work. I was getting good at what I did, discovering I had a sixth sense for the cars carrying drugs. Sometimes I could tell from subtle glitches in the driving. Sometimes furtive motions from the front seat gave the drivers or their passengers away. Sometimes a simple hunch would tip me off.

Soon I led the department in narcotics arrests. I was assigned to AI (accident investigation), but I was still catching so many drug users that I landed myself right back in the crosshairs of Judge Emerson. I had been gracing the L.A. County District Court judges' courtrooms so often to testify that he convinced himself I must be in league with the drug trade. "You've got a whole police department down there," he told my boss. "How come one guy is making all these narcotics arrests?" He couldn't believe the busts were legitimate. He figured I was planting dope, faking probable cause for pulling people over, or getting inside tips from an informant. Finally, he demanded a ride-along.

I was still fuming about the man's barbed comments, but I had no idea he was targeting me. I thought he just wanted to do a ride-along and I had been unlucky enough to get stuck with him.

At around seven P.M. we were sitting next to each other parked on Imperial Highway, working radar and trying to make polite conversation despite the ill will almost palpable in the car, when a black 1959 Ford Fairlane sped past us. I clocked the Ford at twenty miles over the limit. At fifteen over, I would have let him go. But that speed on this road was dangerous. I turned on the overhead lights and tailed the car, spying the familiar hunched pose—the telltale hurried scramble of a user fumbling to stuff his stash under the seat.

When the car finally pulled over, I approached the driver and motioned for him to roll down the window. He cracked it a mere two inches. A pair of bloodshot eyes with pupils so dilated that I could barely make out a rim of iris around them blinked up at me. I glanced back at Emerson and waved him out of the car.

"Could you come over here for a minute, Judge?" I asked him. He walked up to me. "Can you smell that, Your Honor?" Pungent fumes of pot smoke were wafting out of the cracked window. Emerson nodded.

"You're gonna have to step out of the car, sir," I told the driver while Judge Emerson peered over my shoulder. Reluctantly, he swung open the door and stepped out. As he did, I caught sight of something black and shiny peeking out from under the passenger's seat. I ordered the driver to face the car, handcuffed him, and read him his rights.

"Take a closer look in there, Your Honor," I told Emerson, indicating the car's interior. Emerson strolled over to the passenger's side and opened it. Across the top of the Ford, I watched his eyes widen as he spied the half-hidden handgun on the floor.

"Anything else under the seat?" I asked, keeping my voice casual. Emerson bent down for a closer look. Sure enough, there was "jar" after "jar"—a thousand pills each—of colorful "reds" and "yellows" (barbiturates and Nembutal), all neatly divided into plastic bags for sale. We had just nabbed a dealer en route to a delivery, enjoying a joint along the way.

I arrested him for possession with intent to sell, then packed him in the back of the car and we headed to the station. In we walked, with the judge carrying all this dope, a big grin across his face. I booked the dealer, filled out the evidence cards, and typed up my report. Emerson waited until I finished, then left.

"Nice work," he said on his way out.

I had won over the judge at last . . . at least until he got subpoenaed in the case and was accused by the dope dealer's defense attorney of breaching the separation of the judicial and executive branches of government. The case was dismissed because of it, which understandably infuriated Emerson. It frustrated me, too, to think of the dealer back out on the street, but there was nothing either of us could do about it.

A few days later, Jim Shade told me Emerson's true motive for the ride-along: The judge had set me up, sure that I was crooked. Lieutenant Shade had defended me, just as he had in the $8.00 incident, when rapist Robert Thornton tried to get me fired. "Englert's not dirty," he assured Judge Emerson. "He's just got a nose for narcotics and a sixth sense for suspicious cars."

But here's what neither Emerson nor Shade knew: I wasn't a dope cop myself, but I was doing an exemplary job for them—turning loads of drugs over to them and filing flawless reports—because what I wanted more than anything was to join their ranks.

I was at my desk one day, filing yet another report on a drug bust I had made, when the phone rang.

"Englert?"

"Speaking."

"This is Leon Emerson."

What now? I thought.

"Listen," he said. "I owe you an apology."

That was all it took. In the years that followed, Judge Emerson became one of my closest friends. The better I got to know him, the more I admired his dedication. He had taken time out of his own schedule to check up on me, not to be a jerk but because he cared about justice and honesty in the courtroom.

But if you had predicted back on Imperial Highway in 1964 that the stern-faced judge in the passenger seat would become one of my best buddies, bucking hay with me under the glaring sun on my Oregon farm during weekend visits in the years to come, I would have said you were as high as that driver in the 1959 Ford Fairlane.

Going Undercover

I kept busting drug users with Emerson's blessing and eventually made a good enough impression to get assigned to narcotics. In 1966, to my delight, I became an undercover agent in Downey.

In many ways, undercover work was the antithesis of what I had done as a patrolman. You don't go into an office every morning. You don't wear a uniform. You don't worry about keeping your hair short or staying clean-shaven. Your job is to convince criminals that you're one of them.

I still remember what I wore on my first day undercover: a grubby baseball cap, a goatee, a rumpled short-sleeved golf shirt, and—taking a page from old Robert Thornton's book—glasses with big, black frames. The lenses were just clear glass, but they were so thick and heavy that they fooled the bad guys, who figured there was no way I could be a cop. Not with eyesight that pathetic. When a guy I had never met asked if I was on the level, my contacts would dismiss his doubts casually. "That dude?" they would ask incredulously. "The guy's practically blind." For many years I kept those glasses hanging in my lab to remind me of all the frightening places and white-knuckle predicaments they helped me scrape through.

People often raise a skeptical eyebrow when I swear that in all the years I bought drugs I never sampled them, but it's true. I am a master at faking it, though. When a dealer cocks a gun against your temple and threatens to kill you unless you do a line of coke to prove you're not a narc, you get a strong incentive to learn the art of simulated snorting.

"Hey, man," I used to say, "I'm just in it for the money. You can't be gettin' rich if you're gettin' high all the time."

The argument made sense to dealers, so they bought it.

Besides, that stuff was like gold down at the station: You had to account for every bit of it. When you signed out for $50 to buy weed or coke, you had better turn in $50 worth of weed or coke as evidence. Not $45. Not even $49.

I started out simple. My supervisor, Al Soule, and senior narcotics/ vice officer Jerry Gilbert taught me a lot. They gave me a primer on what to say and what to steer clear of to avoid entrapment or tipping my hand ("Where's the action?" is okay; "Can I buy some drugs from you?" is not), then they pointed me in the right direction and offered advice whenever I needed it. At first I just showed up at the bars, streets, and parks where drug trade was heavy. I would hang out for a while, make a buy here, an acquaintance there, but mostly keep a low profile. Gradually, I dug my way deeper into the scene, forging more pivotal contacts and progressing toward the power players—big-money dealers and drug lords.

Soon my hair was long and shaggy, and I had grown a scraggly beard. I looked nothing like the clean-cut young officer in uniform of a few months earlier. Stained T-shirts and grungy ripped jeans had replaced my starched shirts and crisply pleated navy blue pants. By now, my wife and I had three small children, and I looked bi-zarrely misplaced with them, like a drifter who had wandered inad-vertently into a happy family scene. People did a double take when they saw us at the grocery together. What's that shady-looking guy doing with those nice folks? they wondered. I could read it in their expressions.

But disdain from strangers didn't bother me. I loved working undercover. I became another person. I played the part, looked the part of a doper. I've always been gregarious and affable, and that helped me win the trust of the people I needed to convince.

Case Study: The Overdose

Many of my undercover days in Downey were spent chasing a tall, lanky teenager named John Sutherland.* The kid was a pain in the butt, always in trouble. Ostensibly a heroin dealer, he shot up more than he sold. I arrested him repeatedly, but he always made bail and turned up again causing problems. I kept following him, hoping to get him off the streets once and for all. As it turned out, he did that without any help from me.

I was at work one day when I overheard a call on the police radio about a dead body at a familiar address in a run-down neighborhood nearby. John Sutherland's address. I recognized it at once and hurried over.

When I walked in, John was lying in a corner of the living room dead, with a needle sticking out of his arm. There was blood all around him.

A lieutenant I knew well was there with some wet-behind-the-ears rookie patrolman I had never met. In I came, with my long hair and scruffy beard, and pushed right past them toward the body.

"How ya doin'?" I called.

"Hey," the rookie cried indignantly. "What do you think you're doing? This is my crime scene. You're not supposed to be in here."

"He's right, Rod," said the lieutenant, grinning. "You'd better back off."

Chagrined, I apologized and asked if it was okay if I hung around. The rookie grudgingly agreed.

I retreated to an out-of-the-way corner and studied the scene from there. Why was John so bloody? Dark stains had soaked into the carpet and spotted the shabby furniture all around his body.

I had seen enough drug use by that point to draw some preliminary conclusions about the crime scene. It wasn't uncommon to find a user dead with a needle jutting out of some part of his body. Addicts OD'd on hot doses—undiluted ones that they either didn't realize were lethally strong or were too desperate to take time to cut with quinine—all the time. But I had found those bodies before. At most, I had seen a trickle of congealing blood that had run down their arms in their final minutes.

I also knew that the more habitually you shot up, the harder you had to work to find an uncollapsed vein. Smack users were prone to hit an artery now and then in their urgent quest to find an inroad for the drug, and when they did, blood could spurt anywhere. Sometimes you found long, arching lines of it streaked across a mirror over a bathroom sink, and you knew an addict had been gazing in it while searching his neck for a vein to tap. He had pierced an artery by mistake and sent his blood spurting onto the glass. At other times, you spotted a dark red blob beside the body—the telltale sign that a user had found a workable vein, then carelessly squirted his blood onto the floor in order to empty the syringe before refilling it with a liquid he considered more precious to put in his body.

But none of that explained this blood.

Still baffled, I watched them carry out John's body. Later, I read the medical examiner's report and it all fell into place. The ME discovered a large gash on the back of John's head. In the first moments after fixing, as the heroin was flooding his system and doing its irreparable damage, John tried to take a few steps, but he fell down and lacerated his head on the sharp edge of a table. He lost consciousness, but his heart continued beating for several minutes—pumping blood out of the wound in the back of his scalp and onto the floor all around him, leaving him lying in a sticky red pool. The death was ruled an accident. Odds were John didn't feel a thing. He slipped blissfully into a coma, never realizing he was simultaneously overdosing and bleeding to death.

Blood Puzzles

Why am I telling you about this particular case, about this long-dead and forgotten junkie? Because when I recall that day, I am struck by how much police work has changed.

Blood pattern analysis was in its infancy in the United States in the mid-1960s. Looking back, John could have been bumped off by a rival dealer, a reckless junkie who coveted his stash, a thief who knew where he hid his drug money—anyone. The guy had his share of enemies. Frankly, we would never have known if a clever killer had whacked him on the back of the head, shot him up with enough pure heroin to make sure he never woke up again, and vanished, taking the murder weapon with him.

Nowadays, dozens of crime photos would be taken of a scene like that. You would get every angle of the body and the blood on camera. You'd collect samples. You'd photograph the trail of droplets. You'd measure each one and study its shape. You'd do a bloodstain map. In this particular case, you would focus intense attention around the victim's head as the source of the blood. You would conduct a microscopic examination of the table where he hit his head. You would examine John's clothing for touch DNA—places where someone might have grabbed, twisted, or yanked on his clothes and inadvertently stripped off some of their own DNA.

But back then, there wasn't one cop looking for those clues. Everyone just tromped through the blood evidence at crime scenes. Blood was something to be cleaned up. There were no schools studying blood pattern analysis in this country, no textbooks defining terms like "spatter" and "blowback." Even though practitioners in Poland had begun, in 1895, doing research by beating rabbits and studying the bloodstains the blows created, the field wouldn't emerge in the United States for decades.

Blood fascinated me, although I didn't know the first thing about it. As a patrolman, I ran into the stuff almost daily. Fights. Beatings. Dead bodies. They all came with blood. Whenever I was called to a bloody scene, my instincts told me, There's got to be something to this. How did this blood get here? What does it mean?

But I had no answers. I remember shootings where I noticed blood specks on witnesses' clothes. I had no idea that in the years to come, those patterns would prove enough to convict a suspect of murder. I would scrutinize the blood at suicide scenes and traffic accidents, but trying to interpret what it meant was like trying to read a foreign language.

Once, I responded to a call where a woman was lying in a bathtub naked, slashing her wrists. The patterns created by the blood swirling in the hot water intrigued me, but as soon as I set foot in the bathroom she started doing her best to stab me with the butcher knife she was gripping, so I had precious little chance to analyze the watery red pools and ribbons winding over the tile floor.

Another time, we responded to an anonymous call and found a dead teenage girl in a tub full of ice. She had clearly OD'd, and her drug addict friends had injected milk into her veins, then put her on ice before fleeing the scene. (I have never yet seen that trick work, but junkie culture held fast to the belief that cow's milk would dilute the drug and ice would slow its progress to the brain.) Blood was everywhere, most likely because they had jabbed her repeatedly before they managed to get the milk into a vessel. It was the first time I had seen blood mixed with milk. I noticed from the bright red and white swirls that it interacted differently from the way blood did with water.

Around that same time, we raided a heroin den in a heavily Mexican section of town. It was summer in Southern California, which meant the heat was relentless. It made the pavement soft under your shoes and filled the air with a hazy, vaporous shimmer.

It was an oppressive, wiltingly hot afternoon when we pulled up in front of the dilapidated house we were targeting. The users were sprawled around the porch, trying to keep cool with as little clothing and movement as possible. When they saw police cars approaching, they flew into action as if an electric shock had jolted them. We chased them over the lawn and reached the porch just as a shirtless, barefoot man with long black hair slammed the door in our faces. From behind it came panicked yells, the crash of furniture falling over, pounding feet, and someone shouting in Spanish. We heard the distant flush of a toilet, which meant somebody was trying to get rid of contraband in a hurry.

"Open the door! Police!"

We rammed our shoulders into the heavy panels, but the man on the other side of the door was throwing all his weight against it to keep it shut. Finally, we kicked it in. The rip of splintering wood filled the stifling air along with a long and agonized wail from the dark-haired man behind it. He fell backward and began rolling on the ground, his face contorted, screaming and cursing in Spanish.

I looked down and instantly realized why. He had been standing with both hands pressed against the door, one foot back to brace his weight and the other forward to keep his balance. When the door flew inward, the bottom of it caught the top of his foot, shearing off most of the skin and two of his toenails. Blood was spurting out of the open wounds in his foot with each beat of his heart, making long, spattery red lines on the grimy floor. I paused long enough to notice the linear patterns and to register that a heartbeat was causing them. It was the first time I had ever seen an arterial spurt.

In the years that followed, when blood pattern interpretation classes began to crop up in the United States, I was always the first to enroll, despite overwhelming skepticism from my colleagues. I would become a charter member of the first American chapter of the International Association of Bloodstain Pattern Analysts, one of only twenty-five believers doggedly persevering on experiments that most law enforcement professionals ridiculed as a far-fetched waste of time but that would later prove invaluable to the field.

I amassed my knowledge of blood through years spent turning over dead bodies, looking at their wounds, and examining the blood they left behind. Blood pattern analysis is part science, part art. True, you need a solid grasp of math and physics. You have to understand disciplines like trajectory and pathology. And you must be able to apply scientific methods to your work when you conduct experiments. But you also have to put in years of fieldwork to understand it thoroughly. You can't learn what my colleagues and I do from sitting home reading books. You have to be able to read crime scenes. And that's a skill you get only from going to crime scenes. Lots of them.

When I walk into a blood-soaked room with a dead person sprawled in the center, it's like opening a book and starting at the end. The crime scene is the last page. I read that. And then slowly, carefully, often painstakingly, I work my way backward through the chapters—who, what, when, where, and how—until at last I reach the first page and find out how the story began.

Blood, Drugs, and Murder
in Multnomah County

BY 1969, I WAS spending far more time immersed in L.A.'s gritty, treacherous drug culture than I was with my family. I loved undercover work. In fact, I wanted to work all the time. And that was easy to do in a place like Los Angeles, where barbiturates, cocaine, heroin, hallucinogens, marijuana, and hashish changed hands faster than traders swap shares on the stock exchange floor.

But my constant absence was putting a strain on my family. Finally, we decided to move to Oregon, where I hoped to strike a better balance between career and home and where my kids could grow up in a more wholesome, rural environment. I was also eager for them to get a taste of the farm life that had shaped my childhood.

I contacted the sheriff's office in Multnomah County, which covers Portland, and they offered me a job. I left the station in Downey at five P.M. on a Friday afternoon, loaded my family and all our belongings into a moving van, and reported for duty at nine A.M. Monday, where I discovered that I had been assigned once again to narcotics. It wasn't the most auspicious start for someone who had vowed to work less, but we soon felt at home in Oregon and the move proved to be a wise one for all of us.

We settled on five acres of rambling, hilly farmland close enough to Portland that I could travel between work and home easily, but far enough away that Gary, Cherie, and Ron could go to school in a small farm community, enjoy plenty of room to roam and play outdoors, and, in the summer, swim and water-ski at nearby Willamette River.

My first home improvement project was to build a barn. Over the years it held horses, cats, dogs, and a pet sheep named Sammy who would make a break for the house every time he saw the door open and butt poor Ron in the stomach. Mainly, though, it held cattle, which I hoped would prove a lucrative enough sideline to help me cover the costs of raising three children.

I went to a few auctions and bought a handful of skinny three-hundred-pound feeder calves, planning to fatten them up to a robust eight hundred pounds each. It was easy for me to fall back into the familiar routines of farm life still ingrained from my childhood—getting up in the wee hours to feed the cows, mucking out the stalls every night. My kids weren't so easy to convince, though. I was adamant that the cattle were to be a family affair—everybody pitched in, everybody got their hands dirty, and, ultimately, everybody would benefit. From the time they were about nine, the three of them took turns—one week on, two weeks off—handling cow duty. That meant dragging themselves out of a warm bed, puffy-eyed and shivering, at five A.M. to don sweatshirts, knee-high boots, hats, and heavy gloves, then trudging down the hill to the barn to feed the cows, stifling yawns and resentment. The work had to get done even in the rain, sleet, and snow. Sometimes a steer would break out of the barn in the middle of the night and we'd roust the kids at three A.M. to grab flashlights, help us find the runaway, and chase him back home, slipping on the mud and ice. It was tough work for children, but it gave all three of them a sense of discipline and responsibility they've never lost.

The Tortilla Solution

By the end of our first year of farming, we had acquired six head of cattle, slaved over them during countless hours at the drafty barn . . . and made a grand total of $19. My plan was hardly shaping up to be the moneymaker I had hoped for.

The problem was the exorbitant cost of feed. I racked my brain for an answer. Should I give up? Try something else? Not yet, I decided. If police work teaches you anything, it's tenacity. Then I remembered a strategy Phil Weston,* a Los Angeles County deputy sheriff I had known back in Downey, used with his livestock: scrap tortillas. I grabbed the Yellow Pages and started calling every tortilla factory listed within driving distance.

"I've got a question for you," I began. "What do you do with broken tortillas?"

After I had convinced them I wasn't a prank caller, I struck a deal with Reser's Fine Foods: They would give me all their misshapen tortillas and leftover dough from the ton they cranked out daily if my kids and I would pick it up every weekend and haul it all away. In exchange, we promised to keep the factory owners stocked with as much steak and hamburger as they wanted. It worked perfectly. We supplemented the tortillas with alfalfa for roughage, and we made sure the factory owners' freezers never went empty. The kids used to joke that our cows mooed in Spanish from eating all those tortillas, but the cattle couldn't have found more nutritious feed—almost pure corn—and it was restaurant quality. Sometimes I would catch my kids surreptitiously snaking a hand into the barrels and sneaking a tortilla to munch.

As time went on, I expanded my cattle operation to seventy-five head and three hundred regular customers. My children and I spent weekends delivering meat, getting the cattle vaccinated, and scooping manure out of the barn with a front-end loader on a tractor to spread across the pastures as fertilizer. It was backbreaking work, but the proceeds helped to put them through college.

Blood at the Barn

Why am I telling you so much about my cattle business? Because, as farmwork often does, the operation generated a lot of blood—blood that ultimately proved invaluable to my developing career in crime scene analysis.

When the bulls arrived, we castrated them to help them gain weight and to keep them from bothering the heifers. Then we forced them into a squeeze chute, where we cut off their horns with a tool resembling a pipe cutter. That kept them from gouging one another while they vied for space at the feeding trough. The cuts usually created an arterial spurt, and the steer would swing their heads around wildly when their horns came off. Sometimes the blood sprayed over the walls before you could manage to get medicated coagulant on the wound. At other times the steer rubbed their wounds along the sides of the chute, leaving long horizontal red smears and streaks on the walls.

I soon discovered that the patterns bore a striking resemblance to the blood patterns I saw at crime scenes. Since cattle blood has the same properties as human blood, I started studying them more closely, noting the differences between what happened when a steer stood still, shook his head, dragged it along the wall, and so on. Castrations gave me ample opportunity to examine blood-into-blood patterns because cutting through multiple tissue layers as we did meant the steer dripped blood continuously as we worked. That taught me a lot about coagulation, too. Blood starts to get gooey and jellylike as it dries, and the plasma begins to separate, forming a yellow-tinged rim at the edges of the red part. Understanding this process—and knowing how long it takes to occur at different temperatures and in different weather conditions—gave me an effective way to estimate time of death at murder scenes.

But that wasn't what generated the most useful blood.

Every month, the mobile slaughter van would arrive to kill four or five fattened steer. The man who ran the operation shot them in the head before butchering them, a sight that would have turned some folks into vegetarians on the spot. But having grown up on a farm, I had long ago grasped the link between slaughter and supper. I had conquered any squeamish urges as a little kid watching Ernest Braden, a neighboring farmer who did his own butchering back in Wall, slide a coffee cup under the slit he had cut in a steer's throat to catch the blood—and then drink it. Besides, all that cattle blood provided ideal research material for a homicide detective.

Before mopping up the barn, I would study the blood patterns made by the gunshots and the bodies, then I would refrigerate bottles of blood to help me re-create details from cases I was working. Conducting my own experiments using cattle blood often helped me to more effectively unravel puzzling clues in murders I was investigating than I could have done on a crime scene where other people are always tromping around trying to do their jobs, where time can be limited, and where evidence is already cold.

Whenever I had spare time, I would gather up a notebook, a camera, a bottle of cows' blood, and anticoagulant from the barn to further my study of blood patterns. I dribbled blood from my fingertips, from the points of knives, and from holes in plastic garbage bags dragged across the barn floor. I tried the same tests on cement, gravel, dirt, sand, grass, wood, and carpet to find out how the trails of blood differed. Then I did the experiments on ice and snow and watched what happened when it began to melt. I made notes about how the droplets got absorbed or distorted depending on how porous or soft a surface they hit.

In those days, just over half of all the homicides in Oregon were committed with guns, so I spent a lot of time shooting into blood with .22s, .38s, shotguns, and automatic weapons, and studying the fine red mist the impact created. I found out that the more powerful the gun was, the finer the bloody mist it generated. It's common knowledge among blood experts now, but back then it wasn't.

Fortunately, the barn was massive—ninety feet long, thirty feet high, and forty feet wide—large enough to convert to a horseback-riding arena (which is what the people who later bought it from us did). That meant there was plenty of room to experiment without endangering the animals. If I was doing a test that might make bullets ricochet, I stacked phone books or set up plywood around my work area as a protective backdrop. Living in the country—where deer, duck, and pheasant hunting was common—helped, too, because nobody panicked at the sound of a gunshot. I could fire all day long without raising an eyebrow.

Gunshots were just one part of my research. I also hit puddles of blood with bats, hammers, boards, and other blunt objects at different angles, rates of speed, and degrees of force. They generate a coarser mist with larger droplets than guns do—a pattern now classified as "medium-velocity spatter." I also scrutinized the cast-off that various weapons made on wood, metal, fabric, glass, and other surfaces. "Cast-off" is the term crime scene reconstructionists use to describe the blood that flies off a weapon as it's wielded repeatedly.

During the tests, I wore different types of clothes to find out how much blood soaks into certain fabrics and where it concentrates based on the type of attack—swinging a baseball bat, raising one for an overhead blow, and so on. One surprising observation I made was that during a beating, very little blood travels backward onto the attacker—the impact projects most of it forward onto walls, furnishings, and whatever else is in front of both attacker and victim. It's vitally important for homicide detectives, prosecutors, defense attorneys, and jurors to understand this concept, but plenty of them have a hard time believing it.

I filled page after page in notebook after notebook with my findings, documenting the visual effects with photos. Sometimes the experiments were purely theoretical; at other times they sprang from cases I was working and evidence that was puzzling me.

Case Study: The Twenty-Nine Slashes

Take the case of John Lee Hipsher, for example. Hipsher was a longtime transient, well-known in the homeless community that populated some of the parks in Portland. He was found dead one morning in early September 1983 at the end of a secluded hiking trail in Lewis & Clark State Park, lying next to a triangular pool of his own blood. His throat had been slashed twenty-nine times. The lower halves of his arms were covered in the blood-into-blood patterns and satellite spatter that occurs when blood drips repeatedly onto an area.

When I interviewed the other drifters who had been in the park the night Hipsher died, one told me he and Hipsher had been hanging out on a bench when a man and a woman walked by. "Hey!" Hipsher exclaimed. "There's the dude that stole my backpack. I'm gonna go get my stuff back." Hipsher then lumbered off in pursuit of the pair, according to his pal, and that was the last he had seen of any of them.

A few yards down from the spot where Hipsher's body was discovered lay a campsite with a fire pit. I searched it and found a partially eaten pear that someone had tossed away. I overnighted it to forensic odontologist Dr. William Alexander in Eugene, Oregon, to examine before it could decompose, taking vital clues with it. Today, we could most likely have retrieved DNA from the pear. But in the early 1980s, forensic technology was much more limited. Still, Dr. Alexander managed to extract some intriguing information from the fruit.

"Whoever ate this pear was missing a front tooth," he concluded. "The person was probably also wearing a Pendleton shirt, judging from the multicolored threads in the flesh of the pear."

Unfortunately, extensive searching turned up nobody fitting the suspect's description. It would be almost two years before we caught a break in the case—when narcotics agents in our office arrested a woman named Patricia Marcus* for drug possession.

"What if I tell you about a murder you never solved?" she offered, hoping to barter for reduced charges. "I know who did it. I saw it."

As soon as she started talking, I realized she was describing the Hipsher case—and she knew enough details to convince me that she was telling the truth. Marcus claimed she was partying in the park with her ex-boyfriend, Richard Salmon, when a bum approached them. Neither she nor Salmon knew the guy, but a heated argument soon erupted. According to Marcus, Salmon beat up the drifter, then dragged him off into the woods and cut his throat. They were all wasted at the time, she explained, but Salmon was violent even when sober, and she had been too scared of him to come forward until now.

I tracked Salmon down a few days later. Not only was he missing a front tooth, but he actually admitted to killing Hipsher. He insisted, however, that he had done it in self-defense. Hipsher had attacked him, shouting some cockamamie tale about stolen stuff, and he had had no choice but to protect himself. Yes, he was carrying a knife. Yes, he cut Hipsher's throat. But it was pure accident. He swung the blade wildly, trying to fend off the crazed derelict, and inadvertently caught Hipsher across the jugular. Terrified by the sight of all that blood pouring out, he and Patty bolted.

I didn't buy it. Not with twenty-nine slashes. Not with those peculiar blood patterns. I was sure the blood was the key to learning what really went on in that wooded corner of the park that night. My colleagues agreed. But when we dug the crime scene photos out of the files and reviewed them, the bloody triangle in the grass still mystified all of us. Nobody in homicide had seen one like it before.

In the following weeks, as soon as I finished work at the barn I conducted more experiments to re-create the Hipsher murder. I tried angle after angle to determine what would cause the patterns in the crime photos I had tacked up on the wall. No standing position I could think of produced a shape remotely resembling this one. Nor did any seated or prone position. Even if Hipsher had fallen on his side, arms bent toward his head to form a triangle, it didn't make sense. The blood was too evenly distributed between his right and left arms. Besides, Hipsher was found lying on his back, which meant he had bled into that triangle and then rolled or fallen over when he finally died.

At last, I hit on a possibility: What if Hipsher had been on his knees and elbows, with his forearms on the ground, hands clasped together, while his throat was being cut? Blood would have run into blood on the lower half of his arms as multiple wounds were inflicted, while more blood flowed onto the ground between his forearms, creating a gruesome triangle in the grass and dirt.

There was just one hitch: Hipsher's stance was hardly an attack pose. If my theory was right—and I was sure it was—Salmon's tale of self-defense was nonsense. He had forced the transient onto his hands and knees and held him there while he murdered him.

I ran the idea by the other detectives. They agreed, and we presented the evidence to the DA. Despite his efforts to thwart the prosecution by knocking out his other front tooth in his jail cell when he learned that the pear core might be damning evidence against him, Richard W. Salmon went to trial. The prosecutor invited me into the courtroom to reenact the murder and show the jury how a kneeling position would create a triangular pool of blood. They found Salmon guilty in the murder of John Lee Hipsher in 1986. At press time, he was eligible for release in 2010.

At Gunpoint

For most cops, homicide is the pinnacle—the assignment you slog through patrol, vice, robbery, and everything else to reach. Someone asked me recently if it was my favorite assignment as a cop, since my career now revolves around it. In truth, I loved every detail I covered over three decades with the Downey Police Department and the Multnomah County Sheriff's Office. They were all fascinating—and I learned something from each that I could later apply to murder investigations.

The most harrowing by far was undercover work. If you can handle it, you can handle seeing a bloody corpse. Working undercover steels you against the most dangerous and unpredictable aspects of police work.

The closest I came to getting killed was a buy-and-bust in the backseat of a car one night on Beaverton's Watson Street. The area was perfect for a heroin score—dark and deserted apart from myself and the dealer, who had a mop of bushy red hair and a beard to match. I had never met the guy, but I had spoken with him on the phone, and I knew he was hopped up on speed and coke. In person he was even cagier than I had anticipated, fidgeting and tugging at the overalls he wore over a grungy white T-shirt.

I handed him a wadded-up fistful of bills. He gave me a sealed plastic bag of drugs. But then he made an unexpected movement, smooth and swift. The next thing I knew, he was pressing a gun against my forehead.

"You a cop, man?" he demanded.

"Me? No way. I hate cops," I said, trying to stay calm and in character.

"Yeah?" he said, his eyes squinting suspiciously below deep frown lines. "You're lying. I know it."

I played dumb. I rattled off the names of all the users and small-timers from the local drug scene who had vouched for me. I was wearing a wire, and my backup team was listening nearby, but they were too far away to help. The signal to let them know that the deal had gone down was "good shit," but there was no verbal cue for "I'm about to get my brains blown out," so I just kept repeating the code, hoping they'd get the message that something was wrong.

"This is good shit, man. Really good shit. It's the shit. . . ."

The dealer pressed the Saturday night special harder against my head, eyeing me dubiously. A bead of sweat broke loose from my hairline and ran down my temple.

"This shit is the best! I told you, I ain't no cop. . . ."

"Maybe I believe you. Maybe I don't," he said. "But why take chances?"

And he pulled the trigger.

The gun was loaded, but to my indescribable relief, it misfired.

The dealer stared at it in surprise. "Man, you got lucky," he said, just as the sounds of screeching tires and slamming doors filled the air. Sharp as ever, my backup team had realized the deal was souring and raced to my aid. They swarmed over him as I stumbled out of the car, knees trembling. Dave Bishop, my friend and fellow narcotics officer who would go on to become chief of the Beaverton Police Department, looked nearly as shaken as I felt while he cuffed the dealer. Dave told me later that he was close enough to hear the click of the trigger and thought I was a goner.

My would-be assassin cursed and spat and called me every name he could think of. "I shoulda killed you when I had the chance," he growled. "I *knew* you were a cop!"

Ignoring the spate of threats, I read him his rights and shoved him in the back of a police car as the last of my energy drained away, the adrenaline fueling it finally tapped out. Today, a cop would likely get a month's time off to recover mentally from an ordeal like that. He would undergo a battery of psychological tests to make sure he could still function. But in those days, you just showed up for work the next morning and tried to convince yourself that nothing had happened. For years that's exactly what I did—until writing this book brought the memory flooding back in vivid detail and reminded me how very lucky I am to be alive.

The gun that came so close to killing me was admitted into evidence, along with the package of heroin I was "buying" and other incriminating items we found on the red-haired dealer, who turned out to be a Canadian wanted by authorities back home. He was deported with a warning that if he ever showed up in Oregon again, he would be prosecuted for attempted murder.

Code Zero

Another night, I was driving home in my unmarked car after a long shift with Carl Flint,* a partner assigned to me a few months earlier, and an undercover agent named Tina Verdi.* Tina worked for a bail bondsman, and we had recently recruited her to make undercover buys for us. She was a natural and later went on to become a superb policewoman.

We had just dropped off my good friend and undercover colleague Chuck Fessler at his house, and my mind was on the fact that I now had to go home and head straight to the barn. I was ruminating—as I sometimes did in the middle of the night when I was tired enough to keel over and fall asleep in the front seat of my car—about whether the cattle business had been a wise choice of sidelines for a guy whose full-time job already kept him up half the night.

We were passing through an old section of Portland, where the empty streets were lined with modest houses, their windows dark. Then I spied a parked car and the shadowy outline of four men sitting inside it. As we drove past, I spotted a telltale fiery orange flare and the familiar silhouetted profile of someone with a joint pressed to his lips.

"This will only take a second," I assured Carl and Tina. "I'm not going to bust them. I'll just check them out."

Easing my car over in front of theirs, I told the dispatcher I was checking a vehicle at Twentieth and Gladstone. Then I cut the engine and walked back to tap on the car's window. The driver lowered it and looked up at me, the familiar acrid scent of burning marijuana spilling out of the darkened interior. I flashed my badge and told him he and his buddies would have to knock it off or be arrested.

He stared at me blearily, then shrugged. "Okay, man," he said. And he closed the window.

I got back in the car and drove away.

Less than a minute had passed when the glare of headlights suddenly turned my rearview mirror blindingly white and the furious rumble of an accelerating engine filled our ears. I squinted into the mirror, shocked to see the car I had just stopped inches away. It rammed my bumper and sent us skidding down the street. As I struggled to control the steering wheel, the car flew past, spun around, and sped straight back at us as if we were contenders in a late night demolition derby. With no time to move out of the way, we sat helplessly watching the ominous glare of headlights barrel toward us. The impact flung us across the seat, and the ear-piercing shriek of metal on metal ripped through the quiet neighborhood.

"What the hell are they doing?" I asked.

Tires squealed as the car reversed and charged again. Balancing my hands on the steering wheel, I took aim and fired my .38 through my windshield. Across the front seat, Carl did the same. But our bullets missed the men in the car. (I later learned that mine hit the front seat, inches under the driver's arm, and lodged in the back just over the head of one of the passengers, who had wisely crouched down out of the way.)

I had to get Tina out of there. She was an unarmed civilian working for us as a volunteer. If she got hurt, there would be hell to pay.

"One six nine! Shots fired! Code zero," I shouted into the radio. "Shots fired. Repeat, shots fired." It was Multnomah County's equivalent of Downey's nine ninety-nine—a numeric urgent distress call for "Officer needs help!"

Then I grabbed Tina's arm. "I'll be back in a second," I told Carl as I yanked her out of the car. We sprinted through a line of trees toward the nearest house as the dopers' car came careening up on the lawn behind us like a gored bull charging after a matador, sending dirt and debris flying.

We leapt across the porch and banged on the door. "Police!" I cried. "Police! Open up!"

A moment later, the door cracked open and an elderly woman peered out through a sliver of light, clutching at her bathrobe.

"What's going on?" she demanded. "I heard gunshots!"

"I'm a police officer, ma'am," I explained hurriedly, flashing my badge. "We've got some trouble and I need to keep Tina here with you where she'll be safe. I'll come back for her."

"All right," she said, opening the door wider and squinting curiously past us toward the darkened lawn.

"Keep it locked," I warned. Behind me, I could hear the whine of tires on grass and the crunch of metal hitting wood. The crazy bastards were tearing up the lawn, trying to get through the trees to reach me.

I ran back toward them, my gun aimed again at their windshield. When they saw me, all four men stepped out of the car, their silhouettes illuminated in the glare of the headlights. Behind them, I could see their smashed fender dangling precariously.

Where the hell was Carl? Had they knocked him out? Run over him? I peered into the darkness behind the damaged car. Maybe he was lying on the street somewhere beyond my line of vision.

"Man, you picked the wrong car to fuck with," the ringleader said.

I pointed my gun at his head. "Police!" I shouted, holding up my badge. "Nobody move!"

"I don't see a uniform on you," he said. "How do I know you're a cop?"

"Yeah," another chimed in. "How do we know that's a real badge? Let me get a closer look at that thing."

Why couldn't we have run into these guys *before* dropping off Chuck? He and I had improvised our way through life-threatening jams during buy-and-busts. I sure could have used his help now.

"You take one step forward and you're dead," I warned, keeping my finger on the trigger.

He hesitated and glanced at his friend, who was still sizing me up, his head cocked to one side.

At first they made no move toward me, unsure whether to take my threats seriously. Then the ringleader seemed to make his decision. He took a step forward when out of the darkness came the wail of sirens. As the sound swelled, ear-piercing and echoing over the houses, my shoulders sagged with relief. I felt suddenly as if I were back in the parking lot behind Tahitian Village.

A moment later, police cars roared up and county cops leapt out, guns aimed at the men surrounding me. In the commotion, I caught sight of Carl slinking out from behind a cedar sapling thirty yards away. Rage coursed through me as I realized he had been cowering back there the whole time.

Keeping his eyes averted, he slunk over and fell in stride beside me.

"Where the fuck were you?" I demanded.

He mumbled something about running out of bullets.

I'm generally a forgiving person, but I refused to work with Carl after that. We nearly came to blows several times at the sheriff's office.

"You were crazy for going out there! What the hell were you thinking?" he shouted at me, bolder now that he was back in the safety of the station.

"What the hell were *you* thinking?" I yelled back.

Chuck, who learned what happened when he saw the bullet holes in my windshield the next day, stepped in to diffuse the tension more than once.

Partners in any endeavor need a certain level of trust, and when you're a cop, that need intensifies. You have to know beyond doubt that the person who is supposed to be watching your back is going to rush in—not run away.

Carl left the sheriff's office a short time later, and I didn't bother to keep track of his whereabouts. His actions served as a harsh reminder to me that not everybody has the temperament or the stomach for police work, even when there is not a drop of blood involved.

Changing Lives

In my experience, every assignment will help make you a better cop if you're smart enough to put your heart into it and learn from it. The one that taught me the most about human nature was community policing.

Although I have put my share of criminals behind bars, I have always been a proponent of helping people turn their lives around. I spent more than a decade as a youth group leader for my church, counseling troubled teens who would show up at the door begging for shelter in the middle of the night. Perhaps that's why in 1989 I was assigned to spearhead a community-policing effort in Portland's infamous Columbia Villa.

The place spanned only one square mile, but it was a nightmare of squalid, subsidized housing projects, infested with Crips gang members and rife with violence and drugs. Wearing red—the signature color of the rival Bloods gang—was enough to get you killed in Columbia Villa. The rat-tat of gunfire ricocheted off the shabby buildings on a daily basis, from drive-by shootings, bravado "hits" by gang initiates trying to make their bones, and random shots into the air that were as apt to hit a child or senior citizen as they were to hit their intended targets.

Black, white, Hispanic, and other ethnic groups lived shoulder to shoulder in the dilapidated buildings, overcrowded with about seventeen hundred residents. Hardworking single moms and elderly pensioners shared walls and corridors with criminals whose rap sheets went on for pages. Come Friday night, the population would swell to about five thousand as gangbangers poured in like lit matches to tinder, igniting the already dangerous place.

I researched tactics other police forces had used successfully to clean up crime-ridden neighborhoods, flew to several cities to see them firsthand, and then handpicked four deputies to help me. I gave them bicycles to store on racks on the backs of their patrol cars and orders to knock on ten doors during every shift. Gradually we got to know the people, found out what was going on in the community, and built trust. We formed a steering committee of residents, joined forces with social workers, took the kids on fishing trips, helped the unemployed find jobs, and counseled preteens on how to stay in school and out of the gangs that doubled as a fast pass to prison. Gradually, the residents began to stand up to the bad guys and take back their community, and we found ourselves with more informants than we knew what to do with.

I watched dozens of people pull themselves out of poverty and despair and fight their way to happier lives, but the most inspiring was Michelle Thompson.* A longtime dealer, user, and prostitute, Michelle came from a line of drug addicts. Her dad had died of an overdose when she was a kid, and—judging from the apathy she seemed to show the two dirty, disheveled preschoolers I often saw straggling along at her heels—she was bent on continuing the family tradition.

My instinct would have been to write Michelle off as a lost cause.

She was a chronic thorn in our sides—defiant, antagonistic, and back to hustling the moment she got out of jail. But my deputies wouldn't give up on her. They paid her regular visits, always treating her politely despite her foulmouthed belligerence toward them. At last the façade began to crack, and Michelle timidly confessed a desire to change her life. We enlisted some women from my church to revamp her wardrobe and teach her how to handle a job interview. Then we got her part-time filing work at the sheriff's office, checking weekly to make sure her arms were free of track marks.

Life was looking up for Michelle as Christmastime drew near. She was off drugs, getting to the office on time, and—she confided in us—hoping to scrape together enough cash to buy a tricycle for her kids.

But ultimately, funds were too short. Christmas morning arrived, and glancing around the bleak apartment, seeing the crestfallen looks on her kids' faces, was too much. Who was she kidding? None of them would ever get out of this life, she told herself bitterly. Might as well score some dope and escape it for a few hours. She grabbed her coat and told her kids she would be back soon. She was heading to the door when someone on the other side knocked. Figuring it was one of her old junkie customers, she flung it open irritably, ready to tell him to get lost. Instead, she found two deputies in uniform grinning at her.

"What do you want?" she snapped.

"Merry Christmas to you, too, Michelle," said one, still smiling amiably. "Mind if we talk to you for a minute?"

Michelle eyed them cynically. She knew both of them well by now. They had helped her land the filing job. But she was in no mood to be civil.

"It's not a good time," she said brusquely. "You'll have to come back."

"I really think it would be in your best interest to come outside," one persisted.

"And bring your kids," the other added.

She sighed resignedly and motioned the kids to follow her.

When they stepped outside onto the porch, Michelle's children gasped in delight. Hidden behind the deputies was a shiny green tricycle with a bow and a deputy's star painted below the handlebars.

"Merry Christmas!" they told her as the kids rushed eagerly to the bike, running their hands over the polished metal and vying for space on the seat.

Michelle, fighting back tears, learned that one of the deputies was a diver, and while searching for a body in the river that fall, he had discovered a tricycle—rusted, forlorn, and missing a wheel—stuck in mud in a riverbed. He'd wrestled it out of the muck, hauled it home, and spent weeks repairing it, painting and polishing each piece, getting it ready for Michelle's family, knowing how much her kids wanted a tricycle.

Michelle is now employed full-time with a utilities company and attending college. Nobody knocks on her door in the dead of night looking to score, and her kids know their mom isn't going to wander off in search of heroin on Christmas morning.

She became such a believer in community policing that she volunteered to speak at several seminars I ran on our program.

We always had her come in as her old self—leather, tattoos, and stilettos, oozing attitude. I would introduce her, give the "backstory" on her, and ask the audience how they would handle someone like her. We were in Florida when a gruff, middle-aged sergeant slouched in the front row muttered a disparaging remark.

Michelle caught it and, thoroughly in character, spat back, "Fuck you!" loudly enough for the whole audience to hear.

The sergeant sneered, shrugged, and glanced at me.

"What a bitch," he said, rolling his eyes. "I'd put her in jail and throw away the keys. Forget her."

Michelle left, and we spent the next two days in breakout groups discussing community policing. On the third day, she reappeared, this time clad in work clothes, acting polite and professional. Not one person recognized her.

"I'm here to tell you about my relationship with cops," she began. "I'll give you an idea of how to treat people differently, how we can treat you differently, and how we can all help each other."

As she spoke, she strolled over to a blanket that had been draped over an object on a folding table, unnoticed during the entire program.

"My story is under this blanket," she said, and she told them about the holiday gift that changed her life. "That was me. I was at the bottom of the river. I couldn't sink any lower," she said. "But the police put air in my tires. They were there for me. And I surfaced."

By the time she finished, everyone was crying. The irascible old sergeant got up, hugged her, and apologized all over himself, vowing to help implement a program like Columbia Villa's when he got home.

Losing Big

But while Michelle was defying the odds to get her life back on track, some of my brightest colleagues let theirs fall into irreparable shambles. When my phone used to ring in the middle of the night, I knew that if it wasn't a troubled teenager from the church's youth group, it would be my old buddy Phil Weston* from the L.A. County Sheriff's Department—the resourceful, no-nonsense cop who gave me the inspiration for the scrap tortillas that saved my cattle business. He had always had an active life outside the force and logged as many punishing hours on his farm as I did on mine, but when he retired he couldn't move on. Police work had given him an anchor. Now he was adrift.

During Phil's years in L.A., he and I had worked closely with

another great undercover cop named Vic Calzeretta. Vic was a former Chicago Police Department officer who joined the Clark County
Sheriff's Office in Vancouver, Washington, where he headed up narcotics investigations virtually single-handedly when he arrived. In the
early 1970s, the three of us conducted a series of successful multi-
state drug stings together, often with help from other departments. It
was risky, high-adrenaline work—the type of adventure you remember fondly once it's over and you know you survived. But now Phil
was keeping me on the phone for hours, rehashing old cases, his
voice growing more and more slurred, his thoughts more disjointed.
He did the same to Vic, who had left police work to become a lawyer.
Finally the two of us reluctantly checked Phil into rehab, guilt-
ridden but assuring ourselves that it was for the best.

Two weeks later I got a call from Phil's treatment center.

"Rod, ya gotta get me outta here," Phil said. "I'm losing my mind."

"Can't do it, Phil," I told him.

"Our friendship is over if you don't."

Foolishly, I drove back to the treatment center—a top-of-the-line
retreat where celebrities often went to kick the habit—only to catch
Phil mixing cough syrup and gin before noon the next day. A few
years later he killed himself.

Doug Vanderson's* story was just as tragic. Doug was the fair-
haired boy of the Downey police force when I met him—smart, funny,
charming, and a shoo-in to become the next chief of police. He had
a happy marriage and three adorable daughters, but then he fell for
another cop's ex-wife. Rumors started flitting around the office like
gnats that Doug was sneaking off to meet her every night while he
was supposed to be commander in charge of the shift.

Furious, the deputy chief staged a stakeout. Sure enough, he saw
Doug stroll out the woman's front door in his uniform pants and a

T-shirt to pick up the newspaper—all while he was supposed to be on duty. When Doug got back to the station at three A.M., the deputy chief told him, "I've got two pieces of paper. One is your resignation. The other is your termination. Choose."

Doug refused to sign either form. He called me in Oregon, begging for help, so I testified on his behalf at a city council arbitration hearing. I told them we had worked together closely and Doug was a good cop, honest and hardworking. His brother Stan* was a heroin dealer, and I knew Doug was determined to carve out a different path.

But Doug got fired anyway. Out of loyalty and concern for his wife and daughters, I got him a job with the Beaverton Police Department in 1979. His family moved in with ours for three months and then finally bought a little farm six miles from mine. We got together often, just as we had done in Downey.

One weekend while Doug and I were barbecuing as our kids played in the yard, he told me he had landed part-time security work for a diamond dealer. Working overtime to support his wife and kids sounded like a good move to me. But several months later, I was getting ready to go elk hunting with friends early one morning when an article in the newspaper caught my eye:

"A spokesperson for the Seattle police department says that shortly before 5 p.m. yesterday a diamond dealer was approached by three men while exiting a Seattle jewelry store. They robbed him of a briefcase containing a large dollar value of diamonds and cash. The suspects, who escaped on foot, are described as three Caucasian males in their late thirties. . . ."

I read on, more and more convinced that the perpetrators were Doug, Stan, and an ex-con pal of Stan's named Robbie,* whom I had met once back in Downey. Before I left the house, I called the FBI.

As soon as I got back from my hunting trip, I confronted Doug. "I read about that robbery," I told him as we sat parked in his Volkswagen. "I know you're involved." When he opened his mouth to protest, I cut him off. "I don't wanna know. I'm not gonna testify, but you should know I called the FBI."

His silence told me more than a confession. When an undercover FBI agent managed to buy some of the lost diamonds from Stan a few days later, my fears were confirmed.

All three men were arrested and charged, but Doug, with his irrepressible charm, won over the jury and beat the rap. Unfortunately, during the two days he spent in jail before making bail, his cellmate slipped him a phone number for his sister. "You gotta meet Trish*," the guy said.

For reasons I'll never fathom, Doug did. He left his long-suffering wife and moved in with the woman, who was a con and a dealer just like her brother. After that, we all gave up on Doug.

In 1980, less than a year after what was supposed to be Doug's new start, I got a call at three A.M. from Larry Stephens, a friend of mine with Oregon's Salem Police Department. "Rod, I've got some bad news," he said. "We had a shooting tonight. We've got two people in custody, and Doug Vanderson's the victim."

I sat on the edge of my bed, speechless, remembering the undercover operations Larry, Doug, and I had worked before Doug's life came apart—before he traded his wife and daughters for a dope-dealing girlfriend. Apparently, Doug was at Trish's house when several of her "clients" showed up with loaded guns, knowing she kept drugs and cash lying around. Doug heard them crash through the front door and slipped out the back. He started smashing windows to draw their attention and give Trish a chance to escape, but one of them followed him and opened fire to stop the racket. He shot Doug eight times with a rifle.

I broke the news to his estranged wife and daughters, drove the eldest child to the funeral home, and gave Doug's eulogy, sharing memories of my old friend from earlier, happier times.

Though it's no excuse for what happened to Phil or to Doug, juggling police work with family life can admittedly be tough. Nearly everyone I knew on the force went through his or her share of personal struggles. Carolyn and I separated in 1980 and divorced five years later.

Not long after Doug Vanderson's death, I was fortunate enough to give a lecture on blood patterns at a forensics conference. After I had finished speaking, I was putting my notes away when a beautiful woman named Penny approached me and said she had a few questions about my lecture. Penny and I married in 1986, and she has been a great support in both my life and my career. She does plenty of her own fascinating work as well. As a dental hygienist with an interest in forensic odontology, she was part of a National Disaster Medical System (NDMS) Disaster Mortuary Operational Response Team (DMORT) that assisted local medical examiners' offices in identifying bodies through their dental records after the World Trade Center and Hurricane Katrina disasters. She also spent several years designing and perfecting every aspect of my lab, which took me from the drafty, cavernous barn and makeshift garage space of my early consulting days to a state-of-the-art facility where everything is user-friendly and at my fingertips, whether it's case files, slides, high-intensity lighting equipment, or bottles of the luminescent chemicals I use to reveal hidden traces of blood spatter.

Murder Mysteries

By the time I met Penny, I had been investigating murders for a number of years—since 1975, when I became a homicide detective for the

Multnomah County Sheriff's Office. I still remember my first case vividly.

Successful forty-nine-year-old businessman James Turel, a polio survivor, was found strangled and beaten to death with his own crutches in the offices of his company, the Columbia Bookkeeping Service, on August 29, 1974. My partner, Joe Woods, and I inherited his murder investigation from renowned detective Blackie Yazzolino when he retired, and our first step was to review the crime scene photos and the original detectives' notes. Though money was missing from the victim's wallet and the vault was open, the scene looked too neat for a robbery. There was no sign of forced entry, and none of the desks or file cabinets had been disturbed. In fact, all signs suggested Turel had been murdered by someone he knew.

Rod Addicks, a tax accountant and partial owner of Turel's company, drew our attention right away. First, Addicks had refused to take a polygraph test when questioned along with other firm employees after Turel's death. Second, shortly before his death, Turel had confided in his son Stan that he had grown uneasy about Addicks because a house belonging to Addicks had burned down just sixty days after it was purchased. Addicks, he said, seemed downright glib about the fire. Turel suspected arson and told Stan he was checking into the man's background.

Months of investigation proved that James Turel's instincts were on the mark. We dug up a load of dirt on the seemingly clean-cut and mild-mannered Addicks, including allegations of securities fraud and arson in several states. When incriminating evidence surfaced linking Turel's former seasonal tax preparer, Si Cross, to the arson ring, Cross offered to help with the homicide investigation in exchange for immunity. He told us that Addicks had tried on multiple occasions to hire him and several other men he knew, including his cousin, to kill Turel. Cross agreed initially—for a fee of $5,000—but ultimately couldn't go through with the murder. When he backed out, Addicks and a man named Dennis Lee Cartwright—a hunting buddy and childhood friend of Addicks's who was already on parole for assault and battery in Washington—committed the murder themselves. Addicks even bragged about it, Cross said.

After Addicks and Dennis Lee Cartwright were arrested, Cartwright confessed to his part in the murder. His version of events matched Cross's. Cartwright went to prison for murder, though he was paroled after serving thirteen years. Addicks was found guilty of arson, securities fraud, and murder and sentenced to life in prison. While there, he launched a multitude of lawsuits, from a $2 million suit against *Official Detective Stories* magazine for libel to a $5 million suit against the victim's son Stan Turel—who Addicks claimed was secretly a police agent—for allegedly violating his Fourth and Fifth Amendment rights. (The costs of lawsuits launched by prisoners are underwritten by taxpayers.) Though the suits were largely unsuccessful, Addicks was paroled by the states of Oregon and Washington in 1989.

The Deadly Trio

As I investigated more homicides, I learned that most people commit murder for one of three reasons: money, sex, or revenge. If you are astute and you know what to look for at a murder scene, you can often spot clues that reveal which motive inspired the crime—a broken window, a busted lock, or ransacked drawers suggest a break-in; semen on or around the victim indicates that intercourse has recently taken place; and so on. In other cases, delving into the victim's background unearths the motive: Was she a woman with a broken romance and a violent-tempered ex-lover? Was he in a heated struggle with a business partner for control of a company they shared? Were they double-crossing associates in a drug deal? In James Turel's case, Addicks stood to lose a huge amount of money if Turel exposed his shady business dealings and ousted him from the firm.

Sometimes you know instinctively that a killer's actions arose from one of the three common motivations, but you can't prove it. Such was the case in the death of little Larisa L. Wahnita, a six-year-old girl we found stabbed to death in her bedroom in 1977. Her mother's boyfriend, Phyll Mendacino, admitted to killing her, but his story about how it happened would have been laughable if it hadn't been so tragic. Mendacino claimed Larisa was jumping up and down on the bed and he warned her to stop. She didn't. So he tried to stop her while holding his knife, and she jumped into it—more than eighty times.

Child murders have always been the hardest for me to handle emotionally, so it was horrible seeing Larisa's body covered in stab wounds, lying on the floor next to her bed. My gut told me Mendacino had made some kind of sexual advance on Larisa and then flown into a rage at her reaction. I had seen it often enough before to recognize the signs. But there was no way to prove it. Ultimately, he was convicted of murder, and bringing out lurid details about whatever his motive may have been wouldn't have changed anything in the sentence.

Like every other homicide detective, I've made my share of misinterpretations and missed key evidence more than once. I had already been working homicide for eight years when the phone rang at four A.M. one chilly November morning in 1983. My family and I had tickets to the Oregon–Oregon State football game, but instead I got dragged out of bed to respond to a homicide in one of Portland's wealthy, old-money neighborhoods. The scene was a bloodbath. Unbeknownst to his family, Robert Galloway, owner of the successful J&J Construction Company, was on the verge of bankruptcy. Rather than face the humiliation of losing it all, he decided to end it and take his entire family out with him—even the dog. As we soon learned, he told his two older sons he was worried about burglars and needed them to sleep in sleeping bags in the J&J offices. Then he showed up in the wee hours and shot them both. Afterward he drove to Elmer's Pancake House and ate breakfast, before heading home and shooting his wife and his youngest son. His teenage daughter heard the gunfire and called 911. I still have the tape of her screaming, "Dad, Dad, don't!" and the sound of shell casings hitting the floor with a metallic ping like a handful of dimes dropping on hardwood as he jettisoned them. You can hear Galloway reload, then a bang and a yelp as the dog is shot. There is one final shot as he points the gun at himself and fires.

Lucky for me we had the tape to tell us what happened. But I still managed to miss vital blood evidence that I should have noticed on the scene—namely, blood transfers covering the light switch in the daughter's room, which would have proved Galloway's hands were covered in his family's blood before he touched it, had there been any doubt as to who was behind the rest of the Galloway family members' murders.

At other times, I wasn't so lucky. We never solved the murder of elderly Eunice Karr. In 1984, she was found dead, bound and strangled, in her tiny cottage home in a neighborhood known as Parkrose. Her body had been posed on the bed with various objects placed around it, including a paper cross positioned upside down in one of her hands. We suspected the killer or killers were after the numerous antiques that filled her home but were trying to throw us off the trail by staging a bizarre murder scene.

In the months that followed Karr's death, whoever masterminded it started sending notes to us through the personals ads in the local papers with messages like "You're on the wrong track" and "I don't want to work with Detective Pritchard."

We answered them: "Pritchard no longer involved. You are crafty and clever, but time is on our side. Signed, Peterson and Englert."

Karr's niece called me every year on the anniversary of her aunt's death until I retired from the sheriff's office. I always had to tell her the same thing: "I'm sorry, but I haven't found your aunt's killer yet." Advancing technology is at last bringing new hope to unsolved cases like Eunice Karr's. The cords, the paper cross, even the victim's clothing might well be covered in minute traces of her killer's DNA. But when Eunice Karr was murdered, we lacked the science to analyze the evidence we found. Now, as part of Multnomah County sheriff Robert Skipper's special cold case team, we are reexamining unsolved crimes like the murder of Eunice Karr. We can enlist area labs to comb preserved evidence for fragments of DNA and cross-check any samples they extract for matches with criminal profiles in state and national databases.

Case Study: The Pizza Boy's Missing Body

Some of the most compelling cases I ran across while working homicide were those where the body was missing and the only evidence we had to go on was blood. A perfect example was the case of a young man named Daniel W. Pierce in Troutdale. When Pierce failed to show up for his shift at a local Pizza Hut in March 1986, one of his coworkers called his girlfriend. Puzzled, she headed to his apartment, where she found no sign of Pierce, but was alarmed to discover what she thought might be blood in his bedroom. She called the sheriff's office, so my partner, Joe Woods, and I went to the apartment to investigate.

When we searched Pierce's bedroom, the first thing we noticed were wrinkled, uneven bedcovers. The bed had obviously been hastily made. On a hunch, we pulled them back. Underneath the top layers was a large, telltale dark stain. Somebody had bled all over the mattress. I crouched down and took a closer look at the wall. There were a number of brownish red spots up and down it. Smeared sections suggested someone had tried hurriedly to wipe them away.

We collected blood samples, took photographs, and admitted some of the missing man's belongings into evidence.

We also interviewed Daniel Pierce's roommate, a twentysomething by the name of Dan Brown, who claimed he knew nothing of Pierce's whereabouts.

"He probably crashed with some friends," Brown said casually. "He'll turn up." His attitude seemed a little too blasé to be genuine.

Actually, there wasn't much of anything genuine about Brown, as it turned out. First, we ran a DMV check on the car he was driving and found out that it was a stolen vehicle from Seattle. Next, we learned he was using an alias. His real name was Socrates E. Ladner.

We booked Ladner on suspicion of murder and took him down to process him. We searched the apartment thoroughly but found no weapons. Nor did anything suspicious turn up among Ladner's belongings, though we impounded the stolen car he had been driving and towed it to the police lot.

One of the lab technicians concluded that the droplets we had found in Pierce's room were the result of a gunshot to the head. But applying what I had learned from my own experiments and studying blood pattern analysis, I disagreed. The spatter didn't look fine enough to be high-velocity mist. To me, this looked more like the medium-velocity spatter that comes from a beating.

The guys in the crime lab smirked at my theory. "You're way off," they said. "That analysis stuff's nonsense." These were, incidentally, some of the same experts who were scoffing at the relevance of the rapidly emerging field of DNA analysis to forensics. Eventually, we removed a section of the bedroom's blood-spattered east wall to present in court as evidence.

Under questioning at the sheriff's office, Ladner continued to insist that he knew nothing about his roommate's disappearance. He had been hanging out with friends, he said, and come home to find Pierce gone. He hadn't thought much of it—even when the guy failed to turn up the next night—because they led very separate lives.

With no other leads and no evidence to hold Ladner, we were coming to an impasse when we suddenly remembered the impounded car. We hurried out to the lot behind the station, popped open the trunk, and saw an ominous-looking black plastic bag with something lumpy inside. The foul odor emanating from it left little doubt about the contents. Joe and I looked at each other. Neither of us was clamoring to open it.

He shrugged. "You're closest," he said. "You do the honors."

I grasped the edges gingerly and pulled them back so we could peer inside.

"Holy cow!"

I shook my head and looked in the bag again, pulling its edges farther back to let more light fall on the gory contents. I knew I was staring at the severed hands and head of Daniel Pierce, but the face looked just like that of my oldest son, Gary. I closed my eyes, shook my head, and looked again, working hard to steady my breathing and waiting for the features of the decapitation victim to swim into focus. Finally, I managed to convince myself that I was staring into the lifeless face of Daniel Pierce and not my own son.

We went back inside and confronted Ladner about the gruesome discovery we had just made.

"Want to tell us about what's in the trunk of your car?"

At last, he confessed. Yes, he said, he had killed his roommate. He was having money troubles, and Pierce was hoarding enough cash to cover all his debts. Unfortunately, the guy didn't want to part with it.

Ladner went on to explain that he snuck into Pierce's room and beat him to death while he was sleeping, proving my theory about the medium-velocity spatter. Next he decapitated his victim and removed his hands, which explained the large amount of blood soaked into the mattress. Finally, he told us we would find the rest of Pierce's body if we searched a secluded spot on Mount Hood, a favorite local dumping ground for murder victims. He even mapped out where we needed to dig. We followed his directions and soon unearthed the headless body of the missing teenager.

As this and other cases taught me, blood at a crime scene presents an invaluable window into what happened—and what didn't. Even now when I walk into a scene, I focus immediately on the blood. What does it suggest about the victim? What does it say about the killer? About the manner of death? About the motive?

Like footprints, bloodshed leads in a certain direction—toward specific conclusions and away from others. And like fingerprints, it illuminates who did what. It can explain how the attacker struck, reveal what the victim did in his final moments of life, and detail the actions the killer took after the murder. Often the clues to be found in blood yield more vital information than those found on the body itself. Whenever I walk into a crime scene, I glance repeatedly at the blood while I examine other elements of the scene to gauge how each relates to the spatter or pooling patterns I'm seeing. Eventually, the blood almost always reveals its secrets.

Chronicles of a Crime
Scene Reconstructionist

IN THE EARLY 1970S, the field of blood pattern analysis was still developing—and still widely derided—but conferences cropped up here and there. Whenever I heard about them, I signed up. I paid my own way and went on my own time, since most of the men in my department would have scoffed at the subject matter. I disagreed. But I did find myself getting frustrated as I sat in a lecture hall at the Southern Police Institute in Louisville, Kentucky, in 1976, ostensibly expanding my knowledge of how to interpret bloodshed at crime scenes.

For the past twenty minutes, I had been filling my notebook with more unanswered questions than useful information. In the margins I had scrawled a slew of "What about . . ." queries and "Remember to double-check . . ." notes reminding myself to examine photos from my files, refer to my old case notes, and conduct further experiments to find out exactly how the information from this lecture might apply to a real crime scene. I glanced around surreptitiously at some of the cops filling the seats nearby to see whether their faces registered any of the dissatisfaction I felt. Some seemed to be listening intently, but others were gazing off into space or carrying on their own conversations.

What was going on here? At last, I realized what the problem was: The professor lecturing had never actually been on a crime scene. He had never stood over a corpse lying in a puddle of congealing blood, trying to figure out what the plasma collecting at the edges revealed about the time of death. He had never scrutinized blood matted with hair, bone, and tissue fragments on a wall, trying to discern what it told about the murder weapon used. Sure, the speaker knew the *science* of blood. But his lecture was frustratingly far removed from the gritty, real-world contexts in which cops see it. What I really needed—what we all needed—was someone who could combine an academic's knowledge with a veteran detective's field experience.

Yes, blood droplets leave a different shape when they hit carpet than when they hit linoleum. True, they make a teardrop with a pointed tail when they land at an angle. But how does that information help a homicide detective catch a killer? We needed someone who could teach us to read the types of blood patterns you find at murder scenes and how to use that information to solve a crime. We needed someone to show us examples of real blood spatter from real homicides and tell us what they revealed about the weapons used, the motive for the murder, the relationship between the killer and the victim, and so on—and to explain the role those clues played in catching offenders.

After the lecture, I edged my way through the crowd of about 160 attendees to find Raymond Dahl, the ex–chief of police who had organized the conference. He was a gruff, intimidating bear of a man—not the kind of guy anyone strolls up to easily to spout out suggestions that might be misconstrued as criticisms.

"Listen, I've been thinking . . . ," I started tentatively. Then I launched headlong into an unrehearsed explanation of the lecture I wanted to hear at the next conference.

"Why don't you do it?" he asked.

"What? No . . . ," I stammered. "That's not what I was suggesting—"

"Why not?" he said, cutting me off. "You've got field experience. You've been to hundreds of crime scenes. You do crime scene reconstruction, don't you? You could give a talk like that."

A few minutes later, I had gotten myself drafted into giving the seminar I wanted to attend. Dahl thought it was a brilliant idea, and he wasn't taking no for an answer. My name was officially added to the roster for the next conference he was organizing.

By the time my plane landed back in Portland, I was regretting ever having approached Dahl. Why had I shot my mouth off like that? I had promised to stand up in front of dozens of my peers—guys who probably knew just as much as or more than I did—and tell them how to do their jobs better.

At the Podium

Determined not to make a fool of myself, I pored over the notebooks from old cases that filled box after box in my house, culling every point I found related to blood evidence. I combed bookstores and libraries and read every book I could find from medical texts—though there were precious few textbooks on the topic—to true crime paperbacks that mentioned blood patterns.

Months later, dressed for my first homicide investigation lecture, I surveyed myself doubtfully in the mirror. I adjusted my shirt cuffs and tugged nervously at my navy blue suit and vest to smooth out any wrinkles. Maybe this would be like a football game, where the butterflies disappear as soon as you get hit. Maybe my anxiety would vanish when I stepped onstage. I reminded myself of the advice L. D. Morgan, the deputy chief back in Downey, gave me before my first PTA narcotics talk years earlier: "You know more about your subject than they do." Then I forced my feet numbly toward the lectern at the front of a room packed with cops from around the country. I braced myself to hear snores, snickers, or scoffing, unsure which would make me feel worst.

My cousin Ralph, by then detective lieutenant of the San Angelo Police Department; my brother, Mickey, a homicide detective in San Angelo; my friend Fred Dietz, another San Angelo homicide detective, whom we knew and liked so well that he was an honorary member of our family; and some of their fellow officers had enrolled and filled the front rows to give me moral support. They grinned encouragement as I fumbled through the notes and slides I had prepared so painstakingly, doing my best to put all the scientific facts I had culled into the context of actual crime scenes I had handled. I tried to be candid and specific about how blood clues had led and misled me, how they revealed when a body had been moved or manipulated to mislead the police, and when an accomplice or a witness had been on the scene and lied about his actions. I told them about the times blood had helped me catch murderers and the times it might have done so if only I had known how to read it more accurately.

Finally, I stepped gratefully away from the microphone. I gathered up my notes hurriedly, eager to clear out before the criticism started. When I looked up, I was surprised to see Dahl give a thumbs-up from the back of the room. People were forming a line to talk with me.

"I've got this case I've been working on. I wonder if I could get your opinion on it. . . ."

"Would you be willing to take a look at some photos from one of our crime scenes?"

So it went with cop after cop.

"I'm not sure I'll be able to help," I kept telling them.

"Just take a look. See what you think," they said.

Any good cop knows that when you get more minds working on a case, you tend to get more effective results. You bring different perspectives to the puzzle and you increase the accumulated experience exponentially, particularly when you put veteran detectives in the mix. My talk convinced a number of my peers that my particular knowledge might help shed light on the cases where blood evidence was stumping them. So began the most fascinating stage of my career and what has grown into my life's work.

My supervisors in Multnomah County gave me the go-ahead, and soon I found myself lecturing a few times a year as well as consulting informally on weekends, handling what amounted to about four or five cases annually. The sheriff viewed my emerging sideline as good publicity for the work we were doing in the county. As far as he was concerned, it proved how strong our expertise was and how far our reputation reached. We were a midsize department, but we were well recognized for thorough, effective police work. Our achievements stemmed in part from the fact that we were among the first police departments in the United States to require all our officers to hold a bachelor's degree—a strict policy in the Multnomah County Sheriff's Office ever since 1966.

Unfortunately, some of my colleagues were less encouraging, and my sideline inspired a certain amount of jealousy. I got used to sniping, snide comments, and speculations about how much I was gone despite the fact that whenever I lectured, I did it on my days off or used vacation time to cover the absences, often taking my family along and making the speaking engagement double as a family vacation. They used to joke, "Boys, we've got an Englert sighting!" whenever I walked into the office.

One particular colleague made so many disparaging remarks that I finally confronted him. "I hear what you're saying," I told him. "But let me ask you a question: Would you seize an opportunity like this if it was offered to you?"

He thought for a moment. Then he shrugged. "Yeah," he answered. "I would." If he kept criticizing me after that, at least he did it behind my back.

I formed Englert Forensic Consulting in the mid-1980s, though it would be years before I could actually retire from the sheriff's office and devote myself full-time to blood pattern analysis and crime scene reconstruction.

From the start, I made it clear that I didn't have all the answers. I was *not*—and am not—the definitive authority on blood spatter. There is no definitive authority. I stress that point to every client. Even after handling thousands of homicide investigations, I'm still learning. I still run across unfamiliar patterns and mysteries that baffle me. The pattern on the cover of this book is an example.

I knew that if I was going to offer official opinions on cases that had bewildered experienced homicide detectives, I would have to know more than I had learned in my own years on the job plus six months of compulsive research. So I intensified my background reading and my experiments. And I solicited input on my cases from seasoned cops and forensic experts whose opinions I respected. When I lectured, I took along crime scene photos from cases I was working on and, with my clients' permission, tacked them up on the walls, inviting attendees to scrutinize them during breaks. I still do this. I usually combine images from cases I've solved with photos from open homicides. The first group gives attendees a chance to test their skills by analyzing the pictures and drawing conclusions, then finding out if they were right or wrong. The second gives me a wealth of useful insights and tends to spark enlightening discussion. You never know when you'll stumble across someone who managed to crack a case just like the one that's currently puzzling the hell out of you and who can tell you exactly what unorthodox weapon inflicted a series of peculiar wounds or generated a bizarre blood pattern.

Case Study: Horse Hooves and Hammer Blows

One of the first people ever to officially seek my help as a blood spatter consultant was Dr. Bob Keppel, a brilliant criminal investigator who had worked on the Ted Bundy case as a young homicide detective and to whom the infamous serial killer had confessed a number of his murders. Bob was working with distinguished prosecutor Greg Canova, recently appointed senior assistant state attorney general, to head up a newly formed unit of the Washington State Attorney General's Office that was charged with launching independent inquiries into criminal cases at the requests of local prosecutors. The case Bob brought to me in 1981 was one of the most intriguing I had ever encountered.

Donna Howard—a former rodeo trick rider, longtime horse lover, and married mother of two—was found dead on the floor of a stable on her farm in Yakima County, Washington, in January 1975. Donna's husband, Russell Howard, discovered her body and told police that he thought she had been kicked in the temple by one of her horses, judging from the copious amount of blood pooled around her head. The coroner agreed that Donna's head wounds were consistent with blows from a horse's hoof.

But Donna's family was skeptical. Donna's marriage to Russ Howard had long been on the rocks, and Russ, who struggled with a drinking problem and took few pains to hide his affairs with a string of local barmaids, had recently hit Donna so hard in the head during one of their many arguments that she had lost consciousness. When Russ invited his latest paramour, who went by the nickname of Pepper,* to move in and "babysit" his two daughters just weeks after their mother's death, the family saw it as a confirmation of their worst fears.

The death was ruled an accident, but in the years that followed, Donna's sister never stopped hounding prosecutors, begging them to reopen the case. It wasn't until Pepper got fed up with Russ, stormed out, and showed up at the sheriff's office with an unusual "hypothetical" question that anyone began to take Donna's sister's doubts seriously.

"What if," Pepper asked, "I knew about a murder but didn't say anything? If the killer got found out, would I be in trouble for keeping quiet?"

When pressed, she dropped some interesting—and incriminating— tidbits. Toward the end of 1974, Pepper was tired of fooling around with Russ Howard and lowered the boom. "Marry me or we're through," she warned. A smitten Howard eagerly agreed, then hatched a plot to murder his wife with a claw hammer to get her out of the way. He laid it all out for Pepper in hushed tones: He would coax Donna out to the barn, hammer in hand, claiming he needed to talk about some repair work with her. Then, when she wasn't looking, he would hit her with the broad side of the hammer. The death would look like an accident, he assured Pepper. Everyone would think Donna's skull had been crushed by a panicked horse. He even called Pepper the morning Donna died to assure her that he had gone through with the plan.

Pepper's tale was enough to reopen the case, with Keppel and Canova helming the investigation. The problem was, nearly all the crucial physical evidence had long since been burned, buried, tossed out, or painted over. All that was left were some grainy black-and-white photographs. So Keppel and Canova had Donna's body exhumed and sent her skull to a number of forensic pathologists—first in Washington, then at the Smithsonian Institutions, and finally to consultant Dr. Clyde Snow, one of the country's leading forensic anthropologists. All concurred that the damage inflicted—particularly a curious little oval fracture at the temple—looked a whole lot more consistent with hammer blows than horse hooves.

It was damning evidence, but Keppel and Canova needed more to build a shatterproof case against Russ Howard. They needed someone to explain the only other remaining piece of evidence—two dark swaths smeared along the wood on the wall of the stable.

Around that same time in 1982, Keppel attended a one-day class I was teaching on blood patterns. He hovered at the back of the room, then walked up to the lectern after I had completed my presentation.

"I've got a case I'd like to talk to you about," he said, and launched into the details of the Donna Howard death. Intrigued, I agreed to help, and we met a few days later, using a photographer's loupe to scrutinize blowups of every image he could provide of the stained wall and of Donna's body.

Our first task was to confirm that the blackish smears were in fact blood and not oil or mud or some other innocuous substance. The second would be to determine what they proved about the manner of Donna's death.

Part one was relatively easy to prove based on written reports compiled by those who had been on the scene. Numerous sources noted that they had found two large bloodstains on the wall, though the original autopsy report surmised that Donna had been thrown into a railroad tie and cut her head on its sharp edge. We blew up photographs of the tie itself, taken on the day Donna died. Not only was it free of blood, but it was covered with cobwebs.

Part two was trickier. Studying the images, I decided that, like the skull, the blood evidence belied Russ's story and the coroner's original conclusion. All the signs here pointed to homicide. There was no way those smears had been created by Donna's body slamming against the wall from the force of a horse's kick. A kick would have hurled her against the wall in a second or two; there simply wouldn't have been time for that much blood to pool in her hair that quickly. Also, we would have seen a hair impact pattern. Instead, the bloodstains revealed dozens of streaky lines—a classic blood transfer or swipe pattern. (To picture it, think of the marks a paintbrush leaves if you shake off most of the paint, then drag it along a wall; when you look closely, you can discern hundreds of individual thin lines left by the bristles. They can be wavy or straight, depending on how you move the brush—or, in the case of a murder, the bloodied object.) And photos of Donna's body showed that her hair was saturated in blood. If a killer had hit her in the head, then inadvertently allowed her blood-soaked hair to graze the wall as he lowered her body to the stable floor, it would have left precisely the type of pattern visible in the photos.

I did experiments at home in my barn to see if my theories were on track or not. Since I was beginning to give blood pattern analysis lectures several times a year, I also got Bob's permission to take crime scene photos from the Howard case along to my lectures, gradually collecting feedback from detectives who had investigated horse kick–related injuries and deaths, keeping Bob apprised of my findings. I had my students conduct experiments, too, trying their own tactics to see if they could replicate the patterns on the Howards' stable wall.

They reached the same conclusion I had: Lowering a bloody body to the ground would produce the type of pattern in the photo; flinging a body against a wall—particularly immediately after a blow to the head, before blood has had time to pool in the hair—would generate different patterns.

We continued this process over the next three years, slowly amassing solid data to back up our theory about how Donna had really died and eventually giving Bob enough to go on to get a warrant for Russ Howard's arrest.

When the case finally went to trial in 1986, I was invited to join a formidable team of forensic experts presenting their findings in court. Together, our expertise helped to convince the jury that Russell Howard had indeed killed his wife, Donna, with a hammer. He was found guilty of murder in the first degree and sentenced to life in prison. He died in 2002, shortly after being paroled.

Case Study: The Second Shot

A few years later, a consulting case came my way that bore chilling resemblances to the Donna Howard murder. Just after six A.M. on the morning of March 29, 2000, insurance agent David Duyst called 911 to report that his wife, Sandra Anne, had killed herself in their home in Grand Rapids, Michigan. When police reached the scene, they found Sandra sprawled across her bed, dead, with a nine-millimeter handgun lying next to her. Fighting back tears, David Duyst said that he had risen early and gone to another room to avoid waking up his wife when gunshots suddenly shattered the peaceful stillness of the house. He rushed in to find his wife bleeding from the head and gently removed the gun from her hand, laying it beside her on the bed. "I've been afraid something terrible like this would happen," he added, explaining that Sandra had been depressed ever since one of the quarter horses she raised at their nearby ranch kicked her in the head two years earlier.

Like Donna Howard, forty-year-old Sandra Anne Duyst was a mother with young children (two sons and a daughter), an award-winning equestrian, and—investigators soon learned—a woman with a troubled marriage that she did her best to hide from the outside world.

Police doubted David Duyst's grieving-widower act for several reasons. First, forensic experts found two bullet holes in Sandra's skull just behind her right ear. Could a suicide really shoot herself twice in the head? Unlikely. Second, Duyst—who they soon discovered was suffering financial woes and having an affair with his office assistant—had recently taken out a $500,000 life insurance policy on his wife.

If that wasn't enough to raise their suspicions, they got a call from Sandra's sister, who said Sandra had told her she had hidden a note under a drawer in the china cabinet in her dining room. "If anything sinister happens," Sandra instructed her sister, "go find the note when David's not around." Police checked and, sure enough, there was a piece of paper in Sandra's handwriting that read as follows:

"On November 19th, my accident was no accident. David beat me with a hammer/ax. He came from behind while I was in Dexter's stall. He hit me repeatedly.

"If anything has happened to me look first to David Duyst, Sr.," she continued. "He could be my killer. I would never commit suicide. He may have killed me."

Indeed, Sandra's family told police they remembered being a little puzzled about why David's clothes were bloody when they met him in the emergency room after Sandra's "accident" in the horse stall.

Duyst was arrested and arraigned in Michigan's Kent County District Court and charged with first-degree murder in the death of his wife. Prosecutor Greg Boer sought my help to interpret the blood spatter and to find out whether Duyst's version of events was possible. He flew out to Oregon with the evidence, including the bloody sheets and pillowcase and the clothes David Duyst was wearing when he claimed to have found Sandra.

First we examined David's T-shirt under high-intensity lights, using magnifying glasses. (Authorities from the Michigan State Police had issued a report stating that the shirt contained no blood, though Greg later learned that the officers examining the shirt had only eyeballed it—hardly enough to draw a definitive conclusion.) Sure enough, after several minutes of careful scrutiny we found tiny droplets of blood and tissue consistent with the high-velocity mist created by blowback from a gunshot wound not only on Duyst's pants and the front of his shirt, but, most significant, on the back of his right sleeve. Was Duyst right-handed? Yes. There was only one logical way those blood patterns would end up embedded in the fibers of the shirt in that unusual spot: Duyst held the gun in his right hand, extending his arm as he pointed the trigger at Sandra's head. When he fired, the bullet sent minuscule fragments of blood, bone, and brain matter into the air in a fine mist. Some landed on Sandra's body, some on the bedsheets, and some on the underside of his sleeve, toward the back—the part of his clothing closest to and facing the wound he had created.

Next we took the sheet from Sandra's bed outside. We strung it up on a line in the bright sunlight to inspect the patterns, examining it inch by inch. If you looked carefully, you could discern a long, vertical void in the blood spatter—a line that showed where the shooter had stretched out his arm toward his victim as he shot.

Finally, we rented a motel room and re-created the crime scene using measurements and other data from the autopsy. We knew from the fracture pattern in Sandra's skull where each bullet had entered her brain and which had gone in first. Sandra would have had to shoot herself, then reposition the handgun, raising it an inch or so, and fire again. The act would have been physically impossible because the first shot would have incapacitated her. As renowned Texas-based forensic expert Dr. Vincent Di Maio put it in his testimony, the first shot to Sandra's head would have been akin to going into your garage and yanking the electrical panel off the wall. The lights would have gone out, so to speak.

Some suicide victims do manage to shoot themselves more than once if the first bullet barely grazes the skin or misses vital organs. However, you often end up with what cops call a "stove pipe"—a shell casing that gets jammed into the barrel when a shooter's grip on the gun is feeble and his or her wrist and hands are too weak to grip the trigger properly—a phenomenon we did not see in the Duyst case.

To test my theory about how Sandra Duyst died, I turned to my friend Lonnie Ryan, a gun expert with the Clackamas County Sheriff's Office in Oregon. Lonnie suggested we stage an experiment. He asked his wife, Sheila, to come to the gun range and fire the actual nine-millimeter found next to Sandra Duyst's body. Greg Boer and I would be on hand to watch what happened. Sheila knew nothing about the case and had no experience with guns. Lonnie's only instructions to her were to hold the gun in a way that felt natural. We set up a wide ruler to measure the weapon's recoil and a videocamera to film it. When Sheila fired the gun, it recoiled upward by a full four inches. And it stove-piped—in other words, the shell casing got jammed in the chamber instead of ejecting, as it should have. What did that tell us? First, to compensate for the recoil, Sandra Duyst would have needed enough strength and wherewithal to bring the gun back down a considerable distance after her first suicidal shot and reposition it against her head. Given Dr. Di Maio's "lights out" analysis, this seemed impossible. Second, if Sandra had held the nine-millimeter lightly—as most people unfamiliar with automatic handguns do—the gun would almost certainly have stove-piped as it did when Sheila fired it, and that would have prevented the second round from ever loading into the barrel.

I flew to Grand Rapids to present my findings in court, and thanks to Greg's convincing arguments along with solid physical evidence, David Duyst was convicted of first-degree murder and sentenced to life in prison. He requested a new trial five years later but was denied.

Case Study: The Green Thread Mystery

Sometimes the most significant information comes not from the blood itself, but from what's hidden in it. Such was the case in what I call the Green Thread Mystery. Like a number of intriguing cases I had handled as a homicide detective, this one involved a body that was nowhere to be found. In its place was some of the most unusual blood evidence I have ever examined.

Here's what happened: On January 15, 1992, Eric Humbert's wife called local police to report that her husband hadn't returned to their New Albany, Indiana, home in several days and she was starting to get worried. The police filed a missing persons report on Humbert, but with few leads the case stagnated.

Then three months later, they caught a remarkable break: Humbert's Chevy hatchback had turned up in a Housing Authority parking lot just across the Ohio River in Louisville, Kentucky. Police there ran a check on the license plate and realized the car's owner was a missing person. What's more, a police detective had found what he believed was blood all over the back of the interior.

The vehicle was towed back to New Albany for closer examination. Forensic experts determined the substance smeared across the upholstery was indeed a massive amount of blood. And before long, police zeroed in on Humbert's best friend, Jonathan Whitesides, as their prime suspect. Whitesides came under scrutiny for two reasons: First, he turned out to be living with the missing man's wife, as police discovered when they showed up to inform her that her husband's car had been found. Second, he was the last person to see Humbert alive, and he had a rather incredible tale to tell about it.

Whitesides told the police that he and Humbert had been driving home in Humbert's car on a frigid winter afternoon after playing basketball at a local gym. Humbert was planning to drop off Whitesides at an address in the countryside where Whitesides was house-sitting, but he was having car trouble, so instead he pulled into the garage attached to the house to check his engine. According to Whitesides, a heated argument erupted when Humbert started hurling accusations at his friend as he peered under the hood.

"You've been screwing my wife! I know it," he said, glaring at Whitesides.

"I haven't touched your wife!" Whitesides shouted back.

Suddenly, Humbert pulled a knife and launched himself at Whitesides. As the two men struggled, the knife slipped and lodged itself in its owner's neck. Humbert collapsed, and when Whitesides couldn't revive him, he panicked. Thinking his friend was dead and he would get blamed, he shoved the body into the hatchback, drove to the Ohio River, and rolled it in. He ditched the Chevy in the closest parking lot he could find and went home to clean up the blood.

Whitesides insisted that he had acted in self-defense and was guilty of no more than obstruction of justice for having disposed of Humbert's body and his car. His version of events sounded like the far-fetched cover story of a guilty man, but aside from the blood smeared over the car's cargo space, evidence was scant and there was no victim to be found. Murder one would be hard to prove. The task of making a case against Whitesides fell to Floyd County, Indiana, prosecutor Stan Faith. Stan had attended a seminar I gave on blood spatter in San

Diego about a year earlier, so he asked me if I would be willing to examine the scientific evidence and give an opinion on the case.

I flew to New Albany and we conducted a thorough reexamination of Humbert's car to see if any details might have been missed in the initial investigation. It was a good thing we did, for the hatchback yielded a plethora of blood spatter evidence.

First, we examined the blood in the back of the car. Not only was it pooled under the hatch, but there were six distinctive long, thin, wavy streaks of it on the driver's-side wheel well. In reality, we were looking at a transfer pattern not unlike the one we identified in the Donna Howard case, though this time, as we later learned, it was made by fabric rather than human hair.

We continued combing every inch of the car for traces of blood. When we opened the hood, we found something remarkable: Caked all over the filthy, grease-laden engine were minuscule blood droplets of precisely the type you get with high-velocity mist. As in the Duyst case, it was the hallmark of a gunshot wound—not the stab wound Whitesides described. Even more intriguing was the fact that on closer inspection, we found dozens of pristine bright green threads embedded in the blood—threads that matched the color of a wool watch cap Humbert's wife had reported him wearing when he was last seen.

We dug a little further and uncovered a bullet hole in the engine panel under the dashboard, where the windshield wipers are anchored. Using a metal cutter to rip out the firewall that separates the engine from the car's interior, we located three copper fragments and a lead core lodged deep within the engine compartment. When we pieced them back together, they formed a nine-millimeter bullet. We returned to the garage of the house where Whitesides was staying when Humbert vanished, and sure enough, we found a nine-millimeter shell casing, which ballistics experts matched to the bullet fragments in the missing man's car. On the garage floor, we also found bloodstains that someone had obviously tried to wipe away, and there were blood droplets consistent with the high-velocity mist created by a gunshot wound spattered over a collection of wooden drumsticks stored in the garage.

Next we sent the mutilated bullet to Dr. Raymond Grimsbo of Intermountain Forensic Laboratories Inc. in Portland, asking him to analyze the blood on it. We told him nothing about our own findings, but when he called to say he was sending back his report, he told me, "You know, this bullet is very interesting. Did you notice that it had a green thread embedded in the lead core?"

And speaking of those green threads, here is a prime example of how mistakes can hinder evidence collection when people don't understand it thoroughly: I was standing next to Floyd County assistant district attorney Susan Orth and a local evidence collector named Hank* as he removed a section of the plastic radiator housing under the car's hood. In the center of it was a big round drop of blood with scalloped edges that extended out to the sides, suggesting the blood had hit the plastic hard.

We all leaned in to scrutinize the chunk of plastic and spied, perched atop the blackened blood, the first of many bright green threads we would discover.

"Let's get that out of the way," Hank said casually, plucking away the thread with his fingers and shaking them.

Susan gasped and stared at me wide-eyed. Instantly we both fell to our knees, groping over the ground in search of the discarded thread.

"What are you doing?" asked Hank, clearly baffled. "That's meaningless. It's garbage."

"It might be the key to the whole case," I told him, fighting to keep the irritation and incredulity out of my voice.

We never retrieved the thread. We sent the bloody plastic radiator cover to Dr. William Brady, a private forensic pathologist based in

Portland, who found brain tissue and minute bits of skull in the blood as well as pieces of carbonaceous material consistent with gunpowder. Brady's conclusion? "No one could lose brain tissue like that and live."

This gave Stan enough to make a case for murder. But whose?

He didn't have Humbert's body, so how could he prove that was Humbert's blood all over the hatchback? The blood evidence from the engine was in such minute quantities that it would have been impossible at that time to do a classical DNA test. We could conduct one on the blood from the cargo space, but that would only substantiate Whitesides's version of events—a bloody body stowed in the car and then dumped in the river.

So Stan enlisted DNA experts to try a new technique called HLA (human leukocyte antigen) DQ alpha testing, which allowed experts to glean genetic information from very small or degraded tissue and blood samples. Since we had no samples of Humbert's DNA and nothing reliable to cull from his house when other people had been living there for months after his disappearance, Stan ultimately got Humbert's mother and siblings not only to donate samples of their own DNA, but to give the okay to exhume Humbert's father's body and extract bone marrow from a femur to compare with the blood in the car. Experts concluded that the victim whose blood was spattered all over the engine was in fact an offspring of Mr. and Mrs. Humbert and a relative of Eric's brothers and sisters.

The green threads pointed in one direction: Humbert was hunched over his car while the hood was up, wearing his cap in the cold garage and examining the running engine, when Whitesides shot him in the back of the head, sending blood, bone and brain fragments, and minuscule bits of hat into the engine, which sucked them in as it ran.

Using what we knew now, I focused on reconstructing the actual crime scene. I was able to calculate Humbert and his killer's positions relative to each other and to the car when the murder occurred, and to map out the trajectory of the bullet based on the blood spatter and the bullet hole in the engine firewall.

Remember the six bloody transfer streaks under the hatch door? We concluded that they were made by Humbert's blood-soaked watch cap as Whitesides shoved the body into the back of the car; the ribbing would have created a distinct pattern of exactly the sort in the hatchback, with regularly spaced voids between the raised "ribs" of the cap.

Simultaneously, a search of Whitesides's truck turned up a nine-millimeter semiautomatic handgun with bloody blowback on the barrel. The amounts were too small for DNA tests to confirm it as Humbert's, even through DQ alpha testing, though pathologists did confirm that the blood came from a higher primate. As Stan put it, "Jonathan Whitesides either went to the zoo and shot a chimp or a gorilla, or he shot a human being with that gun."

Stan presented the findings in court, with testimony provided by Dr. Grimsbo, Dr. Brady, myself, and other forensic experts, and it took the jury just thirty-five minutes to find Jonathan Whitesides guilty of the murder of his best friend, Eric Humbert. He was sentenced to forty years in prison. He was released with ten years of supervised probation in the spring of 2008.

Case Study: The Bug Case

As word about my consulting business spread, I began to get calls from other states, from representatives of district attorneys' offices and law firms doing defense work, and from a number of police departments. Sometimes my opinions would help to convict a murderer.

At other times they would help to free an innocent person. That's what happened in what I always refer to as the Bug Case.

One afternoon in 2000, I got a call from an attorney in North Carolina named James Cooney. I had met Jim during a case I consulted on involving Dr. Edward Friedland, who was charged with his wife's murder and then sued members of the Charlotte police force—unsuccessfully—for having arrested him after prosecutors dropped the charges against him. In working with Jim on that case, I developed great respect for his dedication and honesty, so when he asked me to give an opinion on the blood evidence for a new case he was handling, I readily agreed.

Twenty-five-year-old Alan Gell had been on death row for the murder of fifty-six-year-old Allen Ray Jenkins since 1998. The case had bounced through a series of inept or uninterested lawyers and languished while Gell's execution date ticked closer. Then it landed on the desks of Cooney and a Raleigh lawyer named Mary Pollard, both of whom the state of North Carolina tasked with reexamining the facts.

As I read through the file and scrutinized the crime scene photos, I shook my head. The evidence against Jim's client seemed convincing. Though there was no physical evidence like fingerprints or DNA tying Gell to the crime, an eyewitness—fifteen-year-old Crystal Morris, the best friend of Gell's fifteen-year-old girlfriend, Shanna Hall—testified that she had watched Gell, a small-time drug dealer who had just been released from jail, step out from behind the bedroom door and kill Jenkins with one of the double-barreled shotguns Jenkins kept loaded in his house.

Morris and Hall were on close terms not only with the alleged killer, but with the victim, who was perhaps not the most stellar of citizens. Allen Ray Jenkins was notorious among the neighbors for loud parties, where he liked to greet guests wearing only a dish towel pinned around his waist, and for his fondness for teenage girls, whom he frequently plied with wine coolers and drugs. When he died, he had already pleaded guilty to two counts of indecent liberties with a minor—a fourteen-year-old girl who was a frequent visitor to a mobile home he owned—and served six months in jail.

Morris, who was a regular guest at Jenkins's house, claimed she had stopped by briefly to repair a VCR for Jenkins when she witnessed his murder, though several empty wine cooler bottles suggested her visit had been more social in nature and, during exhaustive questioning by investigators, she gave six conflicting versions of the events from the night Jenkins died. By the time Gell's case reached Jim Cooney, both Morris and Hall had pleaded guilty to second-degree murder and were serving ten-year sentences for allegedly having helped Gell to rob and murder Jenkins.

I didn't think I could help Jim, so I called and apologized. But a few months later, I was lecturing in France when he phoned me again, asking me to reconsider. Gell's conviction, Jim explained, had hinged largely on when Jenkins died. And Jim had unearthed new evidence suggesting the prosecution had been mistaken about the date.

When the authorities found Jenkins on April 14, 1995, sprawled on the floor of the tidy white house that had once belonged to his mother, his corpse was bloated to four times its size, brown and mottled, with a brittle, paper-thin outer layer of skin already beginning to flake away. The body was also teeming with maggots. How long had Jenkins been lying there to decompose to such a degree?

Forensic experts, lawyers, and jurors debated the question fiercely for one reason: Alan Gell had an airtight alibi for every day after April 3. He had spent some of the days in jail for stealing a truck and the rest with a friend out of state, where he had also run afoul of police when he ducked out of a restaurant without paying the tab.

Prosecutors were adamant that Jenkins died no later than April 3—

so adamant, Jim concluded, that they either downplayed or intentionally suppressed the statements of at least seventeen people who claimed they had seen Jenkins around town as late as April 10. One even swore he had sold him a dozen herring on that date. They also overlooked a taped conversation in which Crystal Morris told her boyfriend that she needed to come up with a story to explain what had happened at Jenkins's house. But witnesses' memories fade, and by the time Jim stepped in to examine Gell's case, five years had elapsed since neighbors gave their initial statements to police. Several witnesses were elderly. Three died before Jim could reinterview them. And Crystal Morris wasn't talking.

Out of respect for Jim, I agreed to take a closer look at the evidence. I flew to Charlotte, North Carolina, to see the house where the murder took place and the creek that ran behind it, where the killer tossed the gun and where the police later retrieved it. Next, we went to the state attorney general's office library, where I examined what was left of the evidence. I laid out each piece on a table on fresh butcher paper under high-intensity lights, photographed it from every angle, then methodically inspected every inch of it with a magnifying glass. First we looked at the gun, then the pellets, and finally, what seemed like the least significant of all, the blue-and-white-striped dish towel Jenkins was wearing as a makeshift loincloth when he was killed. The blood was so old, it looked waxy and smooth, and the deteriorating fabric beneath it was falling to shreds. But hidden in that long-dried blood was one of the linchpins of Gell's case.

There, embedded in the aging blood stuck to the towel, were the bodies of dozens of maggots, one of which had managed to form a nearly finished cocoon before it died. I combed the towel several more times, searching for broken casings of maggots that had hatched out as flies, but there were none.

I could feel my pulse quickening: Here was some of the most

subtle yet definitive data I had ever seen in blood. Based on the wealth of existing research on the blowfly life cycle and what we knew about conditions in Jenkins's house, scientists would almost surely be able to answer the pivotal question in the case: When did Jenkins die?

Crime scene experts had taken temperature readings when they discovered Jenkins's body, so we already knew his house was a veritable hotbox—around ninety degrees—thanks to a gas heater in the living room. Entomologists would know how long it would take blowflies to lay eggs on the body (almost immediately after death) and how many days it would take their larvae to hatch into maggots and start forming cocoons.

"Jim, I think if you get an entomologist to look at this, you'll find out exactly when the murder occurred," I told him.

Jim sought input from famed forensic anthropologist Murray Marks of the University of Tennessee's illustrious Body Farm, which studies human decomposition under a multitude of circumstances and conditions. Marks told Jim that the fly evidence suggested Jenkins had been dead for three to five days—not the eleven days the original prosecutors claimed—before being discovered. The time frame matched up perfectly with neighbors' memories about the last dates they had seen the victim alive. It was just the scientific evidence Jim needed to corroborate evidence from the witnesses who had seen Jenkins alive after April 3 and to make an airtight case.

Jim also asked for my help in interpreting the blood spatter that had drenched the door frame on the side facing Jenkins's bedroom, starting at a height of around five feet and then running down all over the lower part of the wall. Based on the positions of the blood, the body, and the shotgun pellets on the floor and in the ceiling, where was the shooter standing when he or she pulled the trigger? Where was the victim standing? Jim wanted to know whether, in my professional opinion, Morris's account of what she had seen was possible, given the laws of physics.

It wasn't. I studied the photos closely, then went back to the crime scene and strung lines between the blood spatter and the pellet marks to calculate trajectories and angles. There was spatter from blowback and arterial spray in the hallway. If you believed Morris's tale, Jenkins's blood would have had to travel backward around the corner of the door frame. Years of crime scene reconstruction left no doubt in my mind that whoever pulled the shotgun trigger that night stood in the hall just outside the bedroom door and fired through the doorway.

Of course, none of this proved that Morris herself—or even Shanna Hall—killed Jenkins as I suspected one of them did. But it did help to convince the jury that there was reasonable doubt Alan Gell pulled the trigger. Gell was finally cleared of the murder of Allen Ray Jenkins in early 2004 and released from prison after spending more than nine years on death row. He was a troubled young man in many ways— guilty of car theft and drug dealing—but he was innocent of killing Allen Jenkins. No one else has ever been charged in the killing.

Gell went on to get a college education and to become an outspoken anti-death-penalty activist, though he later went back to prison for having sex with yet another fifteen-year-old girlfriend, sentenced ironically by the same judge who presided over the earlier trial that ended in his acquittal.

These are just four of the unique cases I've been privileged to take part in through my consulting efforts. I consider myself fortunate to be in this profession. I enjoy my work immensely. It's fascinating. It's educational. And it helps to ensure that justice is done. I meet some of the most brilliant and dedicated people handling both prosecution and defense around the United States and often outside it, not to mention coming up against a good number of brilliant minds on the criminal side. I learn more about crime scene reconstruction and blood pattern analysis with every new case. Bloodstains can be divided into a few basic categories, and bloodshed itself follows the simple laws of physics. But there is no such thing as routine when it comes to murder, as you will see in the following chapter.

5

Blood Basics

I STARED AT THE reddish brown swirls of blood winding over the wall. In thirty-plus years of police work and crime scene reconstruction, I had never seen anything like them. The case itself was straightforward. Double homicide. The murder victims, a middle-aged man and woman. The weapon, a rifle. The location, the outskirts of Las Vegas. She had been killed first, and he had made the mistake of coming downstairs to see what was going on. The local criminalist, who asked me to consult on the blood evidence, had filled me in on their history, and we were all convinced that the killing was Mob related.

But these bloody spirals were a mystery. They weren't from a victim's hand clutching at the wall for support. They weren't from a murderer's sleeve brushing the wall as he hurried out. They weren't a secret message written cryptically in a dead man's blood. I had seen all of those before, and this was different.

"So, what do you think?" asked one of the local officers.

"No idea," I was tempted to say. But instead, I squinted more closely at the grotesque swirls, trying to force myself to concentrate, to stretch my tired mind beyond the usual causes and conclusions I would determine in more ordinary crime scenes. Nothing.

I scanned the pictures of the crime scene for what seemed like the hundredth time, desperate to catch sight of some sort of clue—some crucial, hidden piece of the puzzle I had overlooked. Then I saw it in the corner of one photo. Lying at the base of the bloody stairs was a large round object partially obscured by a blanket. The pattern looked vaguely familiar to me.

Suddenly the marks made perfect sense. I couldn't help grinning a little.

"Did you figure it out?" asked the cop, watching me closely.

"I did," I told him. "You'll never believe what caused those blood patterns. This couple has a dog, don't they."

"Yeah," he said, surprised. "They do."

"Must be a big dog, judging from the size of that bed," I said, pointing to the edge of the photo, where part of a large, round dog bed was visible. There was a blanket draped over it just like one my in-laws had for a dog at their house back in Oregon.

"As a matter of fact, it is."

"I'm guessing the dog is just about the same height as those blood patterns," I said. The blotches swam into focus as clearly as if a microscope lens had been adjusted. I could see now that they were imprints of a dog's muzzle pressed repeatedly against the wall.

Once you knew what you were looking at, you could even discern the outline of a canine nose in the middle of each. The swirls were tongue marks where the dog had licked its owners' blood off the walls.

Blood Spatter 101

The fact that a family pet's innocent actions could manage to baffle every crime expert scrutinizing the bloody scene just described is less surprising than you might think. It takes years of going to crime scenes to develop skill in interpreting blood patterns, years of encountering bizarre examples like the Las Vegas dog case to build a library of knowledge. My own mistakes have been my best teacher. By now, I've spent decades learning from them. Though academic research has brought invaluable advances to the field, no academic could walk into a room where a murder occurred and reconstruct the crime or use the blood clues to tell whether an eyewitness is lying about what he saw. To do that, you need savvy, street sense, and a lot of experience with witnesses, suspects, and dead bodies.

But I can teach you the basics of beginning blood pattern analysis to help you develop a foundation—one you could never build by watching *CSI* or other crime dramas. If you were a homicide detective, a medical examiner, or another crime-solving professional sitting in on one of my workshops to sharpen your skills of detection, here are some of the bloodstain fundamentals we would cover, along with the basics on bullet trajectories and wound patterns.

As you know from the chapters you've already read, the stains that result when blood spatters are divided into three main categories. These categories are determined by how much force went into the source

A crime scene's combination of blood spatter types.

providing the blood (usually a human body, but in my experiments a puddle of cows' blood) and the size, shape, and number of blood droplets that resulted from the impact. The three basic types of stains you find at murder scenes are low-velocity spatter, medium-velocity spatter, and high-velocity spatter. Being able to distinguish one group from another by the telltale lines, voids, and other calling cards they leave can tell you what kind of weapon was used, how the murder unfolded, and sometimes even the killer's identity.

Low-Velocity Blood Spatter

Low-velocity blood patterns occur when a minimal amount of force is used to spatter blood or when gravity alone causes blood to drip. They are characterized by large drops, much bigger than the ones you see in medium- or high-velocity blood spatter. A trail of blood droplets that dribbled from a murderer's hands, clothing, or weapon as he left the crime scene would qualify as a low-velocity blood pattern. So would blood that dripped or flowed from a victim's wounds as he struggled to get away or reach for a phone to call for help.

Another common low-velocity pattern is **blood-into-blood**—where blood drips repeatedly into an existing pool or puddle of blood, as in the John Lee Hipsher throat-cutting case or the castrations we used to do on the bulls at our farm. One of its hallmarks is **satellite spatter**— smaller droplets that bounce out to the sides of a larger central pool when they hit it. Being able to read blood-into-blood patterns helps you gauge the duration of an attack and the position of both attacker and victim. In the Hipsher case, it told us the victim bled for quite some time before he died and provided a vital clue in distinguishing murder from self-defense.

Blood transfers occur when an object that has wet blood on it

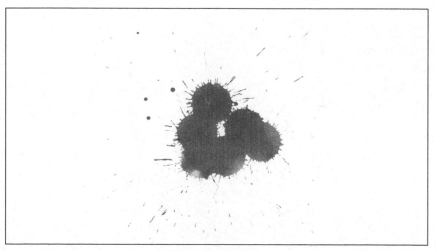

Blood-into-blood

comes in contact with another object. Let's say a killer hoping to hide the evidence of his crime drags his victim's body to his car, leaving a bloody swath behind him in the grass. Then he sets the hammer he used in the murder down momentarily while he hoists the body into the trunk, creating a bloody imprint of part of his weapon on the pavement next to the car. Both marks would be classified as blood transfers.

The sorts of transfers cops find most often at crime scenes are hair transfers, fabric transfers, hand transfers, and weapon transfers. Each generates a distinctive pattern. The blood left on the barn wall in the Donna Howard "horse kick" case, as you'll recall, left a classic hair transfer pattern on the wood—long, thin symmetrical lines that looked almost as if a paintbrush had been dragged over the surface. Blood is often heaviest at the point of contact, with the lines tapering off in the direction the blood source moved. Had Howard's husband's version of events been true, we would have seen a hair impact pattern instead—a much more chaotic, random cluster of thick and thin overlapping lines with some satellite spatter. Blood has to have time to

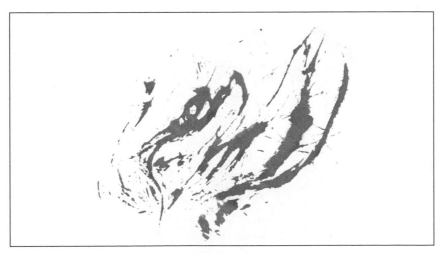

Hair impact

pool in the hair in order to create an impact pattern—something that didn't happen in the Howard murder.

The blood smeared inside Eric Humbert's Chevy hatchback in the Green Thread Mystery left a unique fabric transfer pattern that eventually clued us in to the fact that a body wearing a ribbed winter hat had been shoved into the storage space, the bloodied cap brushing the car's upholstery as it entered. Obviously, different types of hair (straight, curly, short, long) create slightly different patterns, as do different types of fabrics.

Any item soaked or spattered with wet blood can leave a transfer pattern at a crime scene. Say the hypothetical hammer killer was having trouble moving his victim's body, so he wrapped it in a blanket or plastic drop cloth to make it easier to drag. If his victim's blood soaked through the blanket or leaked through a hole in the plastic, investigators would spot a transfer pattern showing that something bloody had been dragged through the grass, assuming the blood was still wet when he moved the body. If he stepped in his victim's blood when he was wrapping up the body, the bloody footprints his shoes made would be classified as a transfer pattern, too.

A **swipe** refers to blood that gets smeared as you move a bloody

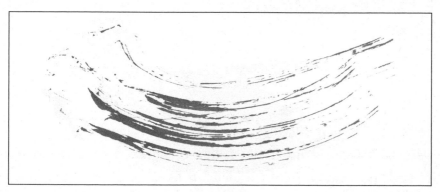

Hair swipe

Hand swipe

Fabric swipe

source across an unsoiled surface. Maybe in his hurry the killer just described slammed his trunk, failing to notice that his fingertips brushed the exterior of his car and left blood on it. If so, he would leave a classic blood swipe on the car. When a swipe is feathered on one side, it usually suggests that whatever or whoever made the mark moved in the direction of the feathering.

You get a **wipe** pattern, by contrast, when you drag an object through an existing bloodstain, removing sections of the blood. For example, the incriminating marks we found on the wall behind the bed in Daniel Pierce's apartment showed wipe patterns—evidence that someone (Pierce's murderous roommate, Socrates Ladner, as we later found out) had rubbed a washcloth through bloodstains in an attempt to clean them up.

Thanks to advances in forensic technology, we can now retrieve a wealth of information from blood transfer patterns that would have gone undetected in the past. Chemical luminescence tests using Luminol and similar chemicals in a darkened lab reveal traces of blood on fabric that would otherwise be invisible. Presumptive tests with amido black and phenolphthalein react with proteins in the blood and trigger a color change. (With amido black, blood shows up purple; with phenolphthalein, it turns pink.) These are followed by confirmatory tests using blood revealers like ABA cards, Hemi-Trace kits, and Takayama microscopic tests. Such methods not only uncover traces of blood hidden on cloth, they also allow us to get identifiable fingerprints from bloody hand transfers, even if the perpetrator was twisting or wadding up the cloth as he gripped it. Blood reagents like Luminol will also unmask flecks of dried blood spatter too small to discern under a microscope, even when the fabrics have gone through a washing machine.

In a criminal case, the police or prosecutor could have experts conduct lab tests to confirm that the blood was human and use DNA-typing technology to pinpoint the blood donor's identity, even if it's decades old or if only minuscule amounts of it remain to test. Scientific data often provide the missing piece of the crime-solving puzzle. They can reinforce or redirect an entire investigation. And they can form the linchpin or the fatal hole in the prosecution's or defense's case.

Case Study: The Knife Prints on the Bedspread

Both weapon and hand transfers played a damning role in the conviction of Brett X. Hartmann for the September 1997 mutilation murder of Winda Snipes in Akron, Ohio. When police discovered Snipes's nude body in her apartment after several anonymous 911 calls, even veteran detectives were appalled at what they saw. The forty-six-year-old woman had been stabbed more than 130 times, gagged, strangled with an electrical cord, one ankle bound to her bed, her throat slit twice, and her hands cut off. Her hands have never been found.

Police soon arrested Brett Hartmann, a cook at the Quaker Square Hilton, who had been hovering around the crime scene, approaching detectives and asking questions when Snipes's body was found. Hartmann told the police he had met Snipes the night before her death at the Inn Between Bar and had consensual sex with her, as he had done on several other occasions, then returned to her apartment a day later and found her body. Panicked, thinking that he would be the prime suspect, he tried to wipe away all evidence that he had been there and then called 911.

That might have explained the bloody fingerprint Hartmann left on the white plastic chair police found on top of Snipes's body, but not the bloody T-shirt detectives retrieved from under his own bed's headboard or Snipes's watch, which they found on his dresser when they searched the apartment he shared with his mother. His bizarre, antsy behavior at the murder scene and references to the victim as a "psycho bitch" and a "whore" who "got what she deserved" didn't help his case, either.

Hartmann claimed he had been at home talking on the phone with his girlfriend at the time of the murder, but prosecutor Becky Doherty believed the evidence suggested otherwise and asked me to give an opinion. She and I examined the bloody bedclothes and T-shirt closely. Both bore the same peculiar bloodstains—a series of linear patterns, each made up of dozens of tiny parallel lines straight as arrows.

"What caused them?" Doherty wanted to know.

I had to confess that I was stumped. Like the dog-muzzle prints, these were a first. Determined to find out what created them, I spent hours at my lab in Portland armed with stage blood, white fabric, and a variety of objects—fabrics, household appliances, knives with unusual blades. One by one, I dipped them in blood and pressed them against the sheet, noting the pattern they made and ruling them out. At last I tried a knife with a serrated blade. The pattern was identical to the one in the blood evidence.

Backing up my theory about what caused the blood transfers was the newly released autopsy report: The medical examiner noted that whoever removed Snipes's hands showed almost surgical precision, cutting through ligament without nicking any bone. The process would have taken considerable time and effort, he observed. The killer would have had to cut a section of flesh, set down his knife while he twisted and pulled the limbs apart to separate muscle and sinew, then pick up his weapon again to continue the laborious effort of severing the hands. He also noted that at least some of the sawing was done with a serrated blade.

The combination of voids, wrinkles, and bloody lines on the shirt suggested that a serrated knife covered in wet blood had been placed on it repeatedly while the garment was lying flat rather than being worn. In fact, when you hung up the bloody bedspread, you could discern a void where an object roughly the same size as the T-shirt had been lying on it. The fact that the vast majority of the transfers from the serrated blade were on the right side of the bedspread, the one next to Snipes's body, bore out the coroner's suggestion—that the woman's killer had set down his knife and picked it up again numerous times while he switched between cutting and tugging at her wrists.

Hartmann had both skill with and access to knives. Local authorities got a search warrant and checked his locker at work. Sure enough, it held a fabric case with knives—one of which was missing. Since none of the remaining cutlery had a serrated edge, it was probable that the missing one did. But like Snipes's hands, the vanished knife from Hartmann's set has never been found.

That wasn't the only incriminating blood evidence, however. When police found Snipes's body, her leg was still draped over her bed, tethered by her fettered ankle. On the bedspread under her calf we found a subtle hand transfer stain. We cut out the bloody section and had it flown to the King County Sheriff's Office in the state of Washington under the watchful eye of a detective. (It's always advisable to have a detective from the local force accompany evidence for safekeeping when it's transported.) When it reached the lab in King County, it was bathed in amido black and revealed a fingerprint.

Using traditional latent fingerprint examination, fingerprint expert Patrick Warrick of King County identified the print as Hartmann's. Warrick also examined the transfer stain using digitally enhanced imaging, which allows an expert to photograph a bloody print, upload it to a computer, subtract the fabric and other extraneous matter from the image electronically, then adjust color and contrast to maximize readability of the fingerprint on-screen. Scrutinizing the digital print, Warrick reached the same conclusion: It belonged to Hartmann. He brought the computer with the digitally enhanced image to Akron with him to exhibit during the trial.

In addition to testimony from Warrick, Doherty called a co-worker of Hartmann's to the stand who claimed the defendant had remarked in August 1997 that O. J. Simpson could have disposed of incriminating fibers, hair, and skin under his victims' fingernails by cutting off their hands. One of Hartmann's fellow inmates at the Summit County Jail also appeared in court and told jurors the defendant had confessed the murder to him and described cutting off Snipes's hands.

The prosecution asked me to testify about the blood evidence. Over the years, I've learned that the best way to help juries understand is to keep things simple and visual. If you present evidence without a reconstruction, it's hard for them to visualize what you're describing and they tend to get confused. So I brought in stage blood and white fabric and dipped a serrated knife in it, then pressed it against the fabric to demonstrate the pattern it made. Doherty and I also hung up the real bedspread covered in Snipes's blood so jurors could compare the two.

On the witness stand, Hartmann claimed he got Snipes's blood on his T-shirt when he tried to pick her up to see if he could revive her. To show the physical impossibility of this, I reenacted it for the jury. I had an assistant prosecutor lie on a blanket on the courtroom floor with one ankle propped on a chair to simulate Snipes's tethered leg while I tried to pick her up. The jury could see how clumsy and awkward it would be to lift a person lying in that position without either kneeling behind them and grasping them under the shoulders or grabbing their forearms and pulling them up, an unlikely choice given Snipes's mutilated wrists. Even if Hartmann had managed to lift the dead woman by pressing his chest against hers, the jurors could see why I concluded that the act wouldn't have left so much blood covering the front of his T-shirt. Nor, in my opinion, would it have created the particular patterns we saw on the garment. Given the estimated time of death and the time Hartmann said he reached Snipes's apartment, the victim's blood would have been dry. Even if he mistook the time and arrived when her blood was still wet, I testified that his actions would have left large smears on his shirt—not long, precise linear patterns.

It didn't take Hartmann long after that to change his story. In his new version of events, he had never tried to lift Snipes's body or revive her. Instead, he said, he had left his shirt behind and the real killer must have set his knife down on it.

In the end, Brett Hartmann was found guilty of aggravated murder with prior calculation and design, tampering with evidence, and kidnapping, which made the crime a capital offense. He was sentenced to death and lost a number of appeals. Days before his scheduled execution in April 2009, Hartmann was granted a stay of execution so that a federal court could reexamine his case, though the Ohio Parole Board recommended against clemency and Governor Ted Strickland had not yet ruled on the recommendation at press time.

Following the Trail

As with other liquids, the shape and size of blood droplets are determined by the surface they land on. When blood falls from a ninety-

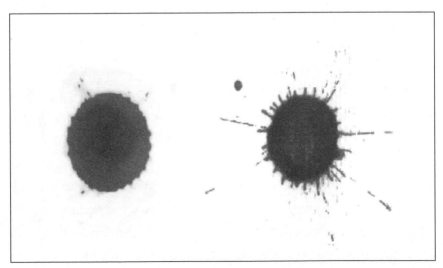

Ninety-degree drops

degree angle, the airborne droplets are perfectly round, like liquid marbles. When they strike a hard, nonporous material such as a pane of glass, they spread out into perfectly round, flat, smooth-edged circles, like coins. Conversely, when blood drops onto a rougher, more porous surface—such as skin or even glass smeared with dirt—the uneven texture ruptures the droplets' surface tension so that they have scalloped edges. The more porous the surface, the more distorted the droplets' edges will be. Drop blood onto plywood or a pair of jeans, for instance, and you will see a dramatic starburst pattern that looks sort of like a drawing of a sun with rays stretching out in all directions—only red, of course.

Satellite spatter occurs when blood falls into blood and bounces or ricochets out to the sides. If blood hits a hard surface like glass, it creates no satellite spatter. But on a more porous or uneven surface—gravel, dirt, even skin—it satellites.

If you tilt the surface the blood lands on, the droplets will start to develop a point. Picture a red teardrop with one rounded end and one pointed end, known in forensics as a "spine" or "tail." What does this mean to a homicide detective or a crime scene reconstructionist in practical terms? Teardrop-shaped blood spatter tells you that blood hit a wall, floor, or whatever other surface it landed on at an angle other than ninety degrees.

If you were to walk into a room where someone had been bludgeoned standing in front of a wall, you would probably see a bunch of blood droplets of various sizes, all with little tails pointed in the same direction. To reconstruct the crime, you would examine the stains to determine what direction the blood was traveling when it hit the wall, then measure the length and width of the bloodstains to pinpoint the **angle of impact**—the angle at which the blood hit the wall—using the ground as your baseline. You could tape a long string through each droplet until you found the point where all those strings intersected,

Angular drops

and that would give you the approximate spot where blood hit the wall first—the **point of convergence** or **point of origin,** in forensic lingo. Now you can also take a digital photograph of the blood spatter, upload it to a computer, and use specialized software to calculate the angle.

The more elongated the blood droplets on the wall, the more extreme the angle of impact. What causes an extreme angle? Standing closer to the wall. If you're scrutinizing blood spatter and you calculate the angle of impact at fifteen degrees (again, using the floor as your baseline), you'll know that the victim had his face practically pressed up against the blood-spattered surface when he was murdered.

To reconstruct the crime, you would also photograph and possibly videotape the crime scene from every angle possible and write down every measurement you took to make sure you didn't distort the scale of the bloodstains. Then you would combine the data you collected with other evidence like the victim's wounds to get an accurate mental picture of what happened. Where was the victim when he was attacked? Was he standing? Kneeling? Lying on the floor? Was he facing his attacker or hit from behind? Was the body moved after death? Does the blood evidence belie or support the suspect's claim that he killed his victim in self-defense? Remember, the truth can exonerate as well as implicate.

Admittedly, there are some limits to reading the shapes in blood spatter. For instance, the smaller the drop, the harder it is to discern directionality. The weave of certain types of clothing and fabrics can influence a blood droplet's shape, too, and mislead a crime scene analyst.

But in the right circumstances, understanding the **directionality** of blood drops can help you determine which way a killer leaving a scene headed and how fast he moved. You would use what the blood trail told you to reconstruct the crime more accurately or, if you were extremely lucky, to follow and catch an escaping killer.

Say you're a cop responding to a 911 call made by a civilian claiming she heard shouts, screaming, and the sounds of fighting in the apartment next to hers. You arrive at the crime scene to find a bleeding, unconscious man who has obviously been in a knife fight. A trail of blood droplets leads out the back door and down a stairwell. You would use what you know about blood patterns to determine whether the attacker walked or ran, how long ago he left (blood starts to dry in three to six minutes), and whether he was bleeding or got his victim's blood on himself—all of which would give you and your fellow officers solid information about what to look for in suspects in the immediate vicinity.

One simple strategy I often recommend to jurors to help them visualize concepts like satellite spatter and teardrop-shaped droplets is to experiment with water. Drip water into a puddle and you'll see the droplets rebound to the sides. Flick water from your fingertips at a fogged-up shower door from various angles and you'll notice that the droplets' tails change as you shift your position.

Medium-Velocity Blood Spatter

If you strike a source of wet blood with a moderate amount of force, you'll produce **medium-velocity blood spatter**. The majority of homicides where you find it involve blunt-trauma attacks such as beatings and bludgeonings or stabbings. But since anything with greater force than gravity but weaker force than a gunshot will generate medium-velocity blood spatter, the possibilities are endless. Remember the old game of Clue? Aside from the rope and the revolver, all of the hypothetical weapons would produce medium-velocity spatter— the wrench, the lead pipe, the candlestick, or the knife. The force ap-

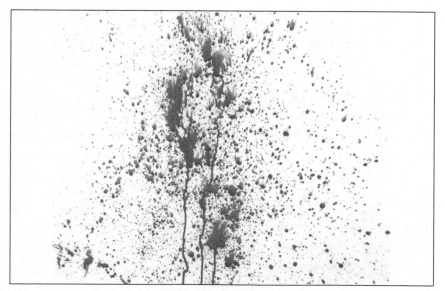

Medium-velocity blood spatter

plied to the blood source (usually the victim's body) means the blood travels faster and produces smaller airborne droplets than it would in a low-velocity pattern. The increased impact of the blood droplets when they land produces a random smattering of large and small drops. They are easier to see with the naked eye than high-velocity spatter, which usually requires magnification.

Here's a key concept in many criminal cases that tends to surprise jurors and lawyers: It requires multiple blows to a victim's body to produce medium-velocity spatter. Say a robber caught in the act hits a gas station attendant over the head with a tire iron and crushes his skull. The first blow would expose the victim's blood but would not send any of it flying onto his surroundings. It's the subsequent blows that would create blood spatter on the walls, ceiling, and nearby objects like the cash register. *The first blow creates no blood spatter.* If there were five blows to the station attendant's head, you will find spatter from four. You won't be able to count the blows by examining the spatter, though, unless victim and attacker moved significantly after each one.

If the hypothetical tire iron murder did involve multiple blows, forensic examination would probably also reveal bits of tissue, bone, and brain matter embedded in the spatter. Detectives could use the stains to calculate the flight path of the blood and the angle of impact and look for voids in the blood spatter to give them an indication of where the murderer and any accomplices were standing when the subject was beaten to death.

Generally speaking, the blunter the weapon, the more blood spatter results. Bigger weapons produce more spatter because a larger surface area is striking the blood, and sharp objects like knives create less spatter than rocks or sledgehammers unless they slice open an artery. When that happens, you get an arterial spurt, where the heart forcefully pumps blood out of the body through the wound, creating a series of long, arced lines of medium-velocity spatter. We call this type of stain a **projected blood pattern** rather than an impact pattern because it's created by blood released under pressure—not by an object striking liquid blood. The bloody puddles junkies leave behind when they jettison their blood after it gets drawn back into a syringe during a fix are also considered projected blood.

Other factors influence the amount of blood spatter, too. What part of the body did the murderer strike? Was the victim wearing heavy clothes? Was he wearing a hat?

As I mentioned in the previous chapter, another concept people find hard to grasp is that assailants often get very little blood on themselves during a beating or stabbing, even if it's an extremely bloody one. That's because in most blunt-trauma attacks, the majority of the blood is directed outward. The blood that lands on the person wielding the weapon is often minimal. You have to examine a killer's clothing under high-intensity lights or apply a blood reagent to it to spot the telltale traces of medium-velocity blood spatter.

If you can read blood evidence well enough to understand what it suggests about the victim's position and the assailant's MO, you'll get an idea of where to look for small deposits of blood spatter on the killer's clothes. Did the victim suffer overhead blows while lying on the ground? The assailant likely got some amount of spatter on the bottom of his pants, socks, and shoes. Did the killer use wide swings to the side like a batter playing baseball? Odds are spatter landed on his sleeves, hands, or gloves during the attack. Did he swing right- or left-handed? The spatter patterns on his sleeves, pants, and shoes will probably reflect that.

If the murder is premeditated and the killer wore protective clothing during the attack, minute traces of medium-velocity spatter can still show up in unlikely spots he's overlooked. I've investigated cases where there wasn't a trace of blood on a suspect's clothes, but minus-

Cast-off

cule flecks of blood on his glasses, his watch, or his belt buckle gave him away.

One other blood pattern that commonly accompanies medium-velocity spatter is **cast-off**—blood that flies off an object while it's in motion. It could result from a person with bloody hair whipping his head around. Or someone with blood-soaked sleeves swinging his arms as he runs could produce it. But usually at crime scenes, it gets inadvertently flung off a weapon being used to make multiple blows. (Think of Lizzie Borden and the infamous "forty whacks" with the ax, for example, though in reality it was fewer than twenty.)

Cast-off can land on items at the crime scene or on a killer's clothing. If two suspects admit to being present at a murder, but each claims he stood by and watched while the other committed it, cast-off blood patterns sometimes provide the only definitive proof as to who actually wielded the murder weapon. (Incidentally, if blood pattern analysis had been well developed in 1892, experts might have been able to determine whether Borden was likely guilty or innocent based on cast-off and impact spatter patterns at the scene, on her clothing, and on the hatchet believed to be the murder weapon.)

Case Study: Secret Lives and Lies

Medium-velocity spatter figured heavily into the case of prominent Massachusetts allergist Dirk Greineder. On the morning of October 31, 1999, sixty-year-old Greineder and his wife of thirty-one years—Mabel, or May, as her friends called her—took their German shepherd for a walk in the woods surrounding Morses Pond near their home in Wellesley. With their three children grown and living on their own, the couple often walked their dogs together for exercise. But according to the story Greineder later told police, May suffered frequent back pain, and when it flared up that day, she decided to go back to the van to wait while he continued walking Zephyr.

When Greineder was returning to the vehicle a short time later, he stumbled upon his wife sprawled across a wooded trail. At first he thought she was resting her back, but bending closer, he discovered to his horror that her throat had been slashed and she had been hit in the head multiple times with what police learned was a blue-handled hammer when they found the weapon along with a pocketknife and a bloodstained glove under the grate covering a nearby storm drain. Further searching turned up a matching bloody glove under a second grate.

Greineder's version of events began to fall apart when lab tests confirmed not only that the bloodstains were May's, but that the pocketknife and one of the gloves bore traces of her husband's DNA. A police sergeant securing the crime scene noted that though the man's Windbreaker, shoes, and glasses were bloody, his hands were spotless—

surprising, considering he claimed to have tried twice to lift May's body and to have checked her carotid artery for a pulse. A trash bag, surgical gloves, and lighter fluid with a label advertising its stain-removing abilities found under a pile of leaves nearby pointed to premeditated murder. When a pair of brown work gloves identical to the bloody ones were retrieved by police from a doghouse at the Greineders' home, suspicion mounted.

Investigators dug deeper into the Greineders' private lives and unearthed the kind of dirt tabloids dream about. Dirk Greineder, it seemed, had a secret Internet sex life, frequenting chat rooms of couples looking for threesomes, ringing up massive phone bills to porn lines, and paying prostitutes for motel sex. In fact, he called one the day after his wife's death. Greineder claimed he was ashamed of his salacious side, but the fact that his wife had lost interest in sex a decade earlier had forced him into it. Police and the DA's office thought it more likely that the doctor longed to get May out of the way so he could pursue his porn obsession freely. They theorized that when she found his condoms and self-prescribed Viagra and started grilling him about them, he snapped.

Prosecutor Richard Grundy asked me to examine the evidence and give my opinion about which side of the story it bore out. I flew to Massachusetts and spent three days studying the bloody items recovered from the crime scene. What I found made a strong case against Greineder. His story just didn't fit the blood on his clothes.

For starters, the front of the yellow Windbreaker he wore in the park that day was speckled with more than ten of the minuscule blood dots characteristic of medium-velocity spatter—precisely the pattern that lands on a killer's clothing during a blunt-trauma murder. They were hardly the superficial blood transfers that might graze a panicked husband who stumbles on his wife's dead body. More of the same spatter dotted his shirt, his pants, and his Reebok sneakers.

We sent the jacket to a forensics lab in King County, Washington, where tests also revealed cast-off stains on the back. That told me Greineder had swung the bloody hammer repeatedly, inadvertently flicking spatter onto himself as he killed May. Though the cast-off evidence was ultimately ruled inadmissible in court, the Windbreaker had plenty more to tell us.

Bloody hair and clothing transfer patterns suggested a dead or unconscious person's head had rested against its sleeves and shoulders— exactly what would have happened if Greineder had dragged his wife's body from behind. Sure enough, drag and heel marks in the woods suggested May had been moved ten feet or more. The shoe size was similar to Greineder's.

Perhaps the most telling evidence of all were the bloody grab marks on the Windbreaker's sleeves—transfer marks in May's blood that would be consistent with the dying woman clutching her husband's clothing as he bludgeoned her to death.

Fortunately, the police took a photograph of Greineder's glasses before he left the crime scene. (He refused to surrender them that morning but turned them in later after they had been wiped clean.) We enhanced the image digitally and saw a large bloody smear with a dimpled dot pattern that matched the surface on the fingers of the bloody gloves.

Grundy called a number of witnesses, including Massachusetts State Police lieutenant Kenneth Martin, a blood spatter expert who provided testimony about the physical evidence against Greineder. My testimony followed Martin's and reinforced his interpretation of the blood patterns in question. For my presentation in court, I dressed a life-size mannequin in the actual clothing Greineder wore on the morning of the murder and conducted a number of demonstrations with it to show the jury the kinds of actions that would most plausibly have produced the bloodstains on Greineder's clothes.

Despite a vigorous defense and a trial that lasted more than five weeks, Greineder was found guilty of first-degree murder and sentenced to life in prison without the possibility of parole in June 2001. He requested a new trial five years later but was denied.

High-Velocity Blood Spatter

High-velocity blood spatter stains occur when something hits blood with tremendous force and atomizes it into a fine mist of airborne particulates. Though it is frequently accompanied by massive amounts of pooled blood from a victim's wounds, the high-velocity mist itself leaves droplets so tiny that they are often imperceptible to the naked eye.

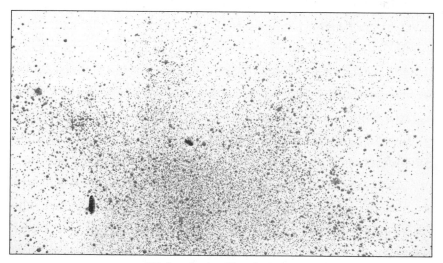

High-velocity blood spatter

Most high-velocity impact patterns you find at crime scenes in the United States are caused by gunshots, but explosives, car accidents, and injuries from heavy machinery like circular saws and chain saws create high-velocity mist, too. Remember the collection of minuscule blood droplets embedded with brain tissue and fiber that we found covering the grease-caked engine of Eric Humbert's car in the Green Thread Mystery? They were a perfect example of high-velocity spatter. Another was the incriminating dot pattern on David Duyst's shirt in the Sandra Anne Duyst "suicide," which, as you know, turned out to be a murder.

To visualize the effect of high-velocity spatter, think of filling an aerosol can with hairspray dyed red and then spraying it onto a mirror or a countertop. The gunshot sends bloody mist traveling through the air even faster than a spray can. If you're a movie fan, picture the wood chipper scene in *Fargo*. The snow sprayed bright red provides a relatively accurate representation of what high-velocity blood spatter stains look like.

Most high-velocity blood spatter will travel in the direction the shot was fired, giving a crime scene reconstructionist solid data to use in understanding who stood where when the gun went off. When a bullet goes through a victim, the exit wound produces a mist of **forward spatter,** too. Exit wounds from gunshots make a conelike shape, as if the blood had been sprayed out through a megaphone.

Depending on the weapon, a sort of amorphous cloud of red mist can also rebound toward the source of the injury. It's called **blowback** or **back spatter.** The Alan Gell Bug Case is a good example. We knew from the high-velocity back spatter in the door frame that the killer fired from the hall, which led us to conclude that suspect Crystal Morris's story about Alan Gell emerging suddenly from behind the bedroom door and firing a double-barreled shotgun was a fabrication.

Because most of the droplets in high-velocity blood spatter are fine and lightweight, they lose momentum quickly in the air. That means they don't travel as far as medium-velocity spatter. No matter how powerful a gun is used, the bloody mist it produces will land only three to four feet from the source of the blood, though there are usually some larger, heavier drops that fall farther away.

Misleading Clues

More than one red herring can throw a seasoned detective off track when it comes to high-velocity blood spatter. Flies love to lay their eggs in blood, for instance. And when they walk around in wet blood, their excrement and their tiny footprints leave a pattern of dark, round specks that to the untrained eye looks a lot like the high-velocity mist from a gunshot. It often gets misidentified. Crime scene investigators will examine it and say, "Well, the killer had to be standing here." But in reality, insects were responsible. How do you tell the difference? Under a microscope, you'll spot the signature Q-shaped marks the insects leave when they regurgitate. Incidentally, scientists can actually pull DNA out of blood that has been through a fly's digestive system to identify a killer or a victim.

Another pattern that often misleads crime scene investigations is expired blood—blood that an injured person has exhaled or coughed out. (Some books on blood pattern analysis mention sneezing as a third source of expired blood, though in more than forty years of crime scene investigation, I have never seen an injured person sneeze out blood.) It can come out through the mouth, nose, or even through severe wounds in the lungs or trachea. It produces a mist very similar to the type a gunshot wound creates. However, the tails of each droplet are blunt, the blood has air bubbles in it, and the pattern it makes is chaotic and random, as if the blood droplets have been spinning through the air in every direction. Gunshot spatter, on the other hand, produces a neat arc or fan of minuscule blood droplets with the sharply narrowed spines of each pointing in the same direction. With experience, you learn to recognize the distinctive little round circles and voids in the blood and to look for mucous strands to confirm that blood was expirated. You can vet your theory by asking a crime lab to test a sample of the blood to see whether there is saliva in it.

I was asked to consult on an interesting case in Yonkers, New York, in the 1990s involving a woman whose husband was released from the penitentiary and then headed straight home to murder her. The man stabbed his wife in the back with a butcher knife, and she died while struggling to get out the front door of her apartment. The positioning of the body and the multitude of bloody hand transfers smeared along the inside of the door frame testified to that. But the DA's office asked me to explain what the rest of the blood spatter meant. There was an abundance of high-velocity mist on the door. Didn't that suggest that the man had shot her in addition to stabbing her? If so, why had the autopsy found no gunshot wound? Fortunately, I knew enough about expirated blood by that point to recognize the turbulent, irregular patterning it creates and to look for telltale mucous strands to confirm my suspicion. The knife pierced the woman's lungs, and in her frantic struggle to escape she was breathing hard, almost panting in her last few minutes of life—exhaling blood all over the door and the wall near it.

It was just one of many cases I've worked on where high-velocity mist could mislead investigators as easily as it could lead them to the truth. Here's another.

Case Study: Suspicious Circumstances

There was no question that Tyler Opperman was dead. The question was how he got that way. His wife, Casey, twenty-seven, swore she had been in the bathtub of their home in Cincinnati, Iowa, at around three o'clock in the morning on January 27, 2008, when she heard a thump in the bedroom outside the bathroom door. She called to Tyler to ask him what had made the noise. When she got no answer, she went to see for herself. There was her twenty-three-year-old husband, lying at the foot of the bed, blood leaking out of his head, still holding the .22-caliber rifle he had just used to commit suicide.

Tyler Opperman's family was hardly the first to have trouble believing that someone they loved had killed himself, though they had more reason for skepticism than many other grief-stricken families—namely, the fact that Casey's first husband, twenty-eight-year-old Brad Tuttle, had also killed himself with a single gunshot wound to the head two years earlier in nearby Green City, Missouri. It didn't help that Opperman's new widow wasn't exactly the sympathetic girl-next-door type, by many accounts. In fact, on the night Tyler Opperman died, Casey fractured her nose in a bar fight with another woman and the couple spent some of their last hours together at the emergency room.

The police and the crime lab couldn't reach a unanimous decision about the cause of death, partly because of the puzzling blood patterns in the couple's bedroom. Opperman's was the only DNA on the gun, and his blood alcohol level was too low to suggest he might have been unconscious when he died. But blood spatter had ended up around the corner of a nightstand. How? Why were Opperman's socks and the floor near his body speckled with what looked like back spatter? What did the voids and pooled blood underneath him mean? And how had he gotten blood transfer stains onto his clothing? Had someone moved his body? Did it suggest an angle of impact that no suicide could manage?

Sheriff Gary Anderson called me. I flew to Iowa and scrutinized the crime scene photos from the minuscule one-story blue cottage where the death occurred. The high-velocity spatter was tricky, but ultimately it all pointed to one inevitable explanation, based on my knowledge of blood patterns: Tyler Opperman sat on the edge of his bed, placed the rifle between his legs, pointing it upward and pinching it between his knees to steady it, then put the end inside his mouth before pulling the trigger.

How could we be sure?

First, the powder deposits and blood stippling on the roof of the dead man's mouth provided concrete evidence that there had been intraoral contact with the end of the barrel.

Second, the distinctive blood spatter on the victim's clothing gave us enough solid data to re-create his position accurately. The inside of Opperman's right sock and pant leg were blood-spattered. So were the outside of his left sock and pant leg. Yet there were blood-free voids on the inside of the left sock and pant leg as well as on the outside of the right ones. This told us that after the .22 discharged, Opperman's head and torso slumped to the left, beyond his left leg and over the edge of the bed. His body remained upright for a number of seconds—blood dripping from his mouth and nose onto his clothing and the floor nearby—until the force of gravity finally caused him to fall and make the thump that his wife heard. (Strange as it might sound, it's not uncommon for a seated gunshot victim to remain upright temporarily as Opperman did.)

During the moments that Opperman's body stayed perched on the bed with his head hanging forward, his blood dripped enough to create a blood-into-blood pattern with satellite spatter on the floor that could easily be mistaken for back spatter pointing away from him. Finally, as he fell he brushed the edge of the swivel nightstand, which spun around so that the spattered side was facing away from him. He fell into his own wet blood and smeared some of it onto his clothing, creating the puzzling transfer stains and explaining how so much blood ended up underneath his body.

We calculated the angle of impact based on Opperman's wound and the blood spatter as well as on the position his body was found in, then we compared this with the dimensions of the tiny bedroom. There simply wasn't enough room for his wife to have shot him. She would have had to sit on the floor with her feet under the bed between her husband and the TV stand, and he would have had to allow her to place the end of the rifle in his mouth. Suspicious circumstances notwithstanding, murder would have been physically impossible in the Opperman case.

Casey Opperman soon moved out of state and married for a third time. Did Tyler mimic her first husband's method of suicide in an attempt to incriminate her as some people have suggested? Did Casey play an active role in her husband's death as others suspected? I have certainly handled cases where one person literally talked another into killing himself. Then again, I have investigated crimes where someone took drastic, tragic actions for the sole purpose of ruining someone else's life. But the blood evidence in the Opperman case told me nothing about the dynamics of their relationship, and I never speculate. Conjecture has no place in crime scene reconstruction.

Web of Lies?

It's not uncommon for people who stumble upon dead bodies to try to find out if the victims might still be alive. They check for a pulse, turn a victim over, shake him, try to resuscitate him, or come in contact with wet blood through any number of other innocent, well-intentioned actions. In most cases they panic, particularly if they know the victim. They might not even realize that they've transferred blood to their own clothing until a police officer points it out. Unfortunately, murderers know this. And, like Hartmann and Greineder, they have an annoying habit of trying to explain away the bloodstains on their clothes by claiming they were the proverbial innocent bystander "trying to help" the victim.

One of the most accurate ways to find out whether such transfers are inadvertent or incriminating is to do a microscopic examination of the fabric. Blood coating only the top layer suggests that the person brushed against wet blood accidentally. However, minuscule droplets of blood spatter embedded more deeply in the fabric's fibers suggest the person wearing the clothing was either the assailant or stood nearby while an attack causing medium- or high-velocity spatter occurred.

Taking this one step further, crime scene reconstructionists would use the position of the blood spatter on the clothing to determine whether it suggests guilt or innocence. The Sandra Anne Duyst murder is a prime example: Not only did an examination of her husband's clothing reveal high-velocity blood spatter, but it showed spatter concentrated behind the right sleeve—precisely where blowback would hit a shooter extending his arm as he pulled the trigger.

Bullet and Wound Trajectories

Firearms are responsible for close to three-quarters of the murders in the United States. They accounted for 68 percent of them in 2006, the most recent year for which the National Institute of Justice has data. They are also the weapon of choice in more than half of the suicides— just over 52 percent, based on 2005 data from the National Center for Health Statistics. So it's not surprising that high-velocity blood spatter interpretation plays a central role in crime scene reconstruction in America today. But it's only one piece of the puzzle.

Understanding **trajectory** (the flight path a moving object takes through space) is equally important. Crime scene reconstructionists work backward from the blood spatter through the victim's wounds and the position of his body to determine the course the bullet or bullets took through the air. Mapping out the bullet's path tells you the shooter's position and distance from the victim, approximate height, right- or left-handedness, whether he or she was stationary or moving when the shots were fired, and more.

Ballistics experts can also piece together what make of gun and type of bullet were used based on shell casings, spent bullets, and bullet fragments. Was more than one gun used? Was the gun a type that leaves residue on a shooter's skin or clothes? If so, detectives will swab any suspects they bring in and lab test their clothing for traces of it. A fired bullet is almost like a license plate—it reveals the distinctive grooves, lands (flat, high points), and other unique markings of the gun that fired it. No two guns create the same markings.

When there is a gun in evidence, experts can use chemicals to reconstruct a serial number that has been ground or filed off. This can then be entered into a state or national database to find out whom it's registered to and whether it has been used in other recent crimes.

Case Study: Ghosts of the Civil War

In 1989, I got a chance to put my knowledge of trajectory to use to help unlock lingering mysteries in a crime that took place almost 150 years ago.

On the morning of July 3, 1863, twenty-year-old Gettysburg resident Mary Virginia Wade rose early and started kneading dough for bread and biscuits she planned to hand out to hungry Union soldiers, as she and her mother had done the previous day. The family had taken shelter at the house of Wade's sister Georgia, who gave birth an hour before Confederate troops rode into town on the first day of what would become the Civil War's most famous battle. Jennie Wade (or Ginnie Wade, according to some sources) and her family hoped the little brick house would provide a safer haven than their own, which was several blocks away. Instead they found themselves caught in a no-man's-land between Northern and Southern sharpshooters.

More than 150 shots hit the façade of the Baltimore Street house before one fatal bullet penetrated the exterior side door. It pierced the interior kitchen door next and then struck Wade in the back under her left shoulder blade. She died instantly, earning the dubious distinction as the only civilian killed in the epic Battle of Gettysburg. Her fiancé, a Union soldier, was wounded, taken prisoner, and died in a hospital less than two weeks later. He never learned of Wade's fate.

The bullet-riddled house where Jennie Wade was shot to death is now a museum and a popular tourist attraction. According to one local legend, it is still haunted by the ghost of the young woman who died trying to serve the cause of patriotism by feeding starving troops. Nearby at Evergreen Cemetery, an American flag flies over Wade's grave around the clock. Betsy Ross is the only other American woman given that honor.

For more than a hundred years, history held that the shooter fired from a building on Baltimore Street just north of the house, where Confederate troops were positioned. When I was attending the FBI National Academy for three months in 1989, my roommate, a captain in a California sheriff's office, was an American history buff, and on weekends I tagged along with him to visit every battlefield within driving distance in that history-rich region. I found Jennie Wade's house especially fascinating and took Penny to see it when she came to visit. There were the famous little round holes in the doors that had left the wood splintered and exposed, the same bullet holes that have drawn countless visitors to the spot over the years. There was the large battered wooden dough tray where Wade was working when she died. I followed an imaginary bullet's trajectory in my mind's eye, as I have done at many crime scenes, from the first through the second hole and on to an imaginary woman standing in the kitchen, trying to calculate the point of origin. Then I read the historical information displayed. Something didn't sit quite right. But it was hard to focus in a room where other visitors were examining the artifacts and intermittently blocking my view. I spoke to the people in charge, explained what I did for a living, and asked if I might be able to come back to examine the bullet holes more closely. They agreed.

It would be several years after I graduated from the FBI Academy, where I was privileged to serve as president and spokesperson of the 159th session and give the commencement speech for my class, but I managed to return with measuring equipment in 2003. I ran a string from one bullet hole to the next and then on to the dough tray. My measurements showed that the hole in the kitchen door was roughly three and a half inches higher than the one in the exterior wall. That meant the bullet was on an upward course when it struck Wade. It also cast doubt on the theory that the sniper who fired it was in a building. He would have been positioned low and firing upward. I stepped outside and scrutinized the area. Based on historical accounts of who was stationed where when Wade died, the bullet most likely came from much farther away than originally believed—probably from a field where Confederate sharpshooters had taken up posts north of the cluster of buildings that included the Wade house. I filmed a short reenactment using an actress dressed in period costume to illustrate how the shooting would have happened based on the trajectory the bullet holes suggested.

In the spring of 2009, Penny and I had the honor of returning to examine evidence at the Jennie Wade House once again with a superb group of investigative pros that included forensic serology consultant

Dr. Ted Yeshion of ClueFinders Inc. as well as former Oregon police officers Amy Dier and Olivia Leon, who now run their own private investigative firm called Blue Line Investigations. Ken Rohrbaugh, who oversees operations at the Jennie Wade House, and house manager Sharon Marcus generously allowed us a full day and evening to conduct tests with phenolphthalein and Luminol for the presence of blood on the dough tray, the wooden floorboards of one of the bedrooms in the house, and a bullet that was donated to the museum recently with the claim that it was the actual bullet that killed Wade. Luminol tests revealed a glowing bright green constellation of what looked like blood spatter patterns on the bottom of the dough tray's center and sides as well as some intriguing reactions with the flooring in the bedroom. We took core samples of the wood and sent them to Dr. Grimsbo for DNA tests to find out whether it was human blood and, if so, whether it belonged to a man or a woman. We were still awaiting results as this book went to press.

DNA Takes Center Stage

As you know if you've watched shows like *CSI* and *Forensic Files,* killers often leave samples of their DNA behind at crime scenes—minute amounts of blood if they cut themselves during the attack, broken fingernails, strands of hair, bodily fluids like semen, and bits of skin that slough off when their hands touch their victims' clothes.

Criminalistics has made phenomenal progress from its first simple forensic applications. In the early 1900s, precipitin tests emerged. They involved extracting the red and white cells from a sample of the blood of a specific kind of animal (deer, rabbit, human, and so on) and then dropping the clear serum that remains into an unidentified sample of blood to see whether it reacted by producing a cloudy "precipitate." The cloudiness indicated that the two samples came from the same species. If nothing happened to the serum, the tester could safely conclude that the unknown bloodstain came from a different species. Investigators used the results of precipitin tests to tell whether a murder suspect was lying or telling the truth when he claimed that the blood smears all over his clothes came from a successful deer hunt and not a human victim. In the mid-1980s, DNA fingerprinting emerged along with PCR (polymerase chain reaction) tests, which allowed for analysis and identification using minuscule DNA samples as well as degraded ones that had been gathering dust in evidence rooms or buried with corpses for decades. Perhaps the best-known early example was the 1985 exhumation of Brazilian rancher Wolfgang Gerhard, whose remains were identified (through PCR DNA testing) by an international panel of forensic pathologists as those of escaped Nazi Angel of Death Josef Mengele.

I've investigated quite a number of cases that hinged on DNA technology. But the one that made the most powerful impression on me is the murder of Helena Greenwood.

Case Study: Better Late than Never

Helena Greenwood, a British scientist-turned-marketer for a California biotech firm on the cutting edge of DNA diagnostics, was at home in her cottage in Atherton, a suburb of San Francisco, on the night of April 7, 1984. She spent the evening catching up on work, then went to bed early since her husband, Roger, was away on business. She wasn't worried about staying alone. Atherton was wealthy and sedate, and crime was virtually nonexistent.

So it was with great horror and shock that she woke up in the darkness to see a tall, athletically built stranger with a gun coming toward her bed through the darkened room. Keeping his hood pulled tight around his face so that all Greenwood could see were his eyes, the stranger ordered her to take off her clothes, then marched her through the house to her purse. After finding little money in it, he forced her back to her bedroom and demanded she perform fellatio on him. Terrified, she complied. A short time later, he pushed her away and fled. Shaking and fighting tears, Greenwood ran to the neighbors' house and asked them to call the police.

Detectives combed the cottage and retrieved a semen-stained pillowcase, several hairs, and a white teapot that had somehow ended up on the deck when the stranger slipped in through the kitchen window. A forensics lab discovered a stranger's fingerprint on it, but it didn't match any in the FBI's criminal database. That gave detectives little to go on, and the case stagnated until women in an apartment complex in the nearby community of Belmont started reporting similar assaults.

By the time a thirteen-year-old girl in the French Village apartments called police in February 1985 to report a man masturbating outside her window, Helena Greenwood had been offered a job with the biotech firm Gen-Probe in San Diego and had gratefully moved south with Roger after assuring the prosecutor that she would return to testify. Police hurried to French Village and apprehended someone named David Paul Frediani on the grounds. Frediani claimed he was in the market for a new apartment and had been looking for the manager of the complex when he was suddenly seized with an urgent need to urinate. Without a bathroom close by, he relieved himself in the bushes and the girl caught sight of him.

Unconvinced, the authorities charged Frediani with indecent exposure and began exploring whether he might have been behind the other Belmont assaults. When an inter-station intelligence report about Frediani crossed the desk of Atherton Police Department Sergeant Steve Chaput, who was overseeing the still open Greenwood assault, he connected the two. He ran a check on Frediani's fingerprints and found that they matched the mystery prints on the Greenwoods' teapot. Chaput approached DA Martin Murray and got an arrest warrant for Frediani for attempted burglary and forced oral copulation in the Helena Greenwood attack.

At the police station, Chaput's suspect vehemently denied any involvement until he heard about the fingerprint match. Then his demeanor changed entirely. According to the officers interrogating him, he started breathing hard, fidgeting compulsively, and claiming to have been so drunk that he didn't know what he was doing when "those things" happened.

Greenwood testified at a preliminary hearing about the assault and the general appearance of her assailant, though she said she couldn't be sure it was the man at the defense table. Bail was set at $25,000, and Paul Frediani's trial was scheduled for September 16.

Then the unthinkable happened.

When Helena Greenwood, the consummate professional who pulled long hours and seldom missed a day of work, failed to turn up for a conference at the office, her colleagues got worried. They phoned Roger, who raced home but couldn't open the gate leading to their rental home near the beach. He peered over the top to find out what was blocking it and saw his wife's blood-covered body slumped on the other side.

Helena Greenwood had been strangled to death and her head smashed against the gate's metal latch, creating a wide laceration in her scalp. Though she hadn't been raped, her skirt had been pulled up over her hips and her legs propped open. Scratches, scrapes, and cuts covered her arms, legs, and face—unmistakable evidence of a violent struggle. Papers she had intended to take to work with her drifted through the yard, caught in the afternoon breeze.

Roger called the police, who carefully bagged and tagged all the evidence at the scene and during the autopsy. But there was too little blood and skin under Greenwood's fingernails to hope to identify her killer. The prime suspect? Frediani, naturally. He was out on bail, and police records revealed that he had gotten into a traffic accident 130 miles from the crime scene a week before it happened. When asked what he was doing so far south of San Francisco, he claimed he had decided on the spur of the moment to get out of town.

Though it certainly wasn't definitive proof of his guilt, Paul Frediani had the size and strength to strangle someone to death, which is harder physically than most people realize. What's more, he had the motive. Eliminating the only witness would have considerably upped his chance of beating the burglary-assault rap. It's worth noting that death by strangulation rarely happens among strangers. More often than not, the assailant knows his victim and channels tremendous rage against him or her into the attack.

Still, it wasn't enough to charge Frediani with the murder.

Come September, the assault case went on as planned minus its star witness. No one was allowed to tell the jurors that Helena Greenwood had been murdered for fear of prejudicing them against Frediani. They weren't even allowed to refer to her in the past tense. No one explained why she wasn't there to give her own testimony. When Frediani took the stand, he explained his fingerprint on the teapot by stating that he had been house hunting (the Greenwoods' cottage was for sale at the time of the assault) and claiming his statements at the police station referred to other drunken acts—not sexual assaults. Nonetheless, the jury found him guilty and he was sentenced to nine years in prison. He won an appeal and was retried and found guilty by a second jury in 1987.

Years passed. Paul Frediani had served out his sentence and been released from prison by the time San Diego detective Laura Heilig was poring over a ream of cold case documents in 1998 and pulled out the file on Helena Greenwood. Practical applications for DNA technology had progressed at lightning speed since the 1980s—when Greenwood herself had been perched on the cutting edge of the field—and Heilig was in luck with this case since the evidence hadn't been tossed out. She sent the fingernail clippings and scrapings to a DNA lab along with samples of Greenwood's hair to make sure any DNA they found wasn't the victim's. Just as Heilig hoped, technicians located foreign DNA in the evidence. Next Heilig obtained a sample of Paul Frediani's DNA from the state Department of Justice lab to test for a match.

Bingo.

It looked as though Laura Heilig had identified Helena Greenwood's killer at last. She met with Deputy DA Valerie Summers and got an arrest warrant for Paul Frediani for the murder of Helena Greenwood.

Frediani insisted he was innocent. He claimed the police, who had ample access to his DNA samples on file with the Department of Justice, had planted them in the Greenwood evidence to close a case that had long rankled them.

Before the trial, Summers sought my help in interpreting the blood evidence that remained from the Greenwood murder. I went down to San Diego and examined more than two hundred photographs of the crime scene as well as the autopsy, then went to see the spot where the murder occurred. I do that whenever it's possible, even if every trace of evidence has long since vanished, because it gives me a more thorough, accurate understanding of the crime and puts it in a solid physical context. Angles, perspective, and minute details you can miss easily even if you're studying hundreds of photos suddenly become apparent when you stand in the spot where someone died.

From what I saw in the photographs, the blood Helena Greenwood lost testified to the tremendous struggle that preceded her death. This woman had obviously fought like hell to stay alive. The multiple cuts and bruises and the low- and medium-velocity spatter told me that she was still fighting hard when her attacker finally forced her to her knees and bashed her head into the latch on the gate to subdue her. Her head wound had been deep enough to bleed freely. It had created a pool on the ground with blood-into-blood patterning and satellite drops in the dirt and on her clothes. The abrasions on her neck, the petechial hemorrhages in her eyes, and the fact that she had bitten the inside of her own mouth were consistent with strangulation.

Greenwood had clearly been posed in that awkward splay-legged position after she died or when she was too weak to resist. The most interesting point about this was the bloody hand transfer pattern on her torn nylons—the handprints of her killer as he gripped her ankles and propped her legs open in his last degrading gesture. We had a lab run tests on the transfer pattern, and Frediani's DNA turned up on the bloody panty hose.

Based on the DNA evidence—primarily from the fingernails, but also from the panty hose—a jury found Paul Frediani guilty of murder in the first degree. In March 2001, he was sentenced to life in prison without the possibility of parole. Helena Greenwood's husband, Roger, had succumbed to cancer by the time the jury returned a verdict. Her mother, too, died of the disease a few weeks before her daughter's death. Greenwood's father, her last close surviving relative, was suffering from cancer throughout the trial. He died sixteen hours after learning the verdict in his daughter's murder.

Brainteasers in Blood

Even those of us who devote our lives to studying blood patterns and manage to stockpile a fair amount of knowledge about them run into crime scenes that leave us scratching our heads. It's inevitable in this line of work. In the years since the unforgettable Vomit Case—when I mistook regurgitation from bleeding ulcers for an ax murderer's handiwork and blithely announced it over the police radio—I've encountered plenty of mystery patterns that left me scratching my head. To save myself chagrin, I keep my theories quiet until I'm sure about what caused them. But I've seen more than one experienced detective identify blood that squirted out of ruptured varicose veins as an arterial spurt from a homicide. It's easy to do. When someone is walking as a leg vein bursts, the pattern mimics an arterial spurt almost perfectly.

I've also seen instances when everyone on the scene missed the obvious, myself included. Case in point: In Santa Monica, California, in the 1970s, police got a call from a distraught woman claiming she had found her boyfriend dead on the bathroom floor. Detectives hurried to the scene and found the body of a man clad only in his underwear, covered in dried blood smears and shattered glass from a broken shower door. (Needless to say, this was before safety glass became a standard feature in bathroom fixtures.)

They photographed every inch of the crime scene and took copious notes. But it wasn't until weeks later that the technician developing the images posed an interesting question: "There's blood all over the room. How come there isn't a drop of it on the victim's briefs?" Blood covered his legs, his arms, and his torso. One bloody hand even rested on the pristine white underwear. Why didn't any of it transfer to the fabric?

The answer? The blood was already dry by the time someone carefully slipped undergarments onto the dead man. The coroner concluded that the victim had died of exsanguination. In simple terms, he bled to death. From that, detectives deduced that he fell through his shower door, severed a major artery, and rolled around in his own watery blood as he struggled unsuccessfully to get up, spreading the blood and sustaining additional cuts and gashes.

When the police reinterviewed the victim's girlfriend and confronted her with the facts, she admitted that she had gone to her boyfriend's house, let herself in, and found him dead in his bathroom. Not wanting him to suffer the final indignity of having police swarm in and see him naked, she put underwear on him before calling the police department. Because the blood was already dry, her hands and feet left no evidence of her actions.

The death was ruled accidental.

I often use the case as a teaching tool in my seminars. I show the photograph and invite attendees to examine it during breaks to see whether they can pinpoint what's out of place in the scene.

Here's a second strange blood pattern from an actual case that took place in the mid-1980s: A young couple in Orange County, California, came home from dinner and were accosted by a pair of armed men at their front door. The men shoved them inside, slammed the door behind them, and marched the couple to the second floor of their home. They led the woman into one room and the man into another. One intruder used surgical tubing and handcuffs to tie the man's hands behind his back and forced him to the floor, where he held him at gunpoint. Meanwhile, his accomplice raped the woman in the next room. Then they switched places. After they finished, they shot the man three times in the head execution style and left him lying facedown on the carpet. The woman survived to call the police but could tell them little about what happened during her husband's murder.

The question officers from the Buena Park Police Department hired me to answer was this: How did a figure eight composed of hundreds of individual blood droplets end up on the carpet next to the deceased's head?

The lab people and the detectives each had a different theory. One camp surmised that he had been picked up and carried to that spot in the room. Another thought the blood had leaked from his mouth and nose. We solved the mystery only through extensive role-playing and reconstruction in a motel room that we rented expressly for the purpose. I worked with the local criminalist, trying scenario after scenario, ruling out various theories. At last we discovered that the truth lay hidden in the dead man's jacket. When you looked at it closely in the photos, you could see that it was all bunched up at the shoulders. That told us one of the killers grabbed the victim's jacket after shooting him and rolled him over onto his shoulder so that his head was off the floor long enough for it to leak blood from the three bullet holes— most likely while he searched the jacket for money. Before they left, they rolled the victim back to his original position facing downward, which created the second loop of the figure eight.

There's a frequently cited Sherlock Holmes quote in which the fictional detective instructs his friend Watson, "Once you eliminate the impossible, whatever remains, no matter how improbable, must be the truth." It's not quite that simple. There's always a chance that you're wrong, that the real explanation lies in some obscure action or unlikely catalyst that has never crossed your mind. Still, the concept of painstakingly ruling out the possibilities one by one is the most valid approach to detective work I know.

6

Celebrity Cases

As word about my work in crime scene reconstruction and blood pattern analysis spread through the legal field, I started to get calls from DAs and defense attorneys seeking my opinion on criminal cases involving names I recognized from TV and movies. I had already seen the cutthroat capabilities of lawyers, and I knew that with a celebrity client or victim, the stakes would be exponentially higher—more media, more potential for a lawyer to make or break his reputation. If I agreed to serve as an expert witness in celebrity trials, I would set myself up for the kind of punishment on the stand that only a masochist could enjoy.

I also knew that my interpretation of the blood patterns at a crime scene wouldn't change, no matter who asked me to analyze them or what they wanted me to find. There are guns for hire out there, but my career is based on my credibility. I go where the evidence takes me. As I tell every client at the outset, "Blood evidence might work in your favor. It might work against you. We won't know until we examine it." That's not the kind of guarantee power players in Hollywood like to hear.

Even when crimes involving the rich and famous turn up intriguing blood evidence and I can shed light on what it means, I can't guarantee that a judge or jury will listen to me. Real life isn't neat and simple like the majority of TV crime dramas. You don't always find out whodunit. You don't always get the bad guy. And the case doesn't always hinge on blood evidence. Sometimes my findings play a pivotal role. Sometimes they play only a minor part in unlocking the mysteries of a murder.

No matter what, my procedure remains the same: I examine the evidence methodically, conduct experiments when they are needed, report my findings, testify about them if I'm asked to, and then leave. I never stick around the courtroom to hear the verdict read out. That would show an undue interest in the outcome of the case, and my job is to be impartial. I have to focus on the evidence, not the characters, even when the rest of the country is obsessed with them.

Case Study: Bob Crane and the Mystery Marks

One of the early celebrity cases I consulted on was the murder of former *Hogan's Heroes* star Bob Crane. In the summer of 1978, Crane was in Scottsdale, Arizona, starring in a play called *Beginner's Luck* at the Windmill Dinner Theatre. When he failed to turn up for a publicity event on June 29, his costar Victoria Berry decided to drop by the Winfield Apartments, where Crane had taken up temporary residence, to make sure he was okay. Finding the door unlocked, she walked in and saw her costar lying facedown in bed, clad only in boxer shorts and partially covered by blankets. His head was covered in blood.

Berry called the police, who rushed to the scene and determined that Crane was dead, his skull crushed by two blows from a blunt instrument. The forty-nine-year-old actor had been hit so hard that his bloodied face was almost unrecognizable, and whoever killed him made doubly sure he succeeded by winding an electrical cord tightly around Crane's neck to strangle him after bludgeoning him.

Police first surmised that the weapon might be a tire iron or jack handle, since a transfer blood pattern of two long parallel lines about two inches apart on a corner of the sheet suggested a long, straight blood-covered object had rested against it.

They also suspected the killer was someone Crane knew because there was no sign of forced entry and neighbors reported having heard no arguments or loud noises. The motive? Police weren't sure, but Crane was famous in certain circles as a womanizer with a penchant for video-taping his conquests, so it seemed plausible that the murder might be linked to his sexual escapades. A camera was perched on a tripod near the murder bed and another lay on the floor, testament to the dead man's favorite guilty pleasure. Investigators also found a veritable library of Crane's pornographic exploits. Perhaps the jealous husband or lover of one of the many women he had captured on tape had killed him or hired someone else to do it.

Detectives soon zeroed in on Crane's friend John Carpenter, a video salesman who often barhopped with the actor and costarred with various women in several of his X-rated home movies. Carpenter claimed to have left Crane outside a coffee shop at two A.M. the night of the murder, which made him one of the last people to see the victim alive. He also made several suspicious moves like leaving town for L.A. the morning Crane's body was discovered and allegedly showing little surprise when he phoned Crane's room and heard a police officer answer. Most significant, when investigators searched the rental car he had been driving at the time of Crane's murder, they found a smear of type B blood—a match with Crane's—on the passenger's-side door. Only 10 percent of the population has type B blood.

Several sources close to Crane told police the actor had been complaining about his perpetual sidekick and wanted to ditch him. Witnesses even reported having seen the two arguing at a nightclub a few nights earlier. Had the prospect of losing his star connection and the endless access to willing women that went with it driven Carpenter into a murderous rage? Prosecutors thought so, but Carpenter denied any involvement in or knowledge of the killing, and ultimately there was simply no evidence to link him to it. No one was arrested or charged, and the case remained unsolved.

It was hardly forgotten, though. According to the trial coverage, prosecutors raked police over the coals for what they deemed sloppy evidence handling and failure to secure a crime scene that might have yielded crucial clues in the highest-profile homicide the city could remember. Local papers quipped that if you were looking for a scenic spot to bump someone off and get away with it, Scottsdale was your best bet.

When Richard Romley took over as county attorney in January 1989, he appointed a special review board of fifteen deputies to reexamine evidence from cold cases. Crane's was at the top of the list. He had the blood sample from Carpenter's rental car retested the following year, hoping advances in DNA technology might link it to the Crane murder, but results proved inconclusive.

Around the same time, I was lecturing in the area and got a call from the Maricopa County District Attorney's Office asking me to analyze the blood patterns in the crime scene photos and give an interpretation of what it all meant. I agreed, and the two lead attorneys met me in Phoenix, then later came to Portland to examine the evidence with me. (I later worked with the same office on another high-profile murder involving the execution of nine people, including six Buddhist monks at a nearby temple.)

It was obvious Crane had been killed with a blunt instrument, judging from the medium-velocity blood spatter evident in the photographs of his body, the bedding, and the bed itself. Linear lacerations were evident in the close-ups, though there was no distinctive pattern in the wounds to help us identify the weapon. Blood smeared all over the electrical cord indicated that the strangulation had followed the bludgeoning, and bloody hand transfers on the curtains suggested a killer with a bloody hand had pulled them aside to peer out before leaving. But it took us several weeks to put two and two together and ask the obvious, overlooked question: What's missing in this picture? The answer: The tripod for the second camera.

Those who knew Crane intimately knew he filmed using cameras on tripods. The missing one could easily have created the head wounds the actor sustained as well as the linear blood transfers on the sheets that were mistaken for marks left by a tire iron or jack handle. It would have been the logical murder weapon, though it was never found.

Not as easy to explain were several other linear blood patterns, some short and some long, as well as a pair of very short, straight lines in blood on Crane's shoulder. Prosecutors wanted to know if I could determine what had caused the marks and whether they might reveal anything about the killer's identity.

The answer came from an unlikely source.

As part of my community-policing efforts, I was working with Portland's David Douglas High School to co-teach and shape the curriculum for a newly created law-related class. David Douglas drew from some of the city's roughest areas and college enrollment rates among its grads were minuscule compared with those of other area high schools, where the student population was more affluent. Our goal was to expose underprivileged students to professions they might not have considered and to broaden their career horizons. We invited judges, crime writers, court reporters, and cops to work with the teenagers and to tell them about their jobs. The class also had parental permission to help me with blood spatter experiments for cases I was handling.

During the Crane investigation, we set up a camp bed with white sheets and purchased a variety of tripods, then had the students conduct blind experiments with the camera stands closed as well as opened to discover what types of imprints each one made on the sheets when dipped in stage blood. (Keeping the experiments blind meant the students were not allowed to see photos from the Crane murder, which might have influenced their efforts and led them to try deliberately to re-create the mystery marks.)

As luck would have it, two of the prosecutors from the Crane case had flown up from Maricopa County, Arizona, to observe some of the experiments my class was conducting and happened to be on hand when something extraordinary occurred. Among my students was a sixteen-year-old girl named Kim Douglas,* whose ambition was to become manager of the Taco Bell where she worked after school. Toward the end of class, she hurried up to us, an excited expression on her face.

"I think I figured it out!" she said. "Look!" And she slapped the plug of an electrical cord dipped in stage blood against her arm. Sure enough, the prongs made a pair of marks just like the ones on Crane's shoulder and the cord left a longer linear pattern near it. She repeated the test on several other students' arms and on the sheets we had brought in for the experiments.

Her solution to the puzzling blood pattern was as brilliant as it was simple. The killer inadvertently slapped the bloodied plug against Crane's skin as he strangled the man. Why didn't we see it before? I asked myself. How had all of us "experts" missed something so obvious? I had been staying up half the night conducting experiments in my lab in an attempt to replicate the bizarre blood prints with no success.

Kim Douglas's discovery is one of the many reasons I encourage input from everyone involved in my cases. I take every source's ideas seriously and try to give them equal weight. You would be surprised at how often it is not a scientist or a seasoned cop but a senior on internship or an office assistant who provides the fresh, out-of-the-box thinking that cracks the case.

The DAs were duly impressed and asked all the students to put their initials on the sheets with the tripod and the electrical plug marks, just as professional evidence collectors would do. Then they photographed the work and took the sheets back with them to Arizona to submit into evidence.

Though the students at David Douglas had no idea whose case they were working on, they knew they had solved a real mystery in a real murder. The triumph on their faces was exhilarating to see. That breakthrough was one of many reasons that a remarkable majority of the students in the class went on to attend college. Kim Douglas gave up on the fast-food industry and set her sights on law school instead.

The plug pattern and the tripod prints put two mysteries to rest, but they hardly revealed the killer's identity. Again, the Crane case stalled. Then, in 1992, a shred of evidence came to light that gave Romley new hope. In examining an old police photograph of the door of Carpenter's rental car, his deputies spied a dark, irregularly shaped blotch, about one-sixteenth of an inch in size. The spot looked just like the spots of brain tissue on the bloody sheets under Crane's body. It was enough to reopen the case.

Evidence collection procedures were very different in the 1970s, however, and nobody had paid any attention to the speck back then. The tissue sample had not been preserved, so there was no way to test it and confirm or deny the theory that it was brain matter.

Undaunted, Romley brought charges of first-degree murder against Carpenter, and he was arrested in Los Angeles on June 1, 1992, fourteen years after Crane's death. At that time he was also facing charges of child molestation, which delayed his extradition to Arizona. He pleaded no contest and got three months' probation. The Crane case went to trial in 1994.

I was called to testify about my theory on the murder weapon and to explain the positions the victim and the murderer would have been in when the attack occurred. The evidence suggested that Crane was asleep under the covers when his assailant snuck up on him, bludgeoned him, and then strangled him.

Not surprisingly, the case hinged on the photograph of the mysterious speck in the rental car. Was it tissue? If so, was it Crane's? Was it proof that Carpenter played a role in the murder? After two days of deliberations, the jury said no. Carpenter was acquitted owing to lack of evidence. He died in 1998, still maintaining his innocence in the murder of Bob Crane.

Case Study: Robert Blake and the *In Cold Blood* Question

A few years later, I was asked to consult on another murder involving a once well-known television name that, like Crane's, had faded from the limelight. This time, though, the celebrity was not the victim, but the accused.

On the evening of May 4, 2001, Robert Blake and Bonny Lee Bakley, Blake's wife of about seven months, went to dinner at Blake's longtime favorite restaurant—Vitello's, in Studio City, California. The onetime *Baretta* star had been a regular for so many years that the popular Italian eatery had named a pasta dish in his honor. Normally he used Vitello's valet parking service, but almost nothing about the night in question could be described as normal for the sixty-seven-year-old actor. Breaking his routine, he parked his black Dodge Stealth down the street behind a construction Dumpster under a burned-out streetlight and walked a block and a half to Vitello's with Bakley, past plenty of empty curbside parking spaces closer to the restaurant.

Around nine-thirty P.M., the couple left Vitello's and walked back to the Stealth. According to Blake's version of events, he suddenly realized he had left the handgun he carried for his wife's protection in the restaurant booth. After assuring Bakley he would be back shortly, he hurried off to retrieve it. When he returned, he found Bakley slumped in the passenger seat, bleeding copiously from two gunshot wounds—one to her right cheek and one to her right shoulder. Blake raced to the nearest house and banged frantically on the door. This being Studio City, the home belonged to someone in show business—filmmaker Sean Stanek. When Stanek answered, a shaking Blake dragged him to the car, where Bakley was barely breathing. While Stanek called 911 on his cell phone and tried to administer first aid, Blake ran back to Vitello's for more help. Bakley died before he returned. She was forty-four years old.

Anyone can panic during an emergency, but a number of Blake's actions raised suspicions among the investigating detectives. The actor told them he had recently started carrying a gun because he feared someone was stalking his wife. If so, why park in a secluded area near a construction site? Why leave her alone in the car with the windows down? The temperature was a chilly fifty-seven degrees, and Bakley was wearing only a lightweight nylon outfit, but Blake took his keys with him so she had no way to close the windows or turn on the car's heater. Blake said he chose the inconspicuous spot assuming that keeping Bakley out of sight would protect her but he wasn't thinking straight when he left her in the car.

Why make reservations and introduce Bakley as his wife that night when he had been showing up for years without reservations and for months with the woman without introducing her? Why hadn't anyone noticed Blake returning to get his gun? Plenty of people remembered him coming in distraught and shouting that his wife had been shot— then drinking two glasses of water before returning to the scene of the shooting.

And there was more: Blake's table had been bussed two minutes after he left—before he and Bakley would have reached the car and noticed the firearm was missing—and none of the busboys had noticed a handgun lying on the seat. Another Vitello's patron reported having seen the actor in the men's room earlier, vomiting, tugging his hair, and mumbling—though that's not so surprising considering that Blake had long been in the habit of throwing up his meals to keep his weight in check, according to those who knew him well. Blake hardly allayed police skepticism about his innocence when he refused to take a polygraph test that night, claiming he was too upset and afraid the dreams he had been having about killing his wife would produce an inaccurate result.

Then again, odds were good that Blake wasn't the only man having dreams about killing Bonny Lee Bakley. She was far from the most sympathetic of victims. As LAPD detectives soon discovered, the woman had a long and lurid history of bilking lonely-hearted men out of money through mail-order scams that involved sending them nude photos (usually of other women) along with promises of a future romance. She had also been arrested for credit card fraud, passing bad checks, and drug possession.

When it came to famous men, she was an aging groupie. She spent several years in Memphis trailing Jerry Lee Lewis in the early 1990s, then sued him for paternity of her third child—a daughter she named Jeri Lee Lewis. Paternity was never proven, though Lewis paid her a settlement. After that, Bakley headed to California, where she had a liaison with Christian Brando, son of Marlon Brando. Next she met Blake, had a fling with him, got pregnant, refused his pleas to abort, and finally talked him into marrying her for the sake of the child, Rose, born in June 2000. By all accounts, Blake was smitten with Rose but repulsed by her mother and the lifestyle she led. He let Bakley live in a cottage on his ramshackle Mata Hari Ranch in Studio City but got a court order barring her from doing anything illegal there.

She ignored it. Among Bakley's belongings, police found a notebook listing Bakley's scam victims, the pseudonyms she used when she wrote to each of them, and the amounts of money they had mailed her. Another notebook contained a list of stars and other rich men she had targeted for romance. Next to their names were notes about their worth and other personal details like the names of their mothers. Nearby was a stash of letters the dead woman had written bragging about her erotic adventures and describing her fondness for everything from sex toys to sadomasochism to meeting strangers in motels for trysts—claims her own friends substantiated. They had warned her to be careful, they said, but Bakley was cavalier. She joked that one day her dangerous games would probably catch up to her, but she didn't stop.

Could another man have been harboring a murderous grudge against Bakley? Possibly. Blake's bodyguard, Earle Caldwell, told police a menacing stranger with a pickup truck and a blond buzz cut had been staking out Mata Hari Ranch for weeks before Bakley's murder.

Police never tracked the man down, but they did unearth the murder weapon—a World War II–era Walther PPK handgun with the serial number partly filed off—in the Dumpster where the Stealth was parked. Attempts to trace it or link it to Blake were unsuccessful.

Still, Robert Blake remained suspect number one. On April 18, 2002, the actor who had once starred as a killer in *In Cold Blood* was arrested. A few days later, he was formally charged with murder, solicitation of murder, and conspiracy to commit murder. Caldwell was arrested, too, and charged with conspiracy to commit murder.

That was when prosecutor Shellie Samuels called my office and asked me to examine the evidence. She and two colleagues flew to Portland with Blake's jeans, boots, socks, belt, and black T-shirt. I examined each of them using my normal protocol. Everyone in the lab dons fresh gloves, then we spread out clean butcher paper for the first piece of evidence, examine it inch by inch, photograph every section of it, make notes on any unusual characteristics that might relate to the crime, and—in Blake's case—test it with Luminol for traces of blood spatter. We then reseal the item, sterilize each piece of equipment used, dispose of the old butcher paper, and change our gloves to eliminate the possibility of cross-contamination. We lay out fresh paper on the examining table for the next item and start the process over again.

Blake's garments revealed no traces of blood. But would Bakley's killer, whether it was Robert Blake or anyone else, have gotten bloody blowback on his clothes? Probably not. Here's why: I went to Los Angeles and examined the blood-covered Dodge Stealth, which had been submitted into evidence there, and measurements showed that when Bakley was shot the blowback traveled only about eight and a half inches. Remember, high-velocity mist is very fine and light, so it never flies farther than four feet from the bullet's point of entry, even when a high-caliber weapon creates the wound.

Next we traced the trajectory of each bullet based on Bakley's injuries. We started by working backward from the termination point of the bullet lodged in the left side of her head to its entry point in her body—a hole low on the right side of her jaw. Then we did the same with the shoulder wound. Both bullets remained lodged in Bakley's body, and both would have been fatal. To understand the path the bullets took, we envisioned an imaginary steel rod running from each termination point back through each entry point. If Bakley had been seated in a normal upright position, the rods would have run downward through the car door to a point of origin on the pavement.

But there were no bullet holes in the Stealth's door. Whoever shot Bakley fired through the open car window. That meant she saw her killer pointing a gun at her and leaned to her left toward the driver's side in a classic defensive posture. She didn't have enough time to do anything else to protect herself. In my opinion, the first bullet struck her in the head and the second hit her shoulder, though I couldn't be certain. Expirated blood covering the gearshift showed that she slumped farther to her left after she was hit and exhaled blood onto it in her last few minutes of life.

To help the jury understand all this, I filmed an actress sitting in a car reenacting Bakley's movements in response to what I judged was the order of the shots. Then I worked with animation specialists to create a computerized video reconstruction of the crime, which we played during the trial.

Of course, none of this implicated or exonerated Blake. It simply helped jurors comprehend exactly what happened during Bakley's murder.

The tensest moment for me came not on the witness stand, but after I testified and the trial broke for lunch. The courtroom was on the eighth floor, so I ducked into an empty elevator and pressed the button for the ground level, intending to grab a quick sandwich. The doors were just closing when someone thrust an arm between them. They slammed on it, then reopened. There stood Robert Blake. We gazed at each other for a second, then he stepped in, the doors closing behind him. Both of us stood there in stone-faced silence, staring intently at the ceiling, the elevator buttons, the floor, anywhere but at each other. It was the longest elevator ride of my life.

Not surprisingly, Blake's case proved a gold mine for tabloids and gossip magazines. The irascible actor went through a revolving door of high-profile defense lawyers, partly because of his insistence on granting jailhouse interviews to famous-name reporters Barbara Walters and Diane Sawyer. When his counsel changed, it sent jury selection back to square one. Then during the trial itself, two colorful former stuntmen from Blake's *Baretta* days, a private investigator, and a hood-turned-minister all stepped forward to say that Blake had offered them money to "whack" or "snuff" Bakley.

On March 16, 2005, Blake was finally acquitted of murdering his wife, though the jury remained deadlocked eleven to one on the solicitation of murder count until the judge dismissed the charge. Blake's longtime bodyguard, Earle Caldwell, was also acquitted.

When he finally walked out of criminal court a free man, Blake was seventy-one. The following year, Bakley's relatives brought a wrongful death suit against him in civil court. I was again asked to provide an analysis of how the crime unfolded based on blood spatter and bullet wounds, though I didn't have to testify. Blake lost the case and was ordered to pay his late wife's relatives $30 million. He declared bankruptcy less than three months later.

Straightforward Evidence: The Cases of Ennis Cosby and Selena Quintanilla-Pérez

Blood doesn't always tell a story. Sometimes it does no more than confirm what is already obvious to police at a crime scene. I've been asked to examine evidence in several high-profile murders to see whether critical clues might lie hidden in the blood spatter but found nothing that would change the direction of an investigation or trial. That was true in the tragic deaths of both Ennis Cosby and Tejano singer Selena Quintanilla-Pérez.

Twenty-seven-year-old Ennis Cosby, son of comedian Bill Cosby, was shot to death on a service road off the 405 Freeway in Southern California as he tried to change a flat tire on his Mercedes around one A.M. on January 16, 1997. Cosby was en route to his friend Stephanie Crane's home when the tire blew and he called her for help. She drove to meet him and used her car's lights to illuminate the roadside, making the tire change easier. While she waited, a man suddenly appeared at her door and in a heavy accent ordered, "Get out of the car or I'll kill you." Instead, she hit the gas. Seconds later, she spun her car around and, to her horror, saw her friend lying in a pool of blood as the man sprinted away.

I was lecturing for the Los Angeles District Attorney's Office when it happened, and LAPD homicide detective Vic Pietrantoni asked me to inspect Cosby's bloody clothing as well as images from the crime scene and tell him whether any signs in the blood pointed to a setup involving Stephanie Crane. Did the victim's split lip suggest a scuffle before the shooting? Did the fact that the shooter stood next to Crane's driver's-side window or the fact that she drove off while Cosby was being shot suggest that she had helped to set him up? Was this a possible dispute between people who knew each other and had arranged to meet off 405 in the middle of the night? Did the fact that Cosby's body had been turned onto his back mean anything?

But the blood patterns bore out exactly what was reported and what the murderer himself later confirmed. An eighteen-year-old opportunist thug from the Ukraine spotted a young African-American man with an expensive car, decided to rob him, and just as casually shot him in the head because he took too long to hand over his wallet, never knowing he was the son of one of America's best-loved actors. Stephanie Crane had no involvement in the crime. The assailant flipped his victim over to pick his pocket, then kicked him in the mouth as a final insult before fleeing. After bragging about the killing to co-workers, Mikhail Markhasev was arrested, tried, and sentenced to life in prison plus ten years. He later apologized to the Cosby family. In one of those odd small-world twists, Detective Vic Pietrantoni's wife, Deputy District Attorney Anne Ingalls, led the prosecution team.

Had there been more to the murder, we would likely have seen evidence of a conspiracy such as additional tire tracks, footprints from co-conspirators' shoes, signs that a struggle took place, or wounds from more than one weapon.

The blood patterns were equally straightforward in the murder of Selena Quintanilla-Pérez, shot to death by her fan club president, Yolanda Saldívar, on March 31, 1995. When the twenty-three-year-old singer discovered that her supposed number one fan was embezzling money from a chain of boutiques the Quintanilla family ran, she fired her. The two met at a Days Inn in Corpus Christi, Texas, ostensibly so Saldívar could hand over some business documents, but as Quintanilla-Pérez was leaving the hotel room, Saldívar shot her in the back. The injured star stumbled to the front desk and told the staff what had happened before collapsing. She died from loss of blood at a nearby hospital a few hours later.

The defense for Saldívar wanted to know if I could find anything unusual in the blood spatter that might mitigate the circumstances or suggest self-defense, but the scene was a simple one to analyze from the crime scene photos. As you know, we work backward in crime scene reconstruction, from point Z to point A. Here, a trail of blood terminated abruptly in front of the hotel desk. The droplets, with their characteristic directional spines, showed that the victim had staggered to the lobby from the hallway. Her path led back to the interior of a guest room doorway, where high-velocity blood spatter on the carpet, walls, door frame, and door showed that the initial injury was a gunshot wound and that—calculating the dead woman's height and the height of the bloodstains—the bullet entered the victim's body in the middle of her back. There was no indication of a struggle, no hint in the blood of any other activity that might have altered my reading of what happened. The police interpretation of events was on the mark from what I could see. I told the defense there was nothing I could add. Saldívar was found guilty of the murder.

In many other homicides, though, blood tells a riveting story. There is no better example than what most Americans call "the O. J. Simpson Case."

Case Study: O. J. Simpson and the River of Blood Evidence

When Nicole Brown Simpson's white Akita wouldn't stop barking late on the evening of June 12, 1994, neighbors in L.A.'s wealthy Brentwood enclave went to see if anything was wrong. They found the dog wandering Bundy Drive in front of Brown's[1] condo around eleven P.M. The Akita was almost frantic—whining, barking, and pacing incessantly. Thinking it might be injured, one man bent down to take a closer look and saw that the animal's fur and paws were caked with something red. Alarmed, another neighbor peeked over the fence that sheltered Brown's condo from the street.

[1]In subsequent references to Nicole Brown Simpson, she is referred to as "Brown" rather than "Brown Simpson" for clarity. In subsequent references to O. J. Simpson, he is referred to as "Simpson."

That's when they saw the blood. Someone had smeared it all over the walkway. Great rivulets of red had run all the way to the front gate from the condo's steps.

Police responding to their 911 call just after midnight spotted the source of all the blood immediately. The body of Nicole Brown Simpson, thirty-five-year-old ex-wife of former pro football star O. J. Simpson and mother of two of his children, was slumped at the bottom of the steps outside her home. Brown had been stabbed multiple times, and her throat had been slashed so deeply that her head had almost been severed from her neck. Her face was swollen as though someone had beaten her, and—as coroners would note in the autopsy—so much of her blood had run down the garden path that there was almost none left in her body.

Lying near her was the body of a man who would soon be identified as Ronald Goldman. The twenty-five-year-old aspiring actor and model waited tables at a nearby restaurant called Mezzaluna Trattoria and had become friendly with Brown, a frequent customer who worked out at the same gym he did. As investigators learned, Brown had dined at Mezzaluna that evening with her parents and children, and when Brown's mother called the restaurant to say she had accidentally left her glasses there, Goldman volunteered to drop them off after his shift. Like Brown's, Goldman's throat had been slashed. He had also been stabbed repeatedly in the torso and thigh. All in all, he had suffered nineteen stab wounds. Autopsies would reveal that the murder weapon was a blade at least six inches long.

Brown's eight-year-old daughter and five-year-old son were still asleep on the second floor and had to be awakened by police. They had slept through the carnage below, mercifully unaware.

As far as blood evidence goes, the crime scene was a bonanza. A trail of bloody footprints next to a line of blood droplets led from both victims to the back of the property. Several objects lay near Goldman's body, including a bloodstained brown leather glove and a blood-spattered white envelope containing a pair of women's glasses.

Within hours, police on the scene received orders from their commander to drive to the home of O. J. Simpson a few miles away on Rockingham Avenue. They were to tell him his ex-wife was dead and ask him to take charge of the children. Among the four homicide detectives who went to Rockingham were Tom Lange and Philip Vannatter, both from the LAPD Robbery/Homicide Division's elite Homicide Special Section, which handles high-profile murder cases and which had officially taken over the investigation, with Lange and Vannatter assigned as the lead detectives. Accompanying them were detective supervisor Ron Phillips and detective Mark Fuhrman, both of the LAPD's West Los Angeles Division. Fuhrman had gone to Simpson's home years earlier as a patrol officer in response to a distress call from Brown— one of many she made when her husband's temper exploded into threats and violence.

When the detectives pulled up to Simpson's walled estate, they saw a white Ford Bronco parked with its wheels on the curb, its back end in the street. While waiting for someone to answer the door, they ran a license check on the vehicle and learned it was leased to Simpson by Hertz. As Fuhrman was shining his flashlight on it, he noticed a reddish smear on the outside of the door. It looked as if it might be blood.

What if the ex-football star, too, were dead or dying inside his mansion? No one answered their repeated knocks and phone calls, so the four concurred and judged the circumstances urgent. That permitted them to enter the property without a search warrant. Fuhrman scaled the wall and unlocked the gate for his colleagues. Again they tried to awaken whoever was inside the main house but got no answer. Next they tried a trio of bungalows on the property. Two of the doors opened. Arnelle Simpson, the ex–NFL star's daughter from his first marriage, peered out bleary-eyed from one bungalow. In the other doorway stood Brian Kato Kaelin, an aspiring actor pal of Simpson's who was a quasi-permanent houseguest at Simpson's estate.

Kaelin told police that he had eaten dinner with Simpson at McDonald's the night before, then spent the evening in his bungalow. He was on the phone with his girlfriend when he heard three wall-rattling bangs and went outside to find the source of the commotion. He saw a limo near the front gate and, remembering that his host was planning to catch the red-eye to Chicago, hurried over to help him load his bags.

While Kaelin talked, Arnelle Simpson found a phone number for her father's hotel in Chicago, and Ron Phillips placed the call. Simpson answered. He sounded horrified at the news of his ex-wife's death and promised to catch the next flight home. He didn't ask how she had died, though, which struck Phillips as odd. It's almost always the first question people ask.

While Phillips was calling Simpson, the other detectives investigated the estate's grounds. Fuhrman trained his flashlight over the area where Kaelin said the loud bumps had originated, and the beam fell on a brown leather glove. It looked just like the one at Bundy Drive, and like that one, it appeared to be stained with blood. He hurried back to the house to get Phillips. About the same time, Vannatter spotted what looked like blood drops in the driveway. He followed them to the Bronco and, shining his flashlight onto the car, spied again the suspicious smear Fuhrman had noticed on the driver's door latch as well as what appeared to be more stains inside the vehicle. The trail led on to the front door of the main house. The detectives left the evidence where they found it, vacated the premises, secured it, and obtained a search warrant to re-enter. The glove and other items would be photographed and collected by criminalists from the lab.

When Simpson returned from Chicago, homicide detectives took him to the Parker Center for questioning and fingerprinting. He wasn't under arrest or charged with any crime. He went voluntarily and answered questions. The officers questioning him noticed a bandage on the middle finger of his left hand and asked if they could photograph the wound. Simpson said okay. He also let a male nurse draw blood for DNA tests. He didn't seem particularly worried, though he contradicted his version of events from the night before several times.

But after lab results showed that the glove found at Rockingham was soaked with both Brown's and Goldman's blood, the Los Angeles District Attorney's Office issued a warrant for Simpson's arrest on June 17. Police went to lawyer Robert Kardashian's home to pick him up. It turned out they were too late. Simpson and his friend Al Cowlings had driven off in Cowlings's white Ford Bronco, also leased from Hertz. (O.J.'s bloodstained white Ford Bronco had already been seized and submitted into evidence.) What followed was a surreal televised slow-speed chase with news helicopters and bystanders shouting from overpasses. The procession eventually led back to Rockingham, where Simpson surrendered and police searching the Bronco found a loaded gun, a passport, and a fake beard and mustache. Simpson was arraigned a few days later but pleaded not guilty to murder charges.

In the months that followed, while "the Juice" cooled his heels in a private cell, an all-star cast of defense lawyers lined up to defend him, including the now familiar names of Robert Shapiro, F. Lee Bailey, Johnnie Cochran, and DNA trial specialists Barry Scheck and Peter Neufeld. The media dubbed them the Dream Team.

At the outset, the case appeared almost airtight. Simpson seemed to have done everything but leave his calling card at the murder scene. Lab tests showed that hairs on Goldman's shirt and inside a navy knit cap found lying on the ground near his blood-covered body belonged to Simpson. So did blood droplets nearby. A pair of socks retrieved from the foot of Simpson's bed tested positive for Brown's blood, and its fibers matched fibers found on Goldman's clothing. Tests of the bloodstains inside the Bronco revealed DNA from all three people—the murder victims and Simpson himself.

Add to that testimony from witnesses like limo driver Allan Park, who said he rang the doorbell at the front gate on Rockingham for twenty minutes, then caught sight of a tall African-American man in dark clothes sprinting toward the estate's side door just before eleven P.M. Simpson answered the intercom moments later, claimed he had overslept, and hurried down to load his bags, drenched in sweat.

Of course, the case turned out to be anything but a slam dunk for prosecutors, who were hardly braced for what the Dream Team had in store. Simpson's defense lawyers launched a furious attack on the credibility of the witnesses, the evidence, and the cops who spotted it. They made mincemeat of criminalist Dennis Fung and his assistant Andrea Mazzola, suggesting the pair had so botched the evidence handling and used such shoddy collection techniques that the blood samples had been irreparably contaminated. Blood samples from Bundy Drive had been stored in plastic bags temporarily, hadn't they? Couldn't plastic bags cultivate bacteria? Wouldn't that destroy test result accuracy?

That was just the beginning. Why had the male nurse at the Parker Center recorded drawing eight milliliters of blood from Simpson when six and a half were in the vial? The nurse said he had estimated the amount, but couldn't someone have filched the "missing" blood to plant evidence around Bundy and Rockingham?

The someone they had in mind was Mark Fuhrman. Why Fuhrman? Fuhrman despised African-Americans, the defense said. For proof, they produced ten-year-old taped interviews made by aspiring screenplay writer Laura Hart McKinney of the homicide detective spouting a slew of racial slurs and lurid descriptions of violent acts against African-American suspects taken in the line of duty. Fuhrman claimed he was acting—creating an exaggerated character of a bigoted cop—but the damage was done. Johnnie Cochran likened him to Adolf Hitler, a genocidal maniac who would stop at nothing to destroy a black man.

As pundits noted, O. J. Simpson was no longer on trial. Racism was. And with the black community still stinging from the recent Rodney King verdict, the issue touched a raw nerve.

To Fuhrman's colleagues who had been on the crime scene, the notion was ludicrous. No matter how distasteful the man's views might be, more than fifteen other detectives had beaten him to Bundy Drive and not one of them had spotted a second glove. It was nearly inconceivable that he or any other cop could have found such a big piece of bloody evidence and surreptitiously pocketed it right under their noses to drop at Rockingham later. Besides, at the time no one even knew they would get orders to go to Rockingham.

Long before the race card surfaced in the courtroom, I got a call from Marcia Clark, Los Angeles assistant district attorney, to analyze the blood evidence from both Bundy and Rockingham. I'll never forget her words: "This crime is a gold mine for a blood spatter analyst. There's blood everywhere."

In the months that followed, I flew to Los Angeles fifteen times to inspect Simpson's Bronco, gloves, socks, and other bloodstained items from the crime. I spent countless hours with Clark, Supervising Deputy DA Bill Hodgman, and their colleagues, poring over hundreds of photos from the crime scene, trying to understand how events had unfolded based on the story the blood told. We discussed different scenarios, challenged one another's theories, and refined our interpretation again and again until we were sure we had it right. We also worked extensively with Dr. Lakshmanan Sathyavagiswaran, L.A. County's chief medical examiner. "Dr. Lucky," as he was known around the ME's office, was instrumental in helping us to understand the positioning of the victims and their murderer based on the wounds and other forensic clues.

Almost all the blood smears and transfers in the crime scene were sixteen inches from the ground or lower. There was no blood on the upper part of the foliage. What did that tell us? Most of the bloodshed occurred when both victims were already down. The autopsy indicated that Brown had been struck on the right temple with a hard object, probably the handle of the murder knife, and either stunned or knocked out so that she put up virtually no struggle. This explained why no one heard her scream, why she had just one tiny defense wound on her hand, and why the soles of her bare feet were blood-free.

Unlike Brown, Goldman put up a monumental fight. His palms and arms were covered with deep defensive cuts—the same type as the one visible on Simpson's knuckle in the photos the LAPD took. The back of his shirt had been ripped by a knife in several places, yet he had no stab wounds in his back. This told us that during their struggle, the killer wrenched Goldman's shirt around almost backward in his effort to hang on to his victim. Goldman also suffered numerous shallow wounds to the sides of his neck in addition to having his throat cut. One early hypothesis held that the jabs were evidence of torture or "teasing" by the killer before he inflicted the fatal, deep wounds. In reality, it showed that Goldman was fighting fiercely—twisting, ducking, turning away, and making it hard for the killer to hit his mark.

After careful and protracted analysis, we determined that the killer moved back and forth between his victims after they were incapacitated, making sure both were going to die by inflicting two mortal blows. He dealt the slash to Brown's throat that almost decapitated her and inflicted multiple deep puncture wounds to Goldman's abdomen, which severed his abdominal aorta and caused massive internal bleeding.

A number of puzzling blood smears on Brown's body confounded us initially. It was only after I borrowed some large dogs from the Multnomah County K-9 unit and from my students at David Douglas, who were still helping me with experiments, that I began to understand what the patterns meant. We poured animal blood on the ground outside the high school, then used a rubber ball to wind up the dogs until they were hyperenergized. As they jumped around in the blood, their claws and the pads of their paws created patterns virtually identical to those in the crime scene photos from Bundy Drive.

Next we dressed an actress with the same build and look as Brown in a dress resembling the one Brown was wearing when she was murdered. We filmed her lying on the concrete at the base of a short flight of stairs outside the school. Then we poured animal blood down the stretch of ground in front of her and brought in one of the K-9 dogs. When he discovered the woman, the dog began to pace and whine anxiously around her limp form. He positioned himself so that his back paws were on one side of her head and his front paws were up on a step on the other side, his body sheltering her in what looked like a protective stance. His actions left transfers, spatters, and bloody paw prints just like the ones on Nicole Brown's body.

As the Las Vegas dog case from chapter 5 showed, animals inadvertently leave their own distinct and misleading marks when they wander into a crime scene. Nicole Brown's Akita clearly became agitated during or after his mistress's murder, particularly when he discovered the massive wound on her neck. This was obvious from the anxious behavior the neighbors noticed and from the paw prints that trailed back and forth over the bloody sidewalk. They indicated that the Akita had paced through Brown's blood numerous times. He created the strange smears on Brown's body by brushing against her when he was already covered in her blood. He also generated quite a lot of the spatter low to the ground and on the bodies by treading repeatedly in the blood running out of Brown's throat wound.

Clark and her colleagues had me prepare several times to testify about the blood pattern analysis we had conducted. In the end, though, I got lucky. I was spared that nerve-racking task. But here's what I told the DA's office and what I was prepared to tell the jury: The blood evidence provided incontrovertible proof that Simpson murdered Nicole Brown and Ron Goldman, in my opinion.

The devil is in the details, however, as the old saying goes. And the prosecution never admitted some of the most crucial details into evidence. Here they are. You be the jury.

The socks: Based on the bloody footprints visible in the crime scene photos, I knew the killer had stepped repeatedly in his victim's blood. That meant he would have medium-velocity blood spatter on the socks he wore during the murder. The LAPD's initial report indicated that no blood was observed on the socks found at the foot of O. J. Simpson's bed at Rockingham. I suspected this was because he was wearing dark-colored socks and no one had examined them under high-intensity lights. I also knew that if Kato Kaelin's description of Simpson wearing sweatpants was accurate, it was likely that the pants had elastic bands around the ankle. If Simpson was the murderer, there would be a precise line where the blood spatter on his socks would end.

But the crime lab kept assuring us that they had already examined the socks. We would be wasting our time to retest them, they said. We kept pushing, and finally, weeks later, they relented. I scrutinized the blue-black cotton kneesocks from the foot of Simpson's bed under high-intensity lights and found nineteen medium-velocity impact spatters of Nicole Brown's blood around the ankle of the left sock. There were thirty-nine spatters of what DNA testing showed was also Brown's blood around the right sock. As you already know, that is precisely the spatter pattern that lands on a killer's clothes during a beating or a stabbing that involves multiple wounds, particularly if he's stepping in wet blood as he attacks his victim. The spatter was around the ankles only—the one section that gets exposed to airborne blood droplets when the killer is wearing pants. It terminated abruptly midway up the ankle, where the elastic bands of the pant legs would have blocked it.

There were also hand transfer bloodstains in Simpson's blood at the tops of the socks and at the toes. Those are the spots you touch when you take off a sock. You push the top down, then grasp the toe to pull it off your foot. The positioning on both was consistent with a cut on the middle finger of the left hand—just where Simpson was injured.

Ron Goldman's white high-top athletic shoes showed the same pattern of medium-velocity blood spatter that Simpson's socks showed. Like those on Simpson's socks, the marks on Goldman's shoes wrapped all the way around, indicating that the two had been locked in a ferocious struggle involving a lot of movement, all the while stomping repeatedly in the wet blood of Nicole Brown and sending it spattering onto their feet and ankles from many different angles.

The car: There was a half-inch-wide knuckle transfer impression in what DNA tests determined was Simpson's blood on the outside of the Bronco's driver's-side door, a matching one on the driver's interior door pocket, and a third on the headlight switch that Luminol revealed. They were all consistent with a bleeding knuckle touching those areas. Of course, that proves only that Simpson was bleeding—not that he murdered anybody—and probably that he was bleeding at night, when a driver would naturally touch the headlight switch. However, a hand transfer stain on the passenger side of the console revealed a mixture of three people's blood—Nicole Brown's, Ron Goldman's, and Simpson's own—just as the leather gloves did. More important, on the right side of Simpson's Bronco, lying against the passenger seat, was a long linear blood transfer—a classic knife pattern—with a blond hair attached to it, though the hair was never tested for DNA.

Tom Lange and I also discovered that the overhead lightbulb had been removed from the Bronco. We found it, in working order, lying on the floor of the car under the right front passenger seat. Removing the bulb would be consistent with someone wanting to approach in stealth. Police officers do it all the time to prevent getting shot at when they respond to night calls. But unless Simpson was ready to admit that he had unscrewed his own car's bulb for the purpose of sneaking up on his ex-wife, this was little more than an interesting observation. Remember, speculation is antithetical to crime scene reconstruction.

Couldn't a clever, devious rogue cop plant blood in a car to frame an innocent man? I certainly couldn't pull off what I saw in the Simpson evidence, and I've spent years in this field. I talked with more than a dozen people who worked on that crime scene, including many of the LAPD officers involved in the initial investigation. Although Tom Lange and Philip Vannatter were great cops, men whose input I'd welcome on a homicide investigation any day, they weren't full-time blood pattern analysts. Nobody there was. Even if he did harbor a grudge against black superstars like O. J. Simpson, Mark

Fuhrman certainly had no extensive expertise in blood pattern analysis. None of the cops at Bundy Drive would have known the first thing about planting evidence effectively enough to trip up an expert. I don't think there is an expert alive who could plant that much evidence so authentically. The bloodstains were too complex, too subtle, and too varied.

If you were hatching a plan to plant blood spatter evidence that would set up an innocent man, you would spatter the whole sock. You wouldn't be able to replicate the precise voids where pants and shoes prevent airborne blood from landing on fabric. If you actually put on the sock, assuming you could find a way to prevent getting your own DNA on it, you would have to reenact the crime itself using the real blood to reproduce the angle of the spatter. You couldn't just flick it onto the sock—the spines of the blood drops and the areas of concentration would give you away. Nor could you dip Q-tips in blood and daub them on upholstery to replicate hand transfers. A blood pattern analyst would know instantly that you had faked it.

To plant the knuckle transfers, you would have had to dip one of your own knuckles in Simpson's blood and then replicate the rounded top and subtle feathering below that are the hallmarks of a knuckle transfer in three spots. Even if you had wanted to implicate O. J. Simpson, you would have had to plant the blood before you knew the man was in Chicago nursing a bloody knuckle on the middle finger of his left hand. The cops didn't know that when they seized his Bronco.

But on October 3, 1995, more than half of the American population watched the famous not guilty verdict read out on national TV.

When I lecture about the blood evidence from the O. J. Simpson case, somebody inevitably asks, "How did it get so screwed up?" Was it payback for acquitting the cops involved in the Rodney King beating? Did the facts get buried under a mountain of hopelessly complex data about DNA testing? Did the Dream Team bombard the prosecution with so many interruptions, so many motions, so many smoke screens, that they broke the thread that would have connected Simpson to the victims? As Bill Hodgman put it, it was a perfect storm. Media. Money. Race. Fame. The truth got lost in the circus.

Like Robert Blake, Simpson fared worse in civil court than in criminal. On February 5, 1997, he was found liable for the death of Ron Goldman and ordered to pay his family $33.5 million. Then came Simpson's bizarre quasi-confessional, *If I Did It: Confessions of the Killer*. The controversial book, ghostwritten by Pablo Fenjves and based on hours of conversations with Simpson himself, describes his relationship with Brown and explains how the murders would have unfolded had he committed them. It was supposed to be hypothetical— a work of pure fiction—but many people took it as an admission of guilt. A Florida bankruptcy court awarded rights to the book to the Goldmans to help settle the damages Simpson failed to pay after being found guilty of their son's wrongful death in civil court.

If that wasn't enough to knock the onetime sports icon off his pedestal, in 2007 O. J. Simpson and several armed friends entered a room in Las Vegas's Palace Station Hotel and Casino and took a collection of sports memorabilia from the occupants. Simpson claimed the items had been stolen from him in the first place. Nonetheless, he was charged with criminal conspiracy, kidnapping, assault, robbery, and use of a deadly weapon. After several of his pals testified against him in exchange for reduced sentences, Simpson was sentenced to thirty-three years in jail with the possibility of parole after nine served. At press time, his lawyers were appealing the verdict.

For me, the most ironic twist of all is the fact that for the past seven years I have lectured about the blood evidence in the Simpson case at the Public Agency Training Council's western states conference. The training seminar is always held at the Palace Station, the hotel where Simpson was arrested. He was sentenced in Las Vegas five days before I gave my annual lecture there on his famous criminal case.

Case Study: A Sad Finale for an Ex-Rockette

The Simpson trial wasn't the only one with lawyers whose celebrity status rivals their clients'. Among the early high-profile cases I consulted on was the death of former Radio City Rockette Alexis Ficks Welsh, stabbed by a homeless drug addict named Kevin McKiever in front of her Upper West Side apartment on June 8, 1991. I testified for the prosecution, but opposing counsel was no less formidable a duo than Ron Kuby and his partner, the illustrious William Kunstler, whose fame dated back to his defense of the Chicago Seven in the wake of the 1968 Democratic National Convention, when my friend Vic Calzeretta was a young cop getting pelted with garbage and worse by protesters in the Windy City.

Welsh, a thirty-year-old retired dancer and M.B.A. student, was coming home from walking her cocker spaniel puppies, Pizza and Pepperoni, early in the morning when someone plunged an eleven-inch carving knife into her back. Few people disputed that it was Kevin McKiever who wielded the weapon.

After all, the man was caught literally red-handed. Hearing screams, one witness looked out her second-floor window to see the tall, gaunt African-American in his red parka, straddling Welsh and jabbing at her. The witness initially thought he was punching her. More neighbors raced to the street at the sound of a woman's screams and arrived in time to see McKiever disappearing down the block toward Central Park. Welsh was still conscious and coherent, the knife handle jutting out of her lower back, though she died on the operating table less than six hours later from loss of blood. She told those who rushed to her aid, "He stabbed me!" and pointed toward McKiever. One neighbor followed the man, flagged down a patrol car, and pointed him out. When police accosted him less than ten minutes after the attack, he still had blood on his hands. Blood analysis and evidence collection being what it was in the early 1990s, the arresting officers allowed him to wash his hands before the homicide detectives stepped in. The blood on his hands was never tested for a match with Welsh's, though McKiever's bloodstained clothes were submitted into evidence.

Still, it made a convincing case. After being twice deemed mentally unfit to stand trial for the murder, McKiever was finally medicated and judged competent in 1993, and the case went to court.

Defense contended that blame for the tragedy should fall not on McKiever himself, but on the woefully inept mental health care system that had allowed him to slip through the cracks time and again. Once a gifted arts student who attended Bard College on scholarship until he started hearing voices, the accused had spent years living on the streets, using crack, and wandering in and out of treatment centers in New York and my home base of Portland, where he lived sporadically to be near his mother.

By the time Welsh died, McKiever had already harassed, stalked, and finally attacked his former neighbor Sarah Kearney with an ice pick, stabbing her repeatedly. Yet he was released after a little more than a month in jail with no more than an injunction preventing him from seeing the woman again. He had also shown up at Bellevue's emergency room a month before the murder, seeking help for the voices in his head. He was released hours later with the number for a cocaine help line.

My job was to explain what the pooled blood in the crime photos showed: The blood patterns indicated that someone had attacked Welsh with a sharp instrument, she resisted, and her assailant wrestled her to the sidewalk while she was bleeding. Using the autopsy report and the blood patterns from the crime scene photos, I concluded that he stabbed her in the right side of her chest and stomach as well as her neck and head as they struggled. Defensive slashes on her arms showed that she put up a fight and that the attack was a lengthy one—long enough to create a pool of blood with more blood dripping into it as the killer gradually subdued his victim.

Welsh rolled away as she lay on the sidewalk in a futile effort to protect herself. The killer's final blow was to drive the weapon hard into her lower back, burying the blade almost to the hilt. She lay on her side on the sidewalk until an ambulance arrived, a massive amount of blood running out of her wounds and forming a triangle as it ran toward the curb.

I explained in my testimony that both low-velocity bloodstains from deep open wounds and medium-velocity impact spatter were evident in the photos. Still, the question arose in court, as it often does, as to why McKiever wasn't drenched in blood given the violent, gory nature of the crime. You know the answer by now. First, the length of the knife enabled him to avoid contact with Welsh's skin and bloody clothes. Only the final, fatal deep wound to her back drove his carving knife in to the hilt, bringing his hand in contact with her body. Second, though she was stabbed repeatedly, none of her arteries ruptured, so there would have been no arterial spurt to spray onto the killer— just the minimal spatter that typically lands on a murderer in an attack that produces medium-velocity blood spatter.

Why wasn't the murder weapon covered in Mr. McKiever's fingerprints? Prosecutor John Martin answered that. Afraid removing the knife would exacerbate Welsh's wounds, doctors left it where it was during emergency surgery, sterilizing it first, which would have made fingerprints undetectable with the technology available at the time. Investigators who retrieved the weapon from the operating room also handled it, which would have corrupted remaining prints.

McKiever himself rejected an insanity defense. But if the jury had any questions about his mental health, he put their doubts to rest by giving a long, rambling statement in court explaining that Welsh was a witch who had to be stopped, though he still maintained that he wasn't the one who killed her. It wasn't the first time he had accused a woman of witchcraft. He had told psychiatric specialists that Kearney (the ice pick victim) and a pair of strangers he saw on a bus were trying to get into his veins and possess him. Doctors who treated him at various hospitals, outpatient clinics, and psychiatric centers had repeatedly expressed concern about his rage toward women.

McKiever was found guilty of felony murder in the second degree and attempted robbery. He was sentenced to life in prison with parole eligibility in thirty years, though the judge recommended he never be considered for parole. Kunstler himself died less than a year later, leaving a legacy of famous and controversial clients.

As a longtime homicide detective, I disagreed with the defense about who was ultimately culpable for the senseless murder of Alexis Ficks Welsh. In my opinion, it was Kevin McKiever. But I didn't doubt that Kuby and Kunstler believed in their argument. In many ways, I respected what they were trying to do to rectify social injustice. I felt the same about Johnnie Cochran—maybe not when it came to O. J. Simpson, but in the many other cases where he represented the underdog. He stood up for the rights of others.

I do the same whenever I fight for the exoneration of men and women I know are innocent based on what I read in blood evidence from the crime scene. The most important thing blood pattern analysis can do is speak for those who can't, whether they are victims of crime or people wrongly condemned.

7

Cold Blood

WHEN I WAS ABOUT to graduate from the Los Angeles Police Academy, an instructor gave me some good advice: "Don't spend all your time with other cops, and don't take your work home with you. Leave it here when your shift ends." I followed his suggestion and built a full life outside my career. But checking my work at the door wasn't always so easy. Certain cases and crime scenes got trapped in my head no matter how hard I tried to shake them out. They wound their way into my nightmares and crept up on me as disturbing memories when I least expected them. Several still do.

What made them stand out? A few cases haunted me because of their sheer savagery. They were hate crimes, thrill kills, murders of children. Others were chilling in their randomness or because they were so complex and sophisticated that the perpetrators nearly eluded us. Just as crime scene investigators learn from one another, so do murderers. They study the mistakes their predecessors made and figure out how to avoid them.

More than one murderer would make the hair on the back of your neck prickle if you strolled past him on the street. But others seem the unlikeliest of killers. As Becky Doherty, prosecutor in the Winda Snipes mutilation case, once put it, "He looks like the boy next door, but he's really the monster under the bed."

The monsters under the bed in this chapter were unique in another way, too. Their crimes left us with unusual mysteries to solve. And the truth lay hidden in the blood they spilled. The men described in the following pages might have gotten away with murder or pinned their killings on other people, had subtle traces of blood evidence not betrayed them.

Case Study: The Telltale Machete Print

In December 1996, Nanette Toder was eager to start training for her new job with Vans Floral Products. John-Campbell Barmmer would be Toder's boss at Vans, and he arranged a flight for his new employee from her home base of Miami, Florida, to Chicago for a series of meetings with the wholesale distribution company's staff and clients. He booked a room for her at the Hampton Inn in the suburb of Crestwood, a mile from Vans's offices. The area was largely industrial and hardly scenic, but Barmmer had stayed at the inn himself and deemed it convenient as well as safe. He couldn't have been more wrong.

As soon as she checked into the hotel, Toder, a pretty thirty-three-year-old aerobics instructor who exercised daily, asked the staff to recommend a safe local gym. They suggested Gold's. So Toder spent the next four days in meetings, then generally declined dinner invitations with her new colleagues in favor of hitting the fitness center. On December 12, the night before Toder was scheduled to check out and fly home, she followed her standard work-then-workout routine. Next, she picked up a salad from Wendy's, stopped by the front desk to request a five A.M. wake-up call, and retreated to her room to eat dinner. At ten P.M., she called her mom in Pennsylvania to say good night. Finally, she checked to make sure her room door was locked and wedged her hefty black suitcase packed with clothes against it, as she did every night for extra protection.

Hampton Inn desk clerk Lisa Dellorto thought it was odd when the hotel's maintenance manager, Christopher Richee, called her just after her shift started at eleven P.M. to ask whether she wanted him to bring her a burrito from a local restaurant. "No thanks," she told him, puzzled. Richee said he was picking up one for himself and would swing by the hotel shortly anyway. That struck Dellorto as even more peculiar, since Richee's shift had ended at three-thirty that afternoon and he never showed up at work during off-hours. Nevertheless, in he strolled around midnight. He told Dellorto he was going to turn on the inn's exterior Christmas lights, but a few minutes later she caught sight of him hunched over the computer that contained guest information. She would not fully understand what Richee's unusual actions meant until much later.

Early the next morning, Nan Toder failed to answer two wake-up calls placed to her room at five A.M. It was just after ten A.M. when Hampton Inn housekeeper Concepcion Dominguez made her rounds of the second floor. She reached room 227 and knocked on the door. No answer. Assuming the room was empty, she inserted her metal housekeeping key and pushed on the door. It budged an inch or so and then stopped, blocked by something heavy on the other side.

Unsure what to do next, Dominguez asked her supervisor, Mirta Arroyo, to help. Arroyo spied the problem immediately: Someone had pushed a big black suitcase against the inside of the door. She knelt and shoved the suitcase back little by little, eventually managing to open the door.

The two women gasped at the sight inside. The bed nearest to them was covered in blood. Terrified, they ran to get hotel manager Brenda Randazzo, who followed them to room 227 and saw the blood-covered body of Nan Toder lying between the beds. She closed the door, called the police, then instructed staff to stay out of the room. A few minutes later, to her annoyance, she caught Christopher Richee using his master key to enter the room where the dead woman lay. She repeated her order that all employees were to steer clear of room 227 until the authorities arrived.

Crestwood police officer John Barolga was the first to reach the Hampton Inn. It was Christopher Richee who led him to room 227 and opened the door for him. Barolga thanked Richee and told him to wait outside. Then he scanned the room carefully. He noticed two things immediately: First, there was a heavy suitcase just inside the door to the hallway. Second, there was a door that connected 227 to an adjoining room.

Barolga turned his attention back to the scene at hand. The pillow and bedspread of the bed closest to the door were soaked with blood. What looked like a bloody towel lay on the bathroom floor. The officer stepped into the bathroom for a closer look when, to his surprise, he saw Richee walk past the open bathroom door toward the center of the guest room. Barolga ordered him to leave—the third time the maintenance manager had been told to vacate room 227—but instead Richee backed into the alcove near the suitcase. "Get out," Barolga barked in no uncertain terms.

Once he made sure Richee had exited, Barolga stepped into the center of the room. Toder was lying on her back on the floor between the two beds, propped up on her elbows. Her head was tipped back and her robe was hanging open so that her breasts and pubic area were exposed. A pair of panty hose was tied tightly around her neck. A phone cord had been used to bind her left wrist and her feet. Miscellaneous items from the room lay strewn over the floor. Though it looked like a sex crime, there was no sign of rape.

An autopsy would soon reveal that Nan Toder had been strangled and slashed on the back of the head no fewer than seven times with a heavy blade that had caused massive bleeding.

The prosecutor's office asked me to examine the bloodstains and offer an interpretation of exactly what had happened during Toder's murder. I read the reports and scrutinized roughly four hundred photographs from the crime scene. I also examined the clothing and bedding taken from room 227. It appeared that Toder was asleep facedown on the bed closest to the door, with her head at the top of the bed, when someone crept up and struck her multiple times in the head. The wounds were parallel, which indicated that she did not fight back. Judging from the blood all over her bindings, the killer tied Toder up and strangled her after the initial attack, then pulled her to the floor and posed her body.

What weapon caused the massive gashes to Toder's skull? On one of the sheets were several large bloody transfer prints of what appeared to be a machete, with its distinctive long, wide blade. Voids in a blood pattern can be as meaningful as blood itself, and here there were definite voids consistent with the brass insets of a machete handle. I conducted a number of experiments that involved dipping machetes and their handles in stage blood and pressing them against a white fabric background to test my theory. The patterns were identical.

Blood transfers on the sheets also suggested that the killer was male and wore gloves. There was the bloody outline of a large hand near one of the machete patterns, but it was devoid of fingerprints—a ghost print. In fact, every scrap of evidence was tested and no fingerprints were retrieved. Nor did investigators find any incriminating hair or fibers. An examination of the bloody towel retrieved from the bathroom floor bore traces of DNA from a previous hotel guest. But police followed up on the lead and soon concluded that Toder's killer had deliberately dipped a used towel from another room in her wet blood and tossed it on the bathroom floor to mislead them.

The exterior of the door that connected room 227 with the hallway had one magnetic key card lock and another lock operated by a metal key. The key-operated lock had been recently damaged with a sharp object, most likely a screwdriver. Metal filings were strewn over the carpet outside the room. But the lock still worked. So did all three locks on the door's interior. Given the position and heft of Toder's suitcase and the struggle the two maids had to move it, it was almost inconceivable that the killer had entered from the hall. Like the bloody towel, the damaged door appeared to be a red herring left by the killer to throw the cops off track. The same held true of the items scattered over the floor of Toder's room: Police concluded that they were staged to suggest a robbery, though nothing was missing.

The windows were all locked from the inside, as was the dead bolt to the vacant room 229, which the inn generally reserved for disabled guests. There was no damage to the ceiling, no secret passage into the chamber. It was the proverbial locked-room mystery right out of an Agatha Christie novel. It looked as if the killer had appeared out of thin air and vanished into it.

In what seemed a terrible twist of fate, the guest rooms at Crestwood's Hampton Inn were set to be upgraded to a new computerized electronic locking system on December 13, the day Nan Toder's body was discovered. The staff had been briefed on the replacement system, which would keep track electronically of whose key was used to enter each room and when.

It wasn't long before Christopher Richee became the prime suspect in the Toder murder for several reasons. First, as maintenance manager, he was one of only four employees with master keys to the guest rooms. Second, Richee was in the vicinity at the approximate time the murder occurred, which was atypical for him, and he seemed to have no legitimate reason for being there. Third, he injected himself into the murder scene, which is common among killers. He just kept hovering around, the same way Brett Hartmann did after the Winda Snipes murder. (Whenever a body is found, a cop will be assigned to take the license plates of cars that drive past and the names of people who approach the scene. The officer will follow up on all these potential leads to find out whether one of the passersby is actually the perpetrator, overcome with curiosity about how investigations are progressing.)

Fourth, and perhaps most significant, Richee had a criminal past that involved arrests for theft and illegal use of weapons as well as allegations of stalking a female co-worker. That was news to hotel management. It turned out the Hampton Inn had hired the twenty-eight-year-old ten months earlier and handed him a key that opened all their guest room doors without bothering to run a criminal background check on him.

But Richee insisted he knew nothing about the crime, and police could find no forensic evidence to link him to it. So the brutal murder of Nanette Toder remained a mystery. It might have gone unsolved forever had one of Richee's pals not gotten arrested in the spring of 1999. Eager to trade information for reduced charges, Michael Duello told police that he had recently helped Christopher Richee break into and enter a building in the area.

Based on Duello's information, Richee was arrested and charged with burglary. He was convicted and sentenced to seven years in prison in March 2000. He soon pleaded guilty to an additional charge of harassing a witness in his burglary case—a woman whose car he asked friends to vandalize—and received another seven years.

But burglary was just the beginning. Christopher Richee had much more sinister secrets to hide, if his onetime pal was to be believed. Duello claimed that on December 16, 1996, Richee called him on his cell phone in a panic to say that police were following him to his home—a room in the garage of his mother's house—to search it. There was a bloody towel in there that he needed to get rid of pronto. Could Duello slip through the window and snatch it? Duello agreed, found the towel, and tossed it into a Dumpster nearby.

He also told police that he was hanging out in Richee's room in late December 1996 when he noticed that the machete Richee always kept in a cargo net was missing. He soon spotted the blade, but the handle was gone.

"What happened?" Duello asked, pointing to the knife.

Richee shrugged. "I was screwing around with it and the handle broke."

Duello watched his friend warily. "Did you kill that girl?" he asked.

Richee shot him a glance. "What do you think?" he replied coyly.

"No," said his friend.

"Stick with that," was Richee's answer.

Duello repeated his question.

Richee first said no, then yes, then no again, leaving Duello unnerved and at a loss about what to think.

Based on Duello's statements, investigators decided to reexamine Christopher Richee's role in the Nan Toder slaying. At last, the pieces began to fall into place.

Richee's former girlfriend Jill Paoletti told police—and later testified in court—that she had been with him at his house on the evening of December 12, 1996, when he suddenly ordered her to leave around eleven P.M., claiming he had a stomachache. The police questioned her at the time, and something they said made her suspect that Richee had lied to get rid of her, then slipped out. She confronted him a few days after her conversation with the cops. Richee said sure, he left. He got hungry and went to get a burrito. That seemed odd for someone with nausea. Besides, Paoletti had never seen Richee eat late at night.

It wasn't the only bizarre behavior he exhibited that week. Paoletti also remembered clearly that her boyfriend had shaved all the hair off his legs, pubic area, armpits, and face the first week of December that year. The only body hair he didn't shave was on the top of his head.

Patricia Yodka, whom Richee was also sleeping with in late 1996, unbeknownst to Paoletti, told investigators and later testified that Richee sometimes asked her to lie on her back, nude, propped up on her elbows with her head tilted back. He even photographed her in the pose—the same pose in which Toder's body was found.

Other acquaintances shared tales that left little doubt about Richee's skill in breaking and entering. Jill Alexejun, yet another one-time girlfriend, stated that when she dated Richee in 1994, she was working as an assistant manager for the Lincoln Property Company. Richee was a maintenance technician there at the time. She often watched him change locks on apartment doors, access vacant apartments, and pick locked knobs deftly with a screwdriver. If the dead bolt was on, he used a drill. She also remembered once watching him unlock a door with a credit card.

Patrick Brennan, a friend of Richee's from 1992, confessed that he had helped Richee break into the Hollywood Park video arcade and mini–golf course in Crestwood, where Richee was a manager, and steal thousands of dollars from the office safe. Before the robbery, Richee showed him a copy of the key armored-car drivers used to open the safe and explained that he had made the dupe by heating up a piece of Plexiglas, sticking it in the keyhole, and then grinding it down.

In at least one robbery, Richee spray-painted graffiti to mislead police into believing gangs were behind his crime. Perhaps more alarming, friends said he viewed himself as a criminal mastermind and boasted that he could easily outsmart any dim-witted cop.

A former manager of Richee's recalled him describing cruel pranks from his boyhood that included tearing the wings off birds and killing cats. And Duello wasn't the only one who remembered Richee's machete. Several former girlfriends confirmed that he kept the weapon in his bedroom at all times.

A chilling picture began to emerge of an arrogant, calculating psychopath who had systematically planned the brutal thrill killing of a complete stranger simply because he thought he could get away with it.

The O. J. Simpson case had saturated American media throughout the year before Nan Toder was murdered, and Richee had apparently learned enough about crime scene investigation from the television reports to know that shaving off his body hair and wearing gloves would reduce the risk of leaving traces of his DNA behind. He left the hair on his head to avoid attracting attention. He even knew enough about DNA to snatch a towel used by another guest ahead of time and plant it at the crime scene.

Investigators concluded that Richee realized he had only a few days to commit his crime before the upgraded locking system would make it impossible. He spotted Toder and checked to ensure that she would be a guest in the hotel for several nights. When he knew she was out of her room, he rigged the dead bolt on the door connecting 227 with 229 so that it would appear locked to Toder. Then he used the hotel's computer to confirm that 229 was empty minutes before entering room 227 to hack Nan Toder to death, most likely wearing only gloves to prevent fingerprints and a shower cap to avoid leaving any of his hair at the scene.

After the murder, he likely got dressed in room 229, then quickly jimmied the lock on the outside of room 227 before escaping through a door at the end of the hallway, where he had already deactivated the alarm. During one of his numerous forays into the room the morning Toder's body was discovered, he managed to genuinely re-lock the dead bolt on the adjoining room door. His two fatal mistakes were leaving a machete print in blood on the bed and failing to notice the huge suitcase that Nan Toder had shoved against her room's exterior door, because the door was in a darkened recess beyond the bathroom.

Christopher Richee was convicted of first-degree murder and sentenced to life in prison in 2002. In 2005, he won an appeal on the grounds that the trial court erred in allowing the prosecution to bring in information about his burglaries. His lawyers claimed that this unduly prejudiced the jury against him and prevented him from receiving a fair trial. The court decided there was no double jeopardy issue, so he was retried for Toder's murder in 2006. That time he pleaded guilty despite having proclaimed his innocence in writing. Why? Because a guilty plea prevented another life sentence. The sentencing judge gave him a forty-year prison term and credited him with six years served. As of the writing of this book, Richee could conceivably be released from prison in ten years.

In the spring of 2003, Sol and Lin Toder settled their multimillion-dollar civil lawsuit against the hotel and devoted the entire sum to lobbying states to pass Nan's Law statutes, which require hotel owners to run criminal background checks on all potential employees who would have access to guest room keys.

A few weeks after Toder's murder, John-Campbell Barmmer was shocked to get a bill in the mail from the Hampton Inn for his late employee's hotel stay. Naturally, he refused to pay it.

Case Study: Cloaks, Daggers, and Debts

To outsiders, the Spiro family might have looked as though they had it all. A sprawling four-bedroom house with a swimming pool in posh Rancho Santa Fe, California. Horseback-riding lessons for the kids. Cocktail parties and country club memberships for the parents. But when the oldest Spiro child failed to turn up for a riding lesson, the neighbors began to get worried. No one had seen the Spiros for three days, which seemed odd. The kids were usually out skateboarding, and the mother was always at the club playing tennis or bridge. Finally, on November 5, 1992, some friends ventured up the drive and peeked in the window. They could see the youngest child clearly, lying motionless on her bed.

Police who responded to their 911 call found the house quiet and locked. Firemen had to break down a door to gain entry. Moving from room to room, they soon located all three Spiro children—sixteen-year-old Sara, fourteen-year-old Adam, and eleven-year-old Dina—lying in their beds, each dead from gunshot wounds to the head. Their mother, forty-one-year-old Gail, was dead in the master bedroom. She, too, had been shot in the head. The medical examiner put the date of death at about three days earlier—November 1 or 2.

The patriarch of the clan, British-born Ian Spiro, was nowhere to be found.

He was suspect number one until he turned up three days later seventy miles north in Anza-Borrego Desert State Park's remote Coachwhip Canyon, slumped over the wheel of his white Ford Explorer. The doors were locked and the keys were inside. An autopsy showed that forty-six-year-old Spiro had died of cyanide poisoning.

To call Ian Spiro a colorful character might be an understatement. When the family moved to San Diego County from southern France a year earlier, Spiro told the locals he was an international commodities broker. But if you believed the stories buzzing around Rancho Santa Fe, the eccentric Englishman was actually a spy with ties to the CIA, Great Britain's MI-5, Israel's Mossad, and some of the Arab world's most feared terrorists.

Rumor had it that Spiro, a longtime resident of Beirut, played a role in negotiations with Lebanese extremists for the release of American and British hostages in the 1980s. By some reports, he introduced negotiator-turned-hostage Terry Waite to the Shiites who eventually kidnapped him. Others said Oliver North mentioned Spiro in his notebooks and suggested him as a go-between in Lebanon during the Iran-Contra scandal.

Could the murders be payback for some shadowy covert action? Were they a government-sanctioned assassination? An underworld hit? The case seemed to combine all the elements of a good murder mystery—wealth, glamour, and intrigue. It captivated everyone from local gossips to London newspaper reporters.

Soon plotlines worthy of a Jason Bourne blockbuster sprang up. According to one, Arab terrorists bent on revenge finally caught up with the Spiro clan. Another had renegades within Israeli intelligence bumping them off. A third pinned the slaughters on Japan's deadly Yakuza Mafia as retribution for some shady Spiro business deals in the Far East. Yet a fourth claimed the family was eliminated by high-ranking U.S. ops because Spiro was hiding incriminating documents that proved Department of Justice misconduct. A rumor even flitted around for a while about a dark-haired stranger with a foreign accent barging into the Spiro household a few days before the murders, then departing abruptly when he learned Ian wasn't home.

But while conspiracy theorists speculated wildly on which sinister ghost had risen out of Spiro's murky spy past to haunt him, another less glamorous possibility began to emerge.

The lead came from unexpected quarters. During the many police interviews with Rancho Santa Fe residents who knew the Spiros, someone mentioned that the family had a housekeeper. Detectives managed to locate the woman, eighteen-year-old Paula Rojas, and asked if she had noticed anything unusual in the family's behavior. Yes, she said.

In broken English, she told them that her husband drove her to work at seven A.M. on the morning of November 2, as always. No sooner did she walk in than she bumped into a disheveled and dazed Ian Spiro, standing in the kitchen wearing a red bathrobe.

"What are you doing here?" he asked.

Rojas said that Mrs. Spiro had asked her to work that day. Spiro told her the family wasn't there and her services wouldn't be needed. There were some "problems," he mumbled vaguely.

Flustered, the maid explained that her husband had left and now she had no ride home. Spiro said he would drive her home, then ushered her out of the main house and into a guesthouse to wait while he got dressed. A short time later, he drove Rojas back to the migrant camp where she spent weekends. It was the last she had seen or heard of the Spiro family.

Around the same time that Rojas's story came to light, investigators poring over mounds of documents in Spiro's office unearthed troubles that had little to do with cloak-and-dagger politics. Despite his family's lavish lifestyle, Ian Spiro was flat broke. He hadn't paid his rent or even his grocery bills in months. Hundreds of lottery tickets were stashed near a Ouija board, suggesting that he had been trying to conjure spirits to pick winning numbers. Though there were notes on countless business schemes, Spiro's main enterprise seemed to be providing 900 numbers for dating services, psychics, and chat lines that advertised on late night television. His business, Home Media Promotions, earned a small amount from every call placed, but records showed Spiro was spending far more to advertise than he was collecting.

At one time, Ian Spiro had been a prosperous entrepreneur. But those days were evidently gone. The catalyst for his downward spiral seemed to be a plan to export Porsches to Japan. He had made money on the first shipment but sank huge profits into the second, which vanished mysteriously en route. Japanese police suspected the Yakuza were to blame but could do little to help Spiro recoup his losses. Since then, the man had been taking more and more desperate measures to stay afloat, luring new investors into his schemes and then paying the furious existing ones with their capital.

Spiro owed thousands of dollars to relatives, friends, and other creditors and millions to a bank that had loaned money to his wife for home repairs several years earlier. The spring before his death, he had taken out a $1.5 million life insurance policy on himself.

Friends from the children's schools said the once tidy Brit had become unkempt and distracted in recent weeks. Always a doting dad who showed up for every class activity, Spiro had lately grown irritable and brusque with his kids.

Next, a local jeweler came forward to say that he had sold cyanide to Spiro, ostensibly for gold processing, two weeks before his death. Spiro's attorney, James Street, added that he had loaned his client a .357 Smith & Wesson revolver because Spiro said he was getting threatening phone calls at all hours and feared for his family's safety. Were the callers mysterious figures from the world of espionage or irate creditors? It was hard to say.

Though investigators were granted access to Spiro's CIA files and confirmed that he had in fact done work for the agency a decade earlier, mounting evidence pointed to a tragic decision made by a man crushed under a mountain of financial pressure.

Then the month after Spiro's body was found, a group of hikers in Anza-Borrego stumbled upon two battered green-and-gold-striped suitcases and a black briefcase, all filled with Spiro family documents, three miles from the spot where Ian Spiro's body was found. Among the reams of papers was a cassette tape with a recording of Spiro rambling somewhat incoherently and referring to himself in the third person. "The house of cards," he said, was "falling down." The investors he had bilked in his failed businesses wanted his head. Gail was going to leave him. The tape seemed to bear out the notion that Spiro had contrived a deadly escape hatch from the debt threatening to engulf his family.

Relatives didn't buy it. Ian Spiro was a devoted husband and father, they said, a gentle man who would never hurt anyone.

Police weren't so sure. In their interview with Rojas, the maid had mentioned a red robe twice. That piqued their interest. They searched the house and found the garment. But when they examined it, they found no trace of blood spatter. After the FBI stepped in to investigate the Spiro murders, they, too, scrutinized the robe and found no blood on it—not even on the white cuffs.

So investigations stalled. The DA's office couldn't get involved because no arrests had been made. Still, pressure to solve the case remained intense. An entire family, a family living in a haven of privilege where violent crime was virtually nonexistent, had been executed. The public wanted closure.

Three years went by before my old pal Tim Carroll—a retired San Diego detective with whom I had worked undercover narcotics operations years earlier—agreed to reexamine the Spiro case as a favor to the local sheriff. Tim called me in 1995 and asked whether I would be willing to take a look at the robe and some other clothes from the Spiro murders as well as the crime scene photos. He also wanted my help finding an unbiased, independent forensics lab to examine the physical evidence.

Tim hand-carried the items to me in Portland. First we took the robe to Dr. Raymond Grimsbo, whom I'd worked with on the Green Thread Mystery. We all examined it under high-intensity lights and a microscope but found nothing.

Then we sprayed it with Luminol and, to our amazement, blood popped up everywhere.

Bathed in the luminescent chemical compound, the robe revealed the high-velocity impact spatter typical of blowback from gunshot wounds all over the right sleeve. It dissipated in the direction of the shoulder. Blood also dotted the front of the robe, and a smaller amount speckled the left sleeve. Spatter was visible even on the white cuffs, though the flecks were too minute to see with a microscope.

Was Spiro right-handed? Yes.

Would the pattern revealed be consistent with contact wounds, meaning the killer held the gun close enough to literally touch his victims when he fired? Yes.

Was there enough spatter to have come from multiple victims? Yes, again.

Confirmatory lab tests bore out our suspicions that the substance embedded in the fibers of the terry-cloth robe was indeed blood. Now we needed to find out whether it belonged to the Spiro victims. Fortunately, samples of their blood had been saved from the postmortems. Dr. Grimsbo conducted DNA tests on the sections of the robe that reacted with the Luminol; experts at a crime lab in San Diego County followed with similar tests.

Both labs concluded that the blood on Ian Spiro's robe came from his wife and three children. The blood on the left sleeve belonged to Spiro's youngest child, Dina, who appeared to have been the only family member to wake up and resist. We already knew this from the crime scene photos. Hers was the only bedroom wall spattered with blood. Hers were the only covers turned back. It appeared that Spiro had started with his wife, then moved systematically to his older daughter and then his son, holding the gun against their heads and firing. Dina heard the noises and came out to see what was causing them. Her father forced her back to her room and held her down on her bed with his left hand while he placed the gun barrel against her forehead and fired with his right, resulting in a concentration of her blood on his right sleeve and a smaller amount on his left.

The solution to a mystery that had captured the imagination of several continents was there all along. It had been sitting on the shelf of an evidence room year after year without anybody noticing.

Tim Carroll filed a report on the homicide-suicide evidence, and police called a press conference to announce the long-awaited answer to the Spiro whodunit in the presence of the family's surviving relatives.

Though the murder weapon was never found, there was strong evidence to suggest that Spiro used the gun his attorney, James Street, loaned him. Gail Spiro's head bore bruise marks with the imprint of a gun barrel with an unusual sight line—a sight line that matched just one particular heavy, thick-barreled model of Smith & Wesson .357—the model Street loaned to Spiro a few weeks before the murders occurred.

There are conspiracy theorists out there who still argue that Ian Spiro was no midlevel conduit with connections in the Lebanese business world, but a full-fledged ace of spies who became inconvenient and got taken out with his family as collateral damage. But blood evidence doesn't lie. Much as crime buffs would prefer a cold war thriller, the blood-spattered red bathrobe told a sadder, less sensational story.

Case Study: Sledgehammers and Finger-Pointing

If the killing of Nan Toder was unsettling for its ice-veined premeditation and random choice of victims, the murder of Betty Lee was equally horrifying for its vicious, spur-of-the-moment fury and targeting of a specific woman because of her race and her vulnerability.

Lee was a thirty-six-year-old single Navajo mother of five living in Shiprock, New Mexico. She had grown up in the town, part of the Navajo reservation, and most of her family still lived there. Lee was taking business courses at a local Navajo tribe–run college, hoping they would help her land a better-paying job to support herself and her kids.

On the evening of June 8, 2000, she joined two female acquaintances making the thirty-mile drive into Farmington for a few drinks. The evening began well, but as the night wore on, her friends started flirting with a pair of Navajo men, and Lee felt like a fifth wheel. The five left a bar together, but the others made it clear they wanted Lee out of the picture and had no intention of driving all the way to Shiprock to drop her off.

It was after two A.M. when, to Betty Lee's dismay, her friends left her at a group of pay phones outside a convenience store and drove away. She was crying openly when a burly stranger approached her and asked what was wrong. Sobbing, she explained that she was stranded in Farmington and was trying to reach someone she knew to give her a lift.

"Well, I hate to see a woman cry," he said kindly. He offered to drive her to a small town halfway to Shiprock.

Another man walked out of the store clutching a pack of cigarettes and joined them. Lee realized he was a friend of the man offering her a ride. The apparent Good Samaritan was twenty-seven-year-old Robert "Bobby" Fry. His pal was twenty-four-year-old Leslie "Les" Engh.

Betty Lee was reluctant to accept a ride from two strange men, but what else could she do? No one was answering the phone, and she was thirty miles from home across barren desert countryside.

The three piled into Fry's Ford Aspire and Fry headed north, while Lee told Engh how her friends had abandoned her. They had driven only a few miles out of town onto County Road 6480 when Fry veered unexpectedly into an unpaved turnoff and stopped the car in a deserted stretch that locals called Twin Peaks. Already apprehensive, Lee jumped out and started to hurry away.

"Where are you going?" Fry called. "I just have to pee."

She ignored him, so he leapt back into the car and pulled up alongside her. Somehow he managed to calm her down, convince her he was genuinely sorry for scaring her, and coax her back into the passenger seat.

At first he seemed to be heading back toward the highway, but then suddenly he cut the car's ignition a second time. He leapt out, darted around to Lee's side, and yanked open her door. Then he grabbed a fistful of her hair and started to drag her out of the passenger's seat.

"Grab her legs!" he told Engh, who obliged as Fry yanked off the struggling woman's shirt and bra. Enraged at her resistance, Fry pulled out an eight-inch bowie knife he had been carrying and plunged the blade into Lee's bare chest as Engh was pulling off her pants. The knife penetrated the breastbone and nearly pierced her heart. Remarkably, she wrenched herself away from her attackers, pulled out the blade, and flung it toward a nearby ravine. Then she ran toward the highway, bleeding profusely, her sandals flopping in the sand.

"Find the knife!" Fry yelled to Engh. Then he reached into the backseat, pulled out a ten-pound sledgehammer, and headed after Lee. He caught up with her easily, stuck out his foot, and tripped her.

Engh would later tell police that he was still searching in vain for the bloody knife with a flashlight when he heard Lee scream. He looked up and saw Fry swinging the sledgehammer over his head repeatedly until the screaming stopped.

Fry returned, panting but visibly exhilarated. He ordered Engh to help him drag Lee, now motionless and bloody, more than a hundred feet to a clump of sagebrush, where they hid her body. Then they kicked her clothing into a shallow ditch nearby where no one driving along the road would spot it.

Eager to flee the scene, Fry gunned the engine, but the Aspire got stuck in the sand only a mile from the murder scene. Despite the fact that it was four in the morning, he pulled out his cell phone and called his parents, with whom he still lived, demanding they come get him.

Gloria and James Fry staggered out of bed, climbed into their red pickup truck, and hurried off to help their son. They dropped Engh at his own house and stopped by theirs so Robert could change his clothes. Then Robert and James headed back to the desert in the pickup, with Gloria following in a second car. By the time she caught up with them, both the Aspire and the pickup were hopelessly mired in the loose sand.

The Frys called a towing service, but as the truck driver spun his wheels in the dried riverbed, his truck became as immovable as the other two vehicles. Humiliated, he called a second tow truck provider—Bloomfield Towing—and driver Charley Bergin headed to the scene with a bigger rig. Bergin got all three vehicles out of the sand but got so irritated with his cell phone's lousy reception that he hurled it out the window before heading back into town.

A few hours passed before a public service worker checking power lines on 6480 spotted a wide swath of fresh blood on the rutted dirt roadway. Thinking someone had hit an animal, he followed the trail with his eyes. With a jolt of fear, he saw what looked like a woman's bare foot jutting out of a bush. He called 911 and waited.

Members of the San Juan County Sheriff's Office, including Detectives Bob Melton and Tyler Truby, followed the trail of blood and found the nude body of Betty Lee. Blood covered her chest, and her skull had been pummeled so hard with blows from a blunt object that portions of her brain were visible. A search soon turned up both murder weapons—a bloody bowie knife and a sledgehammer.

A bloody swath cut through the sand next to several sets of men's footprints, showing that Lee had been dragged to her current position by two assailants. Tracing the drag marks from their termination back to their point of origin, they found more marks in the sand. Footprints suggested that a car had stopped, a woman had walked a short distance, and the same car had pulled up alongside her. Police widened their search of the ground and found a confusion of tire marks from multiple vehicles crisscrossing one another less than a mile away.

While they were still searching the area, Melton and Truby were surprised to see that a probation officer named Gloria Fry had pulled up and was talking with the sheriff. Meanwhile Deputy Matt Wilcox, one of several officers examining the tire tracks, spotted a cell phone lying on the ground. A quick check led back to Charley Bergin at Bloomfield Towing.

Chagrined, Bergin explained to the police that he had flung his phone away while helping to pull James Fry's pickup, his son Robert's sedan, and another tow truck out of the sand in the early morning hours.

Detectives Melton and Truby, who had been following up a series of frustrating false leads, headed to the Fry house as soon as they heard Bergin's story. The Frys, though visibly apprehensive to find detectives converging on their home, agreed to let them search the premises without a warrant. The officers rummaged through piles of dirty laundry covering the floor of Robert's room and found a black T-shirt with a skull-like white face and the logo of the horror punk band the Misfits. The shirt had what appeared to be bloodstains on the front and the back of the right shoulder. They also found a pair of boots with suspicious stains.

Melton and Truby asked the family about their mishap on CR 6480. Robert explained that he had spent the night drinking with his friend Les Engh, then taken a drive along CR 6480, stopping to relieve himself en route. Gloria Fry chimed in with highlights of the towing fiasco that followed.

The detectives made a note to interview Engh as soon as they could track him down. That, as it turned out, couldn't have been easier. The man was already in custody for forgery because an official had caught him falsifying signatures for court-ordered community service, the punishment for a prior offense.

Engh told Melton an innocent tale about partying with Fry, ducking into a convenience store for cigarettes, and walking out to find his pal chatting up a tearful Native American woman. Engh said Fry simply took her number and left. Melton asked Engh what Fry normally kept in his Ford. Among the items Engh ticked off was a sledgehammer. Melton thanked him and left.

Then Truby returned with more questions. In minutes, Engh cottoned on to the fact that the cops had found Betty Lee's corpse. He came clean and started spilling every detail of the gruesome killing.

On June 11, police showed up at the Fry house with a warrant for Robert's arrest. He was charged with the murder, kidnapping, and attempted rape of Betty Lee as well as tampering with evidence. Engh, too, was arrested. Bloodstained items retrieved from his home were submitted into evidence, as was Fry's Ford Aspire, which contained a bloody floor mat and one of Lee's earrings. Lab tests showed the blood on both men's clothing and Fry's car belonged to the murdered woman.

When word of the arrest made the newspapers, those who knew him were hardly surprised. Robert Fry was infamous for a vicious, violent temper that darkened when he drank. And he drank a lot. He was menacing, moody, and prone to picking fights. But he was also a relentless braggart, spinning wild tales about brawls and military adventures. (In reality, he had been dishonorably discharged from the navy after breaking another sailor's nose.)

One of those who read the headlines was his sometime drinking pal Larry Hudson. Fry had long boasted to him about "killing an Indian." Until then, Hudson had dismissed the guy as a blowhard, but now he wondered. Fry had described hitting his victim over the head with a hammer. According to the papers, he had killed this woman exactly the same way. Were Fry's gory, booze-fueled yarns true after all? Hudson figured he had better let police decide. He told members of the sheriff's office everything he could remember of Fry's alleged Indian murder.

When Hudson started talking, detectives realized Fry's stories were no tall tales. Although he didn't realize it, Hudson was relating key details of the still unsolved murder of forty-year-old Donald Tsosie of Ganado, Arizona. Tsosie, a Navajo parent of five just like Betty Lee, had been found beaten to death in the spring of 1998, nearly a month after his murder. The police had deliberately kept certain points out of the newspapers. Only the killer would know them. Now here was Hudson rattling off inside information like the fact that the victim was found barefoot, his cowboy boots tossed over the edge of a cliff on top of his bloodied body.

"Ask Les Engh," Larry Hudson said. "He was with Fry. He'll know more."

Realizing his own fate was on the line when police showed up to grill him about Tsosie, Engh told them everything they wanted to know. He described the murder of a Native American stranger, to whom Fry offered a ride outside a bar one night simply because he was keyed up and wanted to "roll an Indian." Engh remembered Fry chuckling when the stick he was beating Tsosie with kept breaking. He said Fry used the jagged bits to stab his victim in the eyes and genitals.

But by the time the Betty Lee case went to trial, Fry and his lawyer had come up with their own version of events. Engh, they claimed, was the ringleader of the Lee killing and Fry the unwilling tagalong. In their take, he reluctantly followed orders to harm a helpless woman because he was too terrified to defy his psychopathic friend.

The prosecution asked me to examine the evidence and tell them whose story the blood reinforced. Engh said Fry wielded the sledgehammer that murdered Betty Lee. Fry said Engh did it. Somebody was lying.

Analyzing the blood patterns on their clothes, I found it relatively easy to distinguish fact from fiction. Robert Fry's boots were dotted with medium-velocity impact spatter in Lee's blood in no fewer than twenty places. These spatter stains and the stains on the sledgehammer itself were consistent with an attacker who had leaned over his victim and bludgeoned her repeatedly with a blunt instrument like a sledgehammer as she lay on the ground in front of him.

Equally damning was the evidence on the back of Fry's Misfits T-shirt. On the right shoulder was a series of medium-velocity blood spatter dots consistent with cast-off from a bloody weapon being swung overhead in a multiple-blow attack. (The medical examiner concluded that the killer struck Lee in the head between three and five times.) There was also a bloody, sandy impression of the rectangular head of a sledgehammer on the right shoulder, suggesting that whoever wore the shirt slung the weapon over his shoulder and carried it in that position while the blood was still wet. When we placed the murder weapon on top of the indentation, the size and shape were a match.

Close examination of the projected blood spatter revealed that it was mixed with minute granules of sand. I had samples of sand from the section of CR 6480 where the victim's body was found shipped to me in Portland so that I could conduct a series of experiments to help me understand precisely how it interacted with blood. It became apparent that the blood from Lee's injuries created a wet blood-into-blood pattern in the loose, dry sand. As the sledgehammer made contact with it, some of the droplets became airborne on impact and the sand granules projected onto Fry's clothing adhered to the fabric, as did the blood that carried them.

Engh's shirt and black tennis shoes were bloody, too, but there was no impact spatter, no projected patterning, nothing consistent with him having hit anyone over the head with a blunt object. Instead his clothing revealed low-velocity transfer stains in Lee's blood, bearing out his statement that he had dragged the dead woman's body a significant distance immediately after her murder. The front of Fry's T-shirt had similar transfer stains in Lee's blood, reinforcing Engh's explanation of how the two worked together to drag the victim's body to its hiding place.

The prosecutor asked me to stage a reenactment of the murder to help the jury understand how the blood spatter had landed on Robert Fry's boots and shirt and what that meant. So I set up a female mannequin and the actual sledgehammer used in the murder, then demonstrated the blows in slow motion.

I don't take sides in court. I just do my best to educate the jurors on the blood evidence they need to understand. Still, it is impossible to ignore the family members sitting there, watching me re-create the terrifying, final moments of their loved one's life. In the Fry trial, the rows on the right held a smattering of the defendant's kin, while those on the left behind the prosecutor's table were filled with nearly fifty of Betty Lee's relatives. Seeing the pain in their eyes was heart-wrenching.

I very seldom meet with relatives of the victim before my testimony, but I make a point to talk with them after my presentations whenever they are willing. I explain that I am genuinely sorry for forcing them to relive nightmares. I also remind them that my reenactments are done to help ensure justice for the person they have lost, to help give the victim a voice. Usually families understand.

The jury in the Fry case deliberated for seven hours before finding him guilty on all counts. He was sentenced to die by lethal injection. He appealed, arguing that the court violated his right to a fair trial by excusing seven prospective jurors who said their religion made them opposed to the death penalty, but the New Mexico Supreme Court upheld the murder conviction and death sentence. Engh, who testified against Fry, pleaded guilty and got a life sentence for his role in the killing.

After his conviction for Lee's murder, Fry was also tried and convicted for killing Tsosie and sentenced to life in prison. When yet another former friend came forward to give evidence, Fry was tried and convicted of two earlier killings that had long gone unsolved and received two more life sentences for the brutal 1996 slayings of eighteen-year-old Matthew Trecker and twenty-four-year-old Joe Fleming, whose throats were sliced from ear to ear late one night in a Farmington store. At the time, Fry was a frequent customer and ostensibly a friend of both victims, one of whom he attempted to decapitate.

In March 2009, New Mexico became the fifteenth state to abolish the death penalty, though the legislation does not apply to the two men currently on death row, one of whom is Robert Fry. At press time, Fry's case was still in the appeals process. If his appeals prove unsuccessful, his sentence of execution by lethal injection will stand.

A World of Crime

ILOGGED ROUGHLY ONE hundred thousand air miles in 2008, much of it devoted to visiting crime scenes and police departments where I was consulting on blood spatter patterns in homicides. Luckily, I like to travel, and the work I do takes me to fascinating places. I have had the good fortune to lecture in Argentina, Canada, Colombia, France, Russia, and England's illustrious New Scotland Yard, where I got to see some truly pioneering fingerprinting techniques in action. Even when I am supposedly the teacher, every new group I train teaches me something new about crime solving in return. My travels also remind me, continually, that murder finds its way into every kind of community in every corner of the world.

In the Land of the Midnight Sun

One unusual case occurred in the tiny fishing village of Togiak in south-western Alaska. Even now, the population there barely tops eight hundred. In the winter, temperatures plunge to forty below zero. To-giak is one of dozens of Yupik Eskimo villages strung like beads through barren tundra more reminiscent of Siberia than the United States. According to census data, 86 percent of residents are Native Americans. The village perches on the edge of a bay inside a national wildlife refuge that shares its name, and the only way to reach it is to brave nearly impassable roads of ice or mud, depending on the season, or to hire a bush pilot willing to fly anywhere if the price is right.

The homicide in question was an unsettling one involving allegations not only of murder, but of necrophilia. On November 15, 1988, as the bitter Alaska winter set in, the Andrew family hosted a raucous party, where the booze flowed and the revelry lasted until after eight A.M. Most of the celebrants were still recovering from the previous night's bash when two of the host family's younger siblings wandered into the bedroom where twenty-two-year-old Moses Andrew was sleeping during the afternoon. There was Moses, unconscious, lying on top of his girlfriend, Roberta Blue. Something red had stained the pillow under her head. Moses's little brothers took a few steps closer and saw that there was blood all over the bed.

They hurried out to get their aunt, who took one glance into the bedroom and then called the police. By the time a village public safety officer arrived, Moses Andrew appeared to be slowly regaining consciousness. When the officer walked in, according to his later testimony, he found the suspect partially nude and attempting to have sex with Blue's corpse. He pulled Moses off the dead woman, ordered him to get dressed, and arrested him. He also ascertained that Blue had been shot in the head multiple times.

I was asked by the prosecutor in the case to analyze the crime scene photos and give an interpretation of exactly what had happened, since everyone in the house had apparently been too inebriated to remember clearly. The last time anyone recalled seeing Blue alive was sometime around ten A.M. Moses Andrew's defense attorney contended that another resident of the house had pulled the trigger and then set up the unconscious man as the fall guy by dumping him on top of the victim.

The blood in the case told me a story as remarkable as it was disturbing. Blue had been shot in the head three times with a .22 rifle, which was found lying on the floor beside the bed. She had a most unusual blood pattern of thin, crisscrossing red lines—a sort of tic-tac-toe board of blood—across her face. The bed also showed three distinct pools of blood, with thinner trails of blood connecting them all. These components together suggested to me that Blue's body had been moved twice after she was killed. Each time her body was rolled into a different position, more blood leaked out of her wounds and ran down her face from a new angle, creating a pattern of intersecting lines. Blue's body remained in its various positions a relatively long time, long enough for her head to continue bleeding heavily from the gunshot wounds and creating a new pool of blood wherever she lay. The photographs showed the position in which her body was found, with her legs apart and her head hanging over the edge of the bed. Blood had run down the sheets and puddled on the floor. It was gruesome, but an excellent study in flow patterns.

I was asked to testify in the trial. These were the 1980s, when my area of expertise was still a novelty, and the defense attorney requested that the judge bar my testimony on the grounds that blood pattern interpretation had no merit and no basis in science. In this instance, the judge disagreed. Taking part meant that I would need to fly to Anchorage and then board a puddle jumper for the four-hundred-mile journey to Bethel, a remote town forty miles from the Bering Sea, where the trial would be held.

Proceedings were about to get under way and I had my travel plans set when, to my astonishment, my client called to tell me things had ground to a screeching halt because fishing season was starting. At first I thought he was kidding. But many Bethel residents, like their smaller-town neighbors, made their livelihood hunting and fishing in the salmon-rich waters around their homes. The jurors had to earn while they could. So did the alternates. And the salmon didn't stop running, even for a murder trial.

I finally arrived to discover that Bethel boasted a single paved road, which rolled along for about ten miles and branched off into dirt arteries that disappeared into fog and mud and hid treacherous, craterlike potholes. With a population of a little more than six thousand residents, mostly Yupik Eskimos, the place is a rough-and-ready workingman's town, home to more warehouses and dilapidated trailers than hotels and restaurants. It is also the center of government for the many outlying villages, including Togiak.

Since Bethel boasted no courthouse, the trial took place in a drafty one-story building utilitarian enough to serve our purposes. With its narrow confines and bare, battered wooden floor, it might well have been a tavern at one time. In fact, it reminded me a lot of the old watering hole on the outskirts of San Angelo, where I had once wreaked havoc with my cherry bomb many years earlier.

If the setting was intriguing, the jury was downright fascinating. They were the most unusual lot I had ever encountered. One wizened old man sat resolutely staring away from me, avoiding eye contact at all costs, enormous headphones stretching from his shoulders to his chin like a neck brace. The moment the jurors were granted a break, he slipped them on and tuned everyone out in favor of listening to music. The bench never asked him to remove them during the court proceedings.

I wasn't surprised to learn later that jurors had voted to acquit Moses Andrew after a short deliberation. I didn't get the sense that they cared much for my tutorial on the emerging world of blood pattern analysis.

Still, the state had its say. The defendant had already pleaded no contest and been convicted of second-degree robbery in 1986. A state judge ruled that evidence from the unsuccessful Roberta Blue murder case was strong enough to show that Moses Andrew had violated the terms of his probation by possibly killing somebody and to order him to do jail time.

Intrigue and Toasts

In 1994, I got to live out a long-standing dream of mine: I went to Russia. Multnomah County sheriff John Bunnell and I were invited to visit Moscow along with Las Vegas's sheriff and a California state narcotics agent, all of whom were working on a Russian segment of the true crime TV series *American Detective*. I had long romanticized the country as a place steeped in mystery and intrigue, and my ten-day visit lived up to my expectations in every way.

Our hosts from the capital's police department welcomed us with a lunchtime reception at the Moscow Police Training Academy. To break the ice, they served us generous measures of vodka and toasted our arrival. Then they poured more vodka and made another toast. And another. I tried to refuse politely, but to no avail. We raised and downed our glasses again and again to increasingly more expansive toasts, our drinks hoisted to valiant lost fathers and grandfathers from great wars past. Soon tears were flowing as freely as vodka. I stared blearily over at John, who seemed to be clutching the table and working hard not to sway.

"N'thanksh, I don' ushually drink," I slurred as another round came my way. The translator blinked at me in astonishment, then said something in Russian. The local officers grinned and slapped me on the back. Obviously what I had said didn't translate.

After lunch, we toured the academy with an interpreter explaining what was going on in various classes as we peered in. Still struggling to shake off my vodka-fueled fog, I marveled at the fact that every trainee took karate here. I hoped my questions sounded coherent. If not, maybe they would chalk it up to the language barrier. Fortunately, I had recovered fully by the time I was asked to conduct a demonstration about blood pattern analysis and crime scene reconstruction.

Hearing about the crimes, cases, and policing issues our Russian counterparts grappled with every day was riveting. Their problems weren't all that far removed from our own battle against rising violent crime rates and shrinking budgets. (Statistics from the Moscow Bureau of Forensic Medicine later pegged 1994, the year we visited, as the decade's peak for Muscovite murders, with a whopping 2,863.) But in Moscow in the mid-1990s, a police officer wielded more definitive power and authority than in the average American city. If, for example, a cop flagged you down with a red wand at an intersection and you didn't stop, he had the right to shoot at your car. Most citizens knew it and hit the brakes the moment they saw a flash of red.

Though the Russians didn't smile nearly as often as we do, our hosts were warm and convivial, apt to grab you in a bear hug and plant a kiss on your cheek. Some of our new friends were quite candid about their pasts as KGB agents and referred openly to work they did during the cold war, when they didn't officially "exist" during their travels in certain countries. As much as I liked them, I had to admit that they still exuded a vaguely sinister aura.

I didn't appreciate just what an asset that aura could be until one cold night when we were at yet another nightclub, toasting our camaraderie with yet more vodka. I decided to clear my head and naïvely stepped outside around midnight for some fresh air.

As I stood alone on a three-foot cement stoop at the bar's entrance, debating whether to hail a taxi back to the hotel for a little extra rest, out of the deserted street stepped one of the most menacing men I have ever seen. He had hulking shoulders under his heavy jacket, and every visible inch of his skin was covered in tattoos. He muttered something in Russian in a low, guttural voice.

"I'm sorry, I don't speak Russian," I told him amiably.

He stepped up onto the stoop level with me and repeated the sentence.

"I don't speak . . ."

The next thing I knew, he had pulled a knife and was pointing it at me.

I backed up against the outside wall of the building. I wasn't armed. There was nowhere to run. And I couldn't maneuver well enough to dart back inside without risking getting stabbed. All right, I figured. If he wants my wallet, he can have it. I was just reaching into my jacket to retrieve it when the door suddenly swung wide and several of my new Russian pals from the academy staggered out. In less than a second they grasped the situation and surrounded my would-be mugger. An amazing transformation came over him. He seemed to know instinctively who they were, and a look of fear flitted across his face. He jumped off the stoop and hurried away down the street, melting back into the darkness.

"You have to be careful," one of the men said. "It can be dangerous here."

That wasn't my only dramatic encounter. Our hosts guided us enthusiastically from high point to scenic high point, from the Pushkin Museum with its art masterpieces to the Moscow Metro, down escalator after escalator to a subway that seemed miles underground. We also took a number of day trips out of the city, passing bombed-out buildings and run-down nuclear silos until the exurbs gave way to stretches of flat countryside.

Once on the highway, our driver would accelerate to what felt like 170 miles an hour. He darted in and out of traffic, our tiny coupe flying along past a blur of fields and picturesque country villas called dachas. The Russians kept up a steady stream of cheerful conversation, seemingly unperturbed by the fact that the driver was ramping up for the Indy 500. During my first ride, I stared wide-eyed out the window. We're all going to die, I thought, glancing surreptitiously at John to see if his knuckles were as white as mine. He was smiling and nodding at our hosts' comments. Gradually, I relaxed enough to notice that our driver's approach was the norm rather than the exception. In neighboring vehicles, men young and old were applying the same Andretti-like technique behind the wheel, as if they were all bent on winning the Borg-Warner Trophy.

We were flying along at light speed one afternoon, returning from a village famous for its colorful handmade scarves, when our Russian friends decided to pull up at a roadside stand to buy some cold soft drinks and snacks. As we stepped out of the car, the sounds of angry male voices reached our ears. I glanced up. The vendor operating the refreshment stand was having a heated argument with a male customer clad in black. Suddenly, the irate buyer drew out a knife and lunged at the vendor. The man staggered backward with a cry and fell down, clutching his chest. As the victim lay there bleeding, the perpetrator pocketed his knife and strolled off.

I looked around expectantly. Weren't we going to rush him? He was getting away. Realizing we were police, the local people converged on us. But instead of begging us to jump in, they pushed us away, speaking rapidly in Russian. They seemed to be imploring the cops *not* to act. After a minute or so, we piled back into our car and headed toward Moscow. I never knew if that was standard protocol since our colleagues were out of their jurisdiction or if they refrained from getting involved because they had American guests with them.

A year later, we invited our Russian friends to visit us in Portland. We took them on private tours of the Columbia River Gorge and a local steel plant that a friend of mine operated, introduced them to Jerome Kersey of the NBA's Portland Trail Blazers, and hosted a traditional western steak barbecue at my house. Shortly after they arrived for dinner, we were surprised to find them strolling from room to room, lifting comforters to peer under beds and opening doors to peek into closets.

"I hope they don't think we've bugged the house," I whispered to Penny.

"No, no," said one with a grin, realizing our misinterpretation. "We are admiring how much space you have. You have beautiful living conditions here."

My last memorable experience with Russian police officers came when I was lecturing to an international audience of a hundred at the South Carolina Law Enforcement Division. I was discussing the O. J. Simpson case and explaining what might have caused the three loud, distinctive booms outside Kato Kaelin's wall. To simulate the sounds, I bumped my head against the lectern. I didn't see the nail jutting out of it, but I certainly felt it. The second my head made contact with the lectern, a blinding bolt of pain seared through a spot just above my eyebrows. When I straightened back up, blood was blossoming over my forehead. There was a moment of stunned silence and then a burst of applause. I stared out at my audience, dumbstruck. Then I realized they thought it was part of the performance. I was mortified. Luckily, one of the women who had organized the conference rushed in and called a short break. After it, I returned to complete my talk, bandaged and chagrined. It gave a whole new twist to the term *blood spatter lecture*—one I definitely would not want to repeat.

Bienvenido a Bogotá

Although it has long been infamous for its high homicide rate, Bogotá is one of my favorite destinations. I first toured the city as part of an American Academy of Forensic Sciences delegation in 2005.

To help us understand the magnitude of the crime problem they were dealing with, local officials gave us a tour of the city's morgue, where, they told us, an average of fifteen murder victims arrive daily. Technicians work literally twenty-four hours a day, seven days a week. Many corpses come in without identification or next of kin, and finding out the names of the dead lining the corridors is a challenge in itself. When we toured it, the place was brimming with bodies. Corpses in need of autopsies and processing overflowed coolers, freezers, and table space and were tucked into miscellaneous corners simply because there was nowhere else to put them. Medical examiners hurried to and fro in their gowns, concentrating intently and avoiding small talk that would waste precious minutes. The sheer volume they were dealing with triggered memories of the slaughterhouses I had visited in my years of farming.

A few months after my first visit, I was invited to return to Bogotá under the auspices of the International Criminal Investigative Training Assistance Program, which works with the State Department, the Department of Defense, and other U.S. agencies in partnership with foreign countries to help them develop more effective law enforcement. My job was to run an in-depth, multiday training session on blood spatter forensics and crime scene reconstruction.

The Colombian capital exudes enough sheer scariness to give you an adrenaline high, and ours started moments after our arrival. Penny and I landed at El Dorado International Airport at ten P.M., a few minutes later than scheduled. The plan was to meet my longtime friend and colleague Dayle Hinman, an FBI-trained criminal profiler and former homicide investigator whose name you might recognize from *Body of Evidence: From the Case Files of Dayle Hinman* on CourtTV (now truTV).

Dayle was co-chairing the training session, and she had arranged to have a driver on hand to pick us all up. Her flight landed first, and when she inquired about us, even though my wife and I were literally sitting in the plane on the tarmac, airport staff checked the manifest and told her, "There is no Mr. or Mrs. Englert on the plane."

"Are you sure?" Dayle asked, puzzled. "They were supposed to be on that flight."

"Yes, ma'am," they assured her. "They are not aboard."

A few minutes later, Penny and I deplaned and began slogging our way through customs, lugging the enormous trunks of equipment I use to set up hypothetical crime scenes for my students to solve.

Unbeknownst to us, Dayle was beginning to panic. She tried repeatedly to reach me by cell, but got no answer because my phone provider's service range apparently didn't include Bogotá's airport. She had gate agents and other airport officials search for our names repeatedly in their computer system, only to be told that the last flight of the night had landed without us. She scoured the airport, calling Penny's name in the ladies' rooms and combing the baggage carousel for the oversized trunks she had helped me carry many times when we'd taught together in the past. Finally, fearing that we'd had a car accident or some other emergency before even leaving the U.S., she and the driver reluctantly gave up their search. Not knowing what else to do, they pulled away from the airport around eleven P.M.

Just about that time, Penny and I emerged into the arrivals area. Finding no sign of Dayle and discovering that my cell phone wouldn't work, we wandered around the desolate airport and then eventually ventured out the front door to see if Dayle was waiting at the curb.

An unofficial-looking cabdriver approached us. "You want a ride?" he asked.

"No, *gracias*," I said confidently. "We've got one."

He shot me a skeptical glance, then wandered off in search of another fare.

"Let's just wait here," I told Penny, pushing our massive pile of luggage up against a pillar. "I'm sure she'll turn up soon."

The minutes ticked by, and the airport grew quieter. A few slow-moving stragglers trickled out to their cars and cabs, then silence descended as the clock edged its way toward midnight. Maybe my edginess stemmed from all the dire warnings I had been given about Colombia, but a palpable sense of menace seemed to be enveloping the empty building. I knew Bogotá was a city where foreigners are not supposed to walk around by themselves in the daytime. Now here my wife and I were, stranded in the dead of night.

"Maybe I should try to reach her on a pay phone," I began. Penny's eyes widened in horror at the prospect of being left alone on the curb. I glanced ruefully at the heap of heavy trunks and suitcases. It would be ridiculous to lug them all the way to a pay phone and back again. Why hadn't I brought slides instead?

As if we weren't uneasy enough, a female cabdriver spotted us, jumped out of her car, and hurried over. She shook her head vehemently and held up her hands.

"Señor, this is very bad for you to be out here," she said in English.

"We're waiting for somebody," I told her. "We don't need a taxi. . . ."

"You should get back inside the building right now," she warned. "It's not safe here."

Penny and I decided to heed her warning and were starting to drag the trunks back through the doors when a man strolled past and did a double take. "Whoa," he said in an American accent. "You're in dangerous territory. What are you doing?"

"I'm supposed to have a ride, but I can't reach the people I'm meeting," I told him.

"Well, I can't leave you here," he said. "I'm with the American embassy, doing some construction work. I'll give you a lift to your hotel."

"I don't know where my hotel is," I admitted sheepishly. "My colleague has that information."

"Any guesses?"

"Well, it might be the same place we stayed last year."

"Why don't you call and find out?" he said, handing me his cell phone. I did and, to my relief, the desk attendant told me we were registered there.

Our helpful new friend got his pickup, helped me load my equipment, and, though it was a forty-five-minute drive, dropped us off at the hotel I recognized from my previous training session. It was one A.M. when we heaved the trunks through the front doors, bedraggled and drained from the tension and the long trip.

"I'm sorry, but you're not registered here," said the clerk at the desk.

"*What?!*"

The clerk shook his head. "There's no record for you."

By this point, I was desperate. Should we go back to the airport and catch the next flight home? I glanced at Penny, surrounded by mounds of luggage.

"Have you got any vacancies?" I asked.

He checked his computer. "We have one room available."

"We'll take it."

It turned out to be a luxury suite that had been readied for a no-show VIP. Baskets of fruit, flowers, and other luxury amenities covered every table. Ignoring them, Penny collapsed and I got on the room phone and started making calls. At last I reached Dayle, who was still wide awake and trying to locate us. I could hear the worry in her voice. She and our official room reservation were all the way across town.

Some detective. I couldn't even track down my own hotel. After coordinating with Dayle to meet the next morning and transfer our luggage, I gave in to my exhaustion, resolving never to travel internationally again without writing down my reservation information and getting a cell phone guaranteed to work abroad.

We soon realized why people were so stunned to find two lost-looking Americans milling around the airport after dark. Just how seriously Colombians took security became apparent once the conference began and we were all given bodyguards. We spent the rest of the week being escorted everywhere we went in a bulletproof Suburban with two-inch-thick glass in the windows and a professional driver from the American embassy. Our driver never stopped for a red light if he could help it. If a motorcycle he deemed suspicious pulled up behind us, he simply veered over the median and sped off in the opposite direction. Every day when we arrived at the police academy, a thirty-minute drive from our hotel, officers on duty used mirrors to scan the underside of our vehicle, despite the fact that we were invited guests. Armed guards were posted at our hotel at all times.

My students were a sharp and dedicated collection of about twenty-one local pathologists, psychiatrists, intelligence agents, police investigators, and dentists with expertise in bite-mark identification, all handpicked by the Colombian government. In addition to lecturing while students wore earphones for simultaneous translation, I made use of the trunks I had brought by setting up a series of elaborate re-creations of crime scenes with mannequins, stage blood, and other props, all inspired by real homicide cases I had worked. One mannequin was propped up in a bathroom with its head literally shot off using a shotgun. Another setup simulated a hanging, with only the faintest traces of blood as clues.

It took Penny, Dayle, and me long, painstaking hours to set it all up, and whenever we made the smallest mistake, we had to clean up the damaged scene and start all over. We finally finished staging the vignettes at four A.M. Class started at eight A.M. When the students arrived, I divided them into teams, then invited them to rotate from scene to scene, with forty-five minutes allotted to examine each "crime." At the end, the teams gave opinions about the crimes and compared notes, and I explained how the cases had actually unfolded.

We also conducted a number of blood spatter experiments, and as always, I learned something new through teaching. One afternoon, a cluster of my students came hurrying over excitedly. The translator explained that they wanted to show me the work they had done. They dragged me to a gutter and pointed down at a trail of blood they had dropped into the sand-strewn cement channel.

"Which direction does the trail lead?" they asked.

I grimaced. My experience with sand was severely limited. I leaned over to examine it. The blood had soaked into the porous surface, and directionality was almost imperceptible. They watched me expectantly. If I made the wrong deduction, my credibility would be shot.

I crouched down for a closer look. The droplets were round, but I thought I discerned minuscule specks that had broken out of them on one side, creating what's called a "leading edge." I took a deep breath. "This way," I said, and pointed in the direction of the subtle tails.

They erupted into applause.

"Phew. That was a close one," I mumbled.

"What?" asked the translator.

"Never mind," I told him.

On the day before we left, Dayle and Penny decided to squeeze in a bit of shopping. That gave us yet another window into the harrowing aspects of daily life in Bogotá. They were assigned a bodyguard and chauffeured in an armored car to the area's most upscale mall. Before they got out, the driver and bodyguard had them remove all their jewelry, and the driver stashed it in his trunk. Then the bodyguard briefed them on proper mall behavior: "Never separate. Never walk by yourself. Always stay next to each other," he cautioned, slinging an AK-47 over his shoulder in addition to his sidearm. "I will be ten feet behind you at all times." It was more like heading into an undercover narcotics operation than into a department store.

My work in Colombia made me proud of the system we have in America. It's not perfect here, but it's very, very good. I also developed tremendous respect for the men and women who fight crime in Bogotá. Their work is demanding and unending in the face of such high homicide rates. Yet they are passionate about and proud of what they do, and they remain optimistic in spite of the odds. By the time our farewell reception rolled around, we had developed some lasting friendships.

"Weren't you afraid to be here?" asked a female forensic pathologist who had joined with another doctor to serve as my bodyguard team for a portion of the week.

"No. I felt protected by you," I told her.

"Well, we were afraid *for* you," she said.

"Aren't you afraid for yourself?"

"Yes," was the answer, "but what can I do? This is my life."

Not Far from Home

Although I thoroughly enjoy the journeys my work entails, some of the most compelling crimes happen in my own backyard of the Pacific Northwest. One memorable example came early in my consulting career. Let's call it the Case of the Vanished Mariner.

At a glance, Ruth and Rolf Neslund looked like any other retired couple living out their golden years on picturesque Lopez Island, one of the San Juan Islands in the northwestern corner of Washington State. Norwegian-born Rolf had enjoyed a long and largely illustrious career captaining ships for the Puget Sound Pilots Association and was a popular local figure. So when the gregarious octogenarian failed to turn up in any of his usual haunts in the late summer and fall of 1980, his friends at the pilots association got worried and called the San Juan County Sheriff's Department. Deputies paid a visit to his wife, sixty-year-old Ruth Neslund, to see if she could enlighten them on his whereabouts. Ruth said she had no idea where her wayward husband had gone. "Probably ran off with *her*," she said, a bitter edge in her voice. When police asked Ruth to clarify, she explained that Rolf had never broken things off with his mistress of many years earlier.

Police checked out the possibility but soon dismissed it. Rolf's "affair" had long since cooled into a platonic friendship, it seemed. In fact, the woman who had given birth to two sons with Rolf before Ruth had entered the picture and gone from mistress to wife herself was newly married at the time of Rolf's disappearance. When police brought Ruth up-to-date on all this, she shrugged. Well then, she suggested, maybe Rolf left because he was still despondent over a notorious 1978 accident in which he had crashed the *Chavez*—the forty-ton, 550-foot freighter he was piloting—into the east end of the West Seattle Bridge over the Duwamish West Waterway. Fortunately no one was hurt, and Neslund retired two weeks later. But in the process, the old sea captain single-handedly forced the city of Seattle to replace the bridge, a notorious bottleneck, with a new larger, higher $60 million six-lane West Seattle Bridge and freeway that would take seven years to complete. Everyone knew Rolf's name because of the incident. Some had even quipped that the new bridge should be named in his honor. Maybe he just needed to get away for a while.

But the more police delved, the less likely any of Ruth's theories seemed. Rolf was diabetic, yet he had failed to refill his prescriptions for months. On one of their visits with Ruth, detectives noticed Rolf's medicine was still sitting in his home on Lopez Island. Nor had he withdrawn any money from the bank since the previous summer. Even more peculiar, Rolf's glasses were still sitting on the dresser.

Everyone knew the couple was prone to drinking binges that sometimes escalated into violent fistfights. The police had been called to the Neslund residence to sort things out more than once. They noticed it was generally Rolf—not Ruth—who bore the scratches and cuts. Had she finally snapped during one of her benders and done her spouse in, as she had threatened to do so many times after tossing back a few too many?

Circumstances grew even more suspicious when police learned that shortly before his disappearance, Rolf had realized Ruth was secretly transferring money out of his accounts into her own and hiding information about their finances from him. One friend came forward to say that the retired ship's pilot had discussed changing his will and writing his wife out in favor of his two grown sons. People who were close to the tightfisted Ruth knew how she would feel about that: She would sooner see Rolf dead than let him give his boys a penny. She had said so herself.

That was just the beginning. Though Ruth's relatives seemed downright terrified of the pudgy, nondescript middle-aged woman, two of her nieces met privately with investigators to say that Ruth had called them and confessed to shooting Rolf in the head with one of the many guns she kept in the house. She had even told Donna Smith and Joy Stroup that she was burning her husband's body in a barrel in the yard. But she was drunk when she said it, so neither woman took her seriously at the time. Could she have been telling the truth?

In the spring of 1981, police got a search warrant and combed the Neslund home but turned up nothing incriminating. It would take another year and another member of Ruth's own family disclosing even more lurid details about precisely where in the house and how the murder had occurred before a second police search uncovered the blood that had lain hidden in plain sight all along. Ruth's brother Paul Myers claimed he had overheard Ruth describing the killing in sickening detail. Ruth explained how another of her brothers, Robert Myers, had held Rolf still so that she could shoot him in the head. Then Robert dismembered Rolf in the bathtub so his body would be easier for her to burn.

Based on Paul Myers's information about where to look, deputies inspected the living room once more. This time, they noticed that several new sections of carpet appeared to have been pieced together with older ones. When they pulled these back, they found large, dark stains that looked like blood on the concrete. They used a jackhammer to remove them for testing and submission into evidence. There was also what looked like high-velocity impact spatter on the ceiling. They even discerned tiny brownish dots on the edges of the shower doors in the master bathroom—the bathroom where Paul Myers claimed his brother had chopped up Rolf's body for Ruth with an ax and a knife. A .38-caliber Smith & Wesson revolver with what appeared to be a few flecks of blood still clinging to it was also retrieved from one of Ruth's dresser drawers. Though sophisticated DNA testing that could link blood to a specific individual would not appear for more than a decade, the samples were tested and determined to be human blood of type A, the same as both Rolf's and Ruth's.

Ruth stuck to her story. Any blood, she said, came from her own nosebleeds or the injuries Rolf had inflicted over the years. Since there was no body, it would be a challenging case to make, particularly with the department's scant resources. So the San Juan County Prosecutor's Office tapped the attorney general's brilliant team of Bob Keppel and Greg Canova, with whom I worked earlier on the Donna Howard "horse kick" case. As you will recall from the Howard case, Keppel and Canova had been appointed to a special unit designated to help local prosecutors with criminal cases when their offices were understaffed or their resources fell short.

Investigations continued, and in March 1983, Ruth Neslund was formally charged with first-degree murder in connection with her vanished husband. The case would be plagued by countless delays stemming from motions filed by Ruth's lawyers and from her own failing health. During jury selection, she had to be put in intensive care for high blood pressure and suffered delirium tremens from alcohol withdrawal before her release. Ruth's case eventually went to trial in November 1985. By then, her brother Robert was living in a nursing home and suffering from senility. He was never charged in connection with Rolf Neslund's murder.

Canova and Keppel asked me to consult on the evidence and give an analysis of what the bloodstains indicated. So I read all the documents from the investigation to date and visited the Neslund home. The droplets of human blood on the ceiling were indeed consistent with a gunshot wound, particularly with the larger, heavier drops that travel farther than the bloody mist in high-velocity impact spatter. And enough of them were visible to conclude that whoever had been shot had been seriously injured or killed. Even though Rolf's body was nowhere to be found, it looked as though he had left a good deal of his blood at home.

The trial lasted over a month and the jury deliberated for four days before finding Ruth Neslund guilty of the murder of her husband, Rolf. She was sentenced to twenty years to life in prison. She was released while her case was on appeal. But after she got behind the wheel of her van under the influence of alcohol and seriously injured two bicyclists, the judge ordered her to begin serving her sentence. She died in prison of a pulmonary blood clot in 1993 at age seventy-three, still protesting her innocence, still claiming her seafaring husband had sailed off into the sunset somewhere. Rolf Neslund's remains have never been found.

Trials and Errors

MR. ENGLERT," THE DEFENSE attorney began, taking a step forward and regarding me shrewdly, "isn't it true that you once got an F in a high school algebra class?"

"Yes, I did," I replied. "And I was lucky to get it."

A few chuckles emanated from the jury box.

The stern-faced, smartly dressed woman was taken aback but recovered in a flash. "Do you find this funny?" she demanded. "A man's life is at stake."

"No, ma'am," I said. "I don't find it funny."

"Yet clearly you enjoy getting a response from the jury. You like people."

"Yes, ma'am, I do like people. I even like you."

This time, full-fledged laughter erupted from several jurors.

The lawyer's eyes narrowed and her skin deepened to an apoplectic red. This was a high-profile multiple-murder case and she had a lot at stake. She wasn't going to be lampooned by an expert witness whom she fervently wanted the jury to dismiss as a "hired gun."

"Don't you think your struggle with simple high school algebra calls your credibility on mathematical and scientific matters into question?!"

"No, ma'am. It has no bearing on my analysis of the blood evidence in this case."

I wasn't trying to be glib in the courtroom that day. In fact, I admired the defense attorney for doing her homework. She and her colleagues must have gone to some trouble to dredge up my old transcripts from forty-odd years ago in San Angelo. But by the time she went in for the kill in this particular midwest trial, I had already endured so many character assassination attempts on the witness stand that my skin had thickened. If I hadn't learned to deflect the countless slings and arrows criminal lawyers hurl at me whenever I testify as an authority on blood patterns, I would have crawled off to nurse my wounds long ago.

During my years as a police officer, I took the witness stand many times to explain ordinary actions taken in the line of duty. But nothing could have prepared me for going into court to give expert testimony. As a law officer, even jurors who claim to hate cops automatically view you as an authority figure. They assume you know what you're talking about. They listen to you. As an expert witness, you start from scratch. You have to build credibility. The only way to earn the jury's respect is to prove that you know your subject matter.

That's not easy when opposing counsel is deliberately trying to humiliate and discredit you. The first time a lawyer hissed in my ear,

"I'm going to destroy you," it knocked me off balance. The first time one struck up a casual conversation in a corridor, then turned on me in court like a striking rattlesnake spewing venom, I was stunned. I once had a lawyer step resolutely into my path, staring me down and blocking my way to the courtroom until he was certain that I had seen his tie. It was covered with circling sharks.

The symbolism wasn't far off. There are courtroom attorneys out there every bit as ruthless and cutthroat as the criminals, especially when they know their case hinges on a jury's decision to trust or doubt what I say about blood evidence. But by now I've heard almost every threat they can conjure up. I've been told I'll never work in this business again, never eat lunch in this town again, never show my face in public again, more times than I can count. I'm used to it.

I know brilliant, ethical lawyers who ask for no more than an honest analysis of evidence to help them give their clients the best defense possible. But I have also met my share of scoundrels. If my analysis of the blood spatter in a crime scene doesn't work in their favor, they are not above pleading, "Can't you come up with anything better than that for me?"

One memorable experience began a few years ago on my birthday, of all days. The phone rang and, assuming it was a well-wisher, I answered. Instead it was a defense attorney whose name I recognized instantly. He specialized in high-flying power players as clients. I had met him during previous celebrity cases, though we had never been on the same side.

"Rod," he said, "I really need your input on this one. Will you write me a report?"

I was instantly on guard. "I would have to come down and look at the evidence first," I said.

"Great. We'll arrange it."

"Are you really planning to use me on this?" I asked.

"Absolutely."

"You're not just trying to make sure I'm off-limits for the other side, are you?"

"Rod," he said smoothly, a note of hurt indignation in his voice, "how could you even suggest that? My client and I would simply like you to analyze the evidence in his case and let us know what you think."

A few days later, a check signed by the well-known personality in question arrived. I called the lawyer to say that I had received it and to firm up plans for me to examine the evidence. I was surprised when I didn't hear back from him, so I called several more times and left additional messages. No response.

About a week went by before I received a call from the prosecutor in the same highly publicized case. "I think the blood evidence in this case is pretty strong," he said. "Would you be willing to take a look at it and give me an opinion?"

"I can't," I said. "I'm sorry. I've already been retained by the defense."

He seemed surprised, but he thanked me politely and hung up. It got me thinking about the case again, so I decided to do a little research online. A newspaper article popped up touting the fact that the celebrity and his attorney had recently met with their team of expert witnesses in preparation for the upcoming trial.

I should've known. The attorney did precisely what he'd vowed not to do. He knew he couldn't pay me off, so he "hired" me simply to take me out of the game. He had no intention of showing me the evidence. He didn't want my opinion on it in the first place. He just wanted to ensure that opposing counsel didn't hear my opinions. And his client was rich enough to shell out fees simply to keep me out of the picture. In a way, it was flattering.

Of course, neither side has the monopoly on questionable tactics.

I ran into one egregious example of unscrupulous behavior in a case that had nothing to do with murder. It occurred because a woman started hemorrhaging suddenly and called 911. She lost a lot of blood even before the ambulance arrived, and she nearly died en route to the emergency room, partly because she refused to let the EMTs take her to the nearest hospital. She was bent on going to a different one all the way across town. After her recovery, she sued the hospital and the emergency services company that transported her.

I was asked to consult on the case for the defense. The experience had obviously been harrowing for everyone involved, and the woman had been lucky to recover. Still, something about the photos of the blood-soaked mattress in her bedroom looked wrong.

"I can't make a definitive assessment from these images," I told my clients. "I need to examine the mattress itself."

They requested it, but the plaintiff's team was adamant. "Absolutely not," was the answer. "It's not available. And there will be no DNA testing, either."

That was odd. Why should the woman's lawyers oppose DNA testing?

My clients pressed and prodded and appealed to the judge to grant me access to the evidence. At last I was permitted to view the mattress in the woman's home, though opposing counsel showed up literally shouting, screaming, and trying physically to bar us from the premises. The minute I saw the mattress I understood why. There was too much blood. No one could bleed like that and live. Someone had poured an enormous amount of additional blood or another reddish liquid onto the already stained sheets to make the effect more dramatic for jurors in the courtroom.

To test my conclusion, I removed plugs—sample cross sections of the sheets, blankets, and mattress—and showed them to Dr. Grimsbo in

Portland, along with photographs of the bed. We conducted a number of experiments to find out how much liquid had gone into the mattress and bedding. We kept pouring and pouring, but we still weren't matching the levels indicated in the plugs. We concluded that the amount of liquid in the mattress where the woman's hemorrhaging began was well over the total amount of blood in the human body, which is about six quarts. In the end, my clients settled. No one ever determined how that amount of blood found its way into the mattress.

Far-Fetched Speculation

As shocked as I still am at what certain lawyers are capable of, I am equally astounded by some of the statements I have heard over the years from those sworn in as blood pattern interpretation specialists. It's no wonder lawyers, judges, jurors, journalists, and even average citizens tend to be suspicious when "experts" take the witness stand.

I once heard an expert say with a straight face that he could not state beyond a reasonable doubt that high-velocity impact blood spatter was from a gunshot wound. "It could occur if someone dipped a toothbrush in wet blood and ran their finger across the bristles," he explained. "That would create the same type of spray."

Sure. But murderers don't bother to dip toothbrushes in blood and decorate the walls. They're too busy killing their victims.

In the state of Washington many years ago, there was a crime scene where a shooting had projected blood spatter onto the ground. I was asked to consult on the case and gave a report to the DA's office stating that in my opinion, this was high-velocity blood spatter resulting from a gunshot wound. Another expert, who had been called in at the same time I was, told the DA's office that my theory could be right, but that the blood patterns in question could also have come from repeatedly dropping a bloody pencil.

"When the point hits the ground," he theorized, "it would create dots like the ones in these photos."

The entire notion flew in the face of logic. A murder had taken place in the room shown in the photographs. There was a dead body to prove it. The victim's injuries indicated that he had been shot to death. And there were no bloody pencils lying around the crime scene. Pencils don't come into play in murder scenes, unless a killer is jabbing somebody with one. In that instance, the jury agreed. The defendant was convicted.

Was the sole purpose of the pencil expert's statement to throw doubt on the prosecution's case? Did he sincerely believe a pencil was a plausible, possible cause of the blood spatter he was examining? Was he simply playing devil's advocate and pointing out every conceivable hypothetical scenario for the sake of argument? If so, is that an ethical approach in a murder trial? Examples can be used to distort facts as well as to illuminate them. Ultimately, jurors have to sift through what they hear and decide for themselves. More than one panel has voted to acquit a defendant even when the blood evidence proved he was guilty just because an expert testified that blood-spattered clothing could have gotten that way from pencils, toothbrushes, and other innocuous sources.

I have been on scenes where people shot themselves. I have also been on scenes where people got shot and were breathing when I walked in, then stopped after I arrived. And I have been on scenes where I have been personally involved in shootings, though fortunately I have never had to kill anyone. Yet in all my decades of seeing dead and dying people and studying the bloodshed that violent crime generates, I have never, ever seen random household items inadvertently replicate medium- or high-velocity blood spatter around a victim.

I have tremendous respect for the scientific, academic side of forensics, but veteran cops and analysts with years of field experience balk at purely theoretical propositions. Crime is rooted in the real world. It doesn't happen under lab conditions.

Experts who testify in court can be prone to another disturbing characteristic. As America learned from watching the O. J. Simpson spectacle, witnesses in celebrity trials can become famous names in their own right. More than one forensics pro has let the limelight eclipse the work. I caught sight of a remarkable example of this not long ago while my colleagues and I were doing some work on a crime scene. We were flabbergasted to find another analyst literally signing autographs inside the house where a young man had recently met with a violent death. When the family of the deceased asked to pose for a picture with the man, I thought they were joking. Then the cameras came out and I realized they weren't. In the world of crime, abnormal behavior is rampant—and not just among the criminals.

Case Study: A Teen Crush Turns Deadly

One of the stranger things I have done in court is to model a woman's pink bathrobe for a jury. Here is the story behind it.

Sixteen-year-old Sarah Johnson lived with her mom and dad in a well-kept house in the town of Bellevue in Blaine County, Idaho, which counts itself among the nation's wealthiest communities. On the morning of September 2, 2003, Sarah said she awoke around six-fifteen A.M. to the sound of running water and knew that one of her parents was up taking a shower. She was still lying in bed a few minutes later when gunshots suddenly echoed through the house. She raced across the hall to her parents' closed bedroom door and called to her mother. When she got no answer, she tore out of the house and started banging on neighbors' front doors, screaming that her parents had been murdered.

Local law enforcement officers hurried to the scene and found Sarah's mother, Diane Johnson, in bed under the covers, dead from a gunshot wound to the head. Sarah's father, Alan Johnson, lay facedown and naked on the floor nearby, dead from a gunshot to the chest.

Blaine County sheriff Walt Femling had the presence of mind to stop a garbage truck grinding along the Johnsons' street as it made its morning pickups. Then he secured the entire block as part of the crime scene. After getting a search warrant, deputies began to go over the area inch by inch for clues. One of them opened a garbage can near the curb at the Johnsons' house.

What lay inside would unlock the truth about events in the Johnson house that fall morning. But if the trash collectors had been a few minutes faster in their rounds, it would have been whisked away forever. On top of the trash sat a woman's pink terry-cloth bathrobe. Police picked it up, and out fell a left-handed leather glove and a right-handed latex glove.

It was Ian Spiro all over again. Speckling the robe were the familiar traces of high-velocity impact blood spatter. Lab tests also revealed bone fragments and human tissue, deeply embedded in the fibers of the garment. DNA tests showed the blood spatter belonged to both Diane and Alan Johnson. Traces of Sarah's DNA were also present on the robe and both gloves. When questioned, Sarah admitted that the robe belonged to her but said she had no idea how it had ended up in the trash. She vehemently denied having killed her parents. Instead, she accused a housekeeper who had recently been fired by the family for theft.

Police traced the murder weapon, a .264 Winchester Magnum rifle found lying near the bodies, to a man named Mel Speegle, who was renting a garage apartment on the Johnsons' property. But Speegle had an airtight alibi: He had been in another city when the shots were fired, and he had witnesses to confirm his whereabouts. They also followed up on Sarah's accusation of the maid, but she, too, had a legitimate alibi.

Then the sheriff's office found out about Bruno Santos. Santos was a nineteen-year-old illegal Mexican immigrant with a history of drug use and gang ties. He had briefly attended the local high school where Sarah was a student. He was also Sarah's secret fiancé, if the teenager's friends were to be believed.

Sarah's parents had made no secret of their aversion to her taste in sweethearts. In fact, relatives said that when Alan Johnson discovered his daughter had lied to him and spent the night at the Santos family's apartment in a Bellevue housing project three nights before the murders, he had threatened to file statutory rape charges.

Santos looked like the logical killer until DNA tests cleared him. That's when police began to look at suspects closer to home. Sarah had been every bit as enraged as Santos at her parents' efforts to thwart their romance. After dragging his daughter home from her boyfriend's place, Alan Johnson had grounded her, taken away her house keys, and relegated her to the garage apartment while Speegle was out of town. Had she found Speegle's rifle while brooding alone in the guesthouse and hatched a plan to murder the people threatening to separate her from her lover?

On October 31, 2003, Sarah Johnson was arrested and charged with her parents' murders. Because the case had already received such widespread publicity, her trial was moved to Boise. Blaine County prosecuting attorney Jim Thomas and Scott Birch, chief investigator for the Idaho State Attorney General's Office, asked me to examine the blood evidence and help them reconstruct the murders.

That was tricky. The pink robe had clearly been in the room when both shots were fired. But the spatter was in all the wrong spots. Sarah was right-handed, yet the majority of the blood droplets were on the back of the robe and the left sleeve. Did it mean she had assisted someone else in the killings? Local police and I went over various scenarios, but time after time we turned up nothing that made sense.

I pored over the photos and went to the crime scene to inspect the room where the homicides occurred, struggling to piece it all together. The pictures showed a trail of bloody water and footprints leading from the bathroom to the bedside, suggesting that Alan Johnson had been shot in the chest while he was in the shower and had then stumbled out toward his wife before collapsing. His body was naked and wet, and the showerhead was still running when the police arrived, splashing bloody water all over the walls in a scene straight out of Alfred Hitchcock's classic *Psycho*. Diane had been asleep, burrowed under the covers, when she was shot in the head by someone standing no more than three feet away from the bed.

Sarah kept changing her story about how she realized her mom and dad were dead. First she said her parents' door was open a crack when she stood in front of it. Then she said it wasn't. At one point, she said her own door was closed. Then she changed her mind. But airborne blood, bone, and tissue fragments from Diane's head had landed on the outside of Alan and Diane's bedroom door, the hall, and a wall inside Sarah's bedroom. That meant both doors must have been open during the murders, despite what Sarah claimed.

The "open sesame" that finally melted away the cave door and revealed the truth hidden behind it did not come from Jim, Scott, me, or any of the many other investigative specialists working obsessively on the Johnson case. It happened when Sarah's defense attorney, Bob Pangburn, made a guest appearance on Nancy Grace's nightly current affairs program on CNN. While all of us insiders were still grappling with how such atypical blood patterning had gotten onto the bathrobe and Pangburn was maintaining that it exonerated Sarah,

Grace started pondering possible explanations. In the midst of one spontaneous "what if," she mimed putting on an article of clothing backward.

Jim, Scott, and some of their colleagues were burning the midnight oil together in their office and, as luck would have it, took a break to watch Grace's show. It was the eureka! moment in the prosecution's case. Scott grabbed the phone and called me. "Rod, think out of the box," he said. "She wore it backward!" Suddenly it all clicked into place. And once again, the crucial insight came from an unexpected source.

Say you put your clothes on back to front. If you normally shoot right-handed, your right becomes your left and your left becomes your right. What if Sarah had slipped the robe on backward to protect her clothing before firing the rifle that killed both her parents?

Not surprisingly, the Johnson trial was lengthy and emotional. Bruno Santos's links to the drama brought him to the attention of immigration authorities, who first deported him and then brought him back to appear in court. The young man for whose love Sarah, by then eighteen, had apparently sacrificed so much took the stand and testified against her through a Spanish-language translator.

To help prepare his case, the ever-thorough Jim Thomas spoke with a number of experts on parricide. What makes a teenage girl with no prior criminal record and no history of mental illness, sexual abuse, or any other trauma in her life decide single-handedly—with no partner in crime, no accomplice egging her on—to murder both of her parents at point-blank range with a high-powered rifle? It doesn't happen often. In fact, he learned that Sarah Johnson's was the first documented case of its kind since Lizzie Borden's more than a century earlier. There were a few other parallels to the famous ax murders, too. Borden stuffed her dress in the stove and burned it after her parents died. Johnson stuffed her robe in the trash. But, of course, she wasn't quick enough to dispose of it effectively, and that made all the difference in the trial.

The most important task for me was to reconstruct the crime scene according to what I was now certain had happened. I described how events had unfolded step by step, slipping on the pink bathrobe over my own suit with the opening to the back. Then I grasped the rifle to show the jury exactly how the murder had unfolded based on the story told by the blood spatter.

After deliberating for three days, jurors found Sarah Johnson guilty of first-degree murder on March 16, 2005. She received two consecutive life sentences plus fifteen years with no possibility of parole. She appealed the verdict, but she lost.

What Money Won't Buy

Throughout the Johnson trial, reporters converged on anyone who would talk. But they were still no match for the media frenzy the O. J. Simpson case sparked. Before my particular expertise plunged me into the double-murder investigation, I knew there were upstanding journalists and underhanded ones just as there are good and bad members of all professions. But what I saw was still an eye-opener.

During the months I was traveling to Los Angeles and back regularly to consult on the blood evidence in the murders of Nicole Brown and Ron Goldman, Penny and I were having landscaping work done around our house. Glancing out the window one afternoon after she got home from work, Penny was puzzled to notice that some of the workers seemed to be spending an inordinate amount of time around our trash cans. When she spotted them there several days in a row, she stopped the manager of the crew and asked him what was going on. Did they need extra trash bags? A Dumpster, maybe?

He stared at her blankly. "I don't know what you're talking about, Mrs. Englert," he said. "My men haven't been anywhere near your garbage cans."

Penny and I were aghast to discover that the people sifting through the Hefty bags from under our kitchen sink were actually reporters. Somehow they had gotten wind of the fact that I was involved in "the trial of the century" and they were hoping to dig up some front-page dirt. I never knew what they were hoping to find. Crumpled faxes? Discarded notebooks? A pair of blood-covered shoes with "O.J." stenciled inside?

Penny and I didn't wait to find out. We moved our trash bins to a locked location inside our yard and resolved to tell any uninvited guests we found snooping through our garbage to clear off our property.

Around this same time, I went to Seattle to lecture at the American Academy of Forensic Sciences. I had finished my talk and was stuffing my notes back in my briefcase when a woman sidled up to me and whispered an astronomical sum of money in my ear.

"What?" I asked, assuming I had misunderstood her.

"That's what my boss will pay you if we can get our hands on those bloody clothes," she said with a conspiratorial grin.

"Who the hell are you?" I asked, looking for a name tag. All hers said was "Guest."

As my blood pressure rose, she proudly rattled off her credentials. She explained that she represented one of the country's best-known tabloid newspapers. Before joining it, she had made her bones writing for another gossip powerhouse. Now she was hot on the trail of the O.J. case.

"It's worth *a lot* of money to my editor if you can get your hands on that shirt," she said.

"You must be out of your mind to think I would do a thing like that," I hissed, working hard to maintain my composure. "How did you even get in here?"

"Think about it," she said confidently.

Without another word, I turned my back on her and stalked off to complain to the conference organizers about their attendee-screening procedures.

In the years since then, I have run across that same reporter a number of times. These days, we are cordial when we see each other. I know that's how she earns her living. And she knows I will never answer any questions she asks beyond where the restroom is located and what time the seminar ends.

Case Study: One Drop Is All It Takes

One murder that garnered little interest from national tabloid reporters but that sticks in my memory more than many higher-profile trials was the case of eighteen-year-old Mark Sells in Tipp City, Ohio. On January 5, 2003, Sells and two younger friends smoked a little pot and tossed back some vodka to steel their nerves, then headed for the home of sixty-five-year-old city activist Sharid Gantz.

Sells, who knew Gantz and had done yardwork for him, was armed with a baseball bat and keyed up for a robbery. He barged in while his fourteen- and seventeen-year-old pals waited outside to act as lookouts. Before long, the pair heard raised voices and peered through the window. Sells was in a sort of frenzy, bashing Gantz in the head over and over with the baseball bat, turning the room bright red, they would later testify. It took the shell-shocked youths only a few days to roll over on Sells and spill the details about what they had watched.

You could tell by the blood arcing over the wall that the batter had swung from right to left, and Sells was right-handed. But that was hardly enough to tie him to the murder. Even the testimony of two eyewitnesses might not be enough. Why? First, Sells had a charmingly sweet and childish face, which could predispose a jury to believe him innocent. Second, there was the issue of his clothing. It had been thoroughly examined and only one drop of the victim's blood had been found on the collar of Sells's red Windbreaker. Yet the murder scene was a horror show. Bits of skull, tissue, and brain matter had reached the ceiling. Prosecutor Gary Nasal knew that this would be no easy win. If he and his colleagues were struggling to believe a killer could walk away from a scene so bloody without his jacket and pants looking like a butcher's apron at the end of a long shift, how would he convince a jury?

Gary asked me to visit the crime scene with him to see the house and the creek that ran behind it, where the bloody bat was thrown and later retrieved. We also examined the evidence together and scrutinized the photographs. He was hoping I would be able to provide an analysis of what it all meant and to explain why more blood hadn't landed on Sells. By now, you know the answer: Because all the blood was projected forward, away from the attacker.

"Look at the victim's legs below his waist," I said, pointing to an image of the dead man's bare white legs protruding helplessly from his bathrobe. He had been kneeling on the floor when he died. There were no traces of blood on the lower part of his body. "And look at this." I pointed to dozens of pristine white sheets of typing paper strewn over the floor around the victim's feet. They had obviously scattered during the murder, yet there was no blood on them. Nor was there blood on the floor. I combed over every inch of the clothing the police had collected from Sells many times, but there were no additional flecks of blood.

Gary asked me to testify to help the jury understand what happens to blood in a blunt-trauma attack involving multiple blows, so I set up a three-section panel of cardboard about three feet high in front of the jury. Then I poured stage blood onto a sheet of paper and positioned myself to strike it with a rolled-up newspaper in lieu of a bat. Gary stood on the other side of the cardboard display, pale and tense. I hadn't given him a chance to watch the demonstration beforehand, and I knew he was expecting us both to be dripping in scarlet in a few seconds.

I smacked the "blood" and it spattered the cardboard dramatically but left Gary and me without a trace of red on our clothes. The jurors suddenly understood—and believed—that medium-velocity blood spatter really does travel forward because they saw it for themselves.

The two lookouts in the Sharid Gantz murder got plea agreements, thanks to their youth and their testimony. They admitted to guilt in juvenile charges including delinquency and complicity to aggravated burglary. Sells, however, was found guilty of aggravated murder and aggravated robbery. And a single droplet of blood made all the difference.

The Intimidation Factor

Unethical behavior isn't the norm, but if you spend enough time in the world of criminal trials, you're bound to run into it. So is unmerciful grilling on the witness stand. That makes many people who work in criminal justice dread giving testimony. Some of them don't want to be there any more than the accused does. A number have been subpoenaed or ordered by their boss to show up. Others get so paralyzed with stage fright that they come across as bumbling novices even though they are widely respected authorities in their fields. Some take lawyers' humiliating barbs and innuendos to heart and slink away devastated. I have seen seasoned professionals literally break down in tears on the stand. A few resent having to take time away from their "real" jobs to appear in court and, to show their resentment, don't bother to prepare, which does a disservice to the jury and the court proceedings.

From my point of view, enduring a vicious attack from opposing counsel is a small price to pay to help jurors understand a crucial piece of the puzzle—a piece that will allow them to reach a more informed and accurate verdict. Whenever I give testimony, I believe absolutely that what I am saying is the truth. I do my best to stay calm and focused even when the other side is trying to rattle me. I state my findings with confidence, in simple terms, and I never stretch the facts to reach a conclusion. Jurors are smart. If you stretch it, they know.

I also remember that I am there only to educate—never to advocate. I am not trying to get anyone convicted or exonerated. It is not my job to justify or excuse anyone's actions.

So why do I continue to testify as an expert witness in homicide cases despite skepticism from jurors, ego battering from lawyers, and countless hours of grueling prep work? Why put myself through it?

Because in the end, it is worth it. And because ultimately it is my responsibility. Victims can no longer speak for themselves, but they leave a pure and candid account of their final, tragic moments written in their blood. If the people who can read that blood do not tell their stories, who will?

Afterword: A Glimpse of the Future

BLOOD PATTERN ANALYSIS HAS come a long way since those early years when I was studying puddles of cows' blood on the floor of my barn and saving up vacation time to attend conferences. Gone are the days when lawyers asked judges to bar blood pattern analysts' interpretation on the grounds that our expertise had no proven basis in science or fact. Over the past twenty-five years—thanks to the tireless work ethic and selfless dedication of researchers, detectives, criminalists, students, and many other talented people—blood spatter forensics has become an essential and respected element of law enforcement and criminal justice. I feel privileged to have played a small part in that development.

But science changes fast. The landscape today is entirely different from the one we saw a decade ago. DNA advances have revolutionized the way we look at blood and the information we can extract from each precious drop of it. It can identify the guilty, exonerate the innocent, speak for victims, and crack cases that would have been hopelessly unsolvable in an earlier era.

And the frontier of forensics is expanding at a remarkably exciting rate. As you read this, robotic processors at the FBI's nuclear DNA lab are flying through hundreds of minuscule DNA samples, analyzing them thoroughly and effectively dozens of times faster than a human scientist could. At the same time, researchers are coaxing crucial new clues out of fingerprints, perfecting cutting-edge technology that can detect, isolate, and retrieve prints buried beneath other prints. They are also using miniaturized mass spectrometers to detect minute amounts of substances such as explosives, drugs, and biohazards like anthrax in the prints, which could provide the missing link that connects dangerous substances to those who spread them.

Computerized developments are under way that promise to refine bite-mark identification by amassing a data bank of dental characteristics like tooth width and spacing between teeth. Audio forensic systems are using GPS technology to help cops pinpoint when and where shots are fired almost as soon as the trigger is pulled. Laser facial reconstruction technology is allowing technicians to scan a skull and simultaneously render a three-dimensional image of its owner's face with extraordinary detail on screen, bringing new hope to the daunting task of identifying victims' remains.

Yet as fast as these breakthroughs appear, so do new challenges. As of the writing of this book, scientists in Israel had announced that they had discovered a way to fabricate DNA evidence in a lab, which could create huge problems for crime solvers. Experts were also grappling with the ramifications of a new generation of detergents on blood evidence collection. The cleaning products contain sodium carbonate peroxyhydrate, which produces oxygen bubbles that threaten to eliminate the telltale proteins in blood that have pointed a damning finger at killers in otherwise baffling crimes for years.

When it comes to the public's obsession with forensics, those of us in the field face a double-edged sword. Criminals study crime shows and court proceedings, then invent new and sophisticated ways to circumvent the latest methods of detection, as the tragic murder of Nanette Toder in Illinois demonstrated. On the other hand, jurors become ever better informed and more demanding. That raises the bar for all of us providing information in the courtroom to help them reach an accurate and just verdict. America's tremendous fascination with crime solving may also have been one of the catalysts behind an in-depth two-year review of forensic techniques in the United States by the National Academy of Sciences and an energetic new movement to push Congress to establish an independent governing body that would enforce standards, oversee education, and elevate quality in forensic practices nationwide.

What does all this mean to you? Crime costs the United States in excess of $450 billion a year, according to the most recent National Institute of Justice data available at press time. That's more than half of the 2009 economic stimulus package. If you converted the amount into one-dollar bills, it would fill forty-four miles of train cars with money. You could stack them to the moon and back 168 times. Are all the efforts to advance detection and forensic capabilities worthwhile? You bet. But most of us do not appreciate how worthwhile they are until a member of our own family or someone else we love becomes a victim of violent crime. And as the heartbreaking story of every victim recounted in these pages shows, violent crime does not discriminate. It can happen to any of us anytime.

What lies ahead? Is there hope for a safer future? Speculation is a dangerous business when it comes to criminal analysis, so I won't hazard a guess. But one thing is certain: As long as bad guys continue to shed blood, the field of blood spatter forensics will keep evolving and improving to help the good guys catch them.

Acknowledgments

There is an ancient African proverb that goes, *"Umtu ngumtu ngabantu."* It translates roughly to, "A person is a person because of other people." In other words, we derive our dignity and worth from one another. In my case, that is certainly true. Without the following people, this book would still be at the bottom of my bucket list.

First and foremost, I am grateful to my wife, Penny, who has devoted her time and energy to this project, patiently reading every page and sharing her thoughts, ideas, insights, and editing suggestions. Our children, Gary, Ron, Cherie, and Jeb, too, have given me valuable input, which helped me tremendously in shaping the book.

Sincere gratitude also goes to those without whose early encouragement and support *Blood Secrets* would never have grown from the kernel of an idea to the reality of a printed book. Many thanks go to Dayle Hinman, Vernon Geberth, Jim Cooney, and especially to Ann Rule, who not only walked me through contract information in the beginning, but shared her vast writing experience, explaining how true crime readers want to experience the "richness" of a book. Her support along the way was like filling my tank with superunleaded. I was always upbeat after conversations with her. Then came her foreword. Words cannot express how much I appreciated her written and verbal moral support throughout this project. I am glad she chose to collect her stories from the Multnomah County Sheriff's Office so many years ago.

I am deeply indebted to my literary agent, Frank Weimann, who suggested the idea for this book more than three years ago. His persistence, determination, and faith in my story paid off, and he is greatly appreciated. Frank's talented and dedicated staff—in particular, Jaimee Garbacik and Elyse Tanzillo of the Literary Group—were also instrumental in making a longtime dream of mine a reality. I am grateful to Peter Fields and Larry Logan as well, who shared their considerable expertise and walked me through the key points of book publishing contracts in the early phases of the project.

My special thanks go to Kathy Passero, who made magic out of stories I always considered somewhat boring, with little human interest value. Kathy's talent, enthusiasm, and dedication to the project gave me strength to push through the countless hours we poured into *Blood Secrets*. Her tireless research, her willingness to delve into sometimes complicated subject matter, and her ability to master the technical aspects of blood pattern analysis and crime scene reconstruction helped not only to make the stories in this book come alive, but to ensure that the fine points would be understandable to readers.

Kathy's husband, Greg, an editor, was super with small but powerful suggestions. So were Kathy's parents, Dick and Ginny Passero, who became the book's first official fans.

Editing plays an enormous part in any book because it ensures accuracy, attention to detail, pacing, and much more. Our editor, Peter Joseph, of Thomas Dunne Books is a master already at his young age. His encouragement and expertise guided us from rough manuscript to final pages seamlessly. We would recommend him to anyone.

A number of people who played key roles in the real-life cases and crimes discussed in these pages agreed to be interviewed by Kathy during the many months she spent researching my cases and my years as a police officer in both Downey and Multnomah County. They generously donated their time and tapped their memories to ensure accuracy and to add vivid detail. Kathy's and my deepest gratitude go to Aminah Ali, Jim Alsup, Gary Anderson, Dave Bishop, Greg Boer, Victor Calzeretta, Tim Carroll, Becky Doherty, Mickey Englert, Ralph Englert, Stan Faith, Chuck Fessler, Tom Hallman, Keith Henderson, Buck Henry, Bill Hodgman, Cheryl Kanzler, Bob Keppel, Gary Nasal, Jim Newsom, Brian Robertson, Shellie Samuels, Valerie Summers, Jim Thomas, Stan Turel, and Nelson Word.

Ken Rohrbaugh and Sharon Marcus, of the Jennie Wade House in Gettysburg, were very accommodating and graciously allowed my colleagues and me entry into Jennie's historic home on more than one occasion so that we could conduct our research. Cindy L. Small, author of the book *The Jennie Wade Story*, generously shared her time and considerable expertise on the case. Dr. Ted Yeshion of ClueFinders Inc. along with Amy Dier and Olivia Leon, both of Blue Line Investigators, pooled their considerable expertise and energy into a formidable on-site team for our 2009 forensic investigations at the Jennie Wade House. Dr. Ray Grimsbo, too, lent his time and talents to the project, and these proved invaluable in our research.

My gratitude also goes to gifted photographer Mike Gaffney, whose portrait work is featured on this book jacket, and to my good friend Joanna Johns, who wisely recommended Mike to me.

This list would be incomplete without a nod of gratitude to my former homicide partners, Joe Woods and Chris Peterson, who were there with me on a number of the cases highlighted in *Blood Secrets* and who taught me a great deal.

I would also be remiss if I failed to mention the dedicated cold case team I work with in Multnomah County—Bob Boertien, Karl Hutchison, John Ingram, Jim McNelly, Lane Sawyer, Quinton Smith, Piete VanDyke, and Kathy Allen, who keeps us all organized. These individuals donate countless hours of what would otherwise be their own free time to re-examining old cases that have remained unsolved, sometimes for decades. I am perpetually awed by your dedication and determination to uncover the truth, to find those who have evaded justice too long, and to at last bring closure to family members who have lost loved ones.

Many other family friends contributed their editing talents and eagle eyes for catching typos and inconsistencies. Among them are Larry and Lilly Logan, Stacey Stuart, Sammie Thomas, and Keith and Amy Henderson. Finally, I want to extend a heartfelt thanks to my stalwart longtime friends Scott Birch, Bruce Bischof, Steve Ells, Denise Ferreira, Clayton Handy, Melissa Handy, Tom Lange, Melinda Lewis, Alison Mann, Jim Shade, Wendy Stefani, Debbie Welser, Stacy Welser, and Judy Witthuhn.

I am sincerely grateful and truly blessed to have all of you in my life.

Bibliography

Chapter 1

Anthony, Paul A. "2 Former Chiefs Show Problems with Both Systems." *San Angelo Standard Times* online, November 3, 2007. http://www.gosanangelo .com/.

Harden, Kevin. "Retired Detectives Hope Public's Help Thaws 'Cold' Cases." *Portland Tribune,* March 3, 2009. http://www.thebeenews.com/.

Chapter 2

Los Angeles Dodgers official Web site. "Dodger Stadium History." http://www .dodgers.com/.

Los Angeles Police Academy, official Web site. http://www.joinlapd.com/ academy.html/.

Mcgreevy, Patrick. "New LAPD Digs, Old Name?" *Los Angeles Times,* March 19, 2006.

North County Times, Escondido, CA, November 14–30, 2005. http://www .nctimes.com.

"Oceanside CA.—Death Penalty for Killing Police Officer, Then Stealing His Patrol Car." December 1, 2005. http://www.tremcopoliceproducts.com/articlesdet.htm/.

U.S. senator Dianne Feinstein, official Web site. "Senator Feinstein Urges Border Patrol Investigation and Reforms in Wake of Police Officer's Fatal Shooting by Deported Criminal Alien." July 25, 2003. http://www.feinstein.senate.gov/03Releases/r-camacho.htm/.

Whatcom County Sheriff's Office Law Enforcement Code of Ethics. http://www.co.whatcom.wa.us/sheriff/ethics.jsp/.

Chapter 3

Glaister, Dan. "U.S. Police Replace Codes with Plain English; 10-4?" *The Guardian,* November 14, 2006. http://www.guardian.co.uk/.

Hallman, Tom Jr. "Detectives Still Seeking Clues to 1984 Murder." *The Oregonian,* June 16, 1985, page 1.

Turel, Stan. *A Plague of Justice.* Newport, Ore.: Dancing Moon Press, 2008.

Chapter 4

Charlotte, North Carolina, *News & Observer.* Numerous articles by staff writer Joseph Neff and other reporters about the Alan Gell case. December 10, 2002–November 28, 2007. http://www.newsobserver.com/.

DiBiase, Thomas A. (Tad). "No body" murder trials in the United States. http://www.nobodymurdercases.com/.

Donovan, S. E., M. J. R. Hall, B. D. Turner, and C. B. Moncrieff. "Larval Growth Rates of the Blowfly, *Calliphora vicina,* over a Range of Temperatures." *Medical and Veterinary Entomology* 20, no. 1(March 2006): 106–114. Published online, January 9, 2006, by the Royal Entomological Society. Abstract: http://www3.interscience.wiley.com/journal/118628204/abstract/.

Englert, Rod, and Ray Grimsbo. "Trace Evidence and Crime Scenes—Pulverized Green Threads, Brain and High-Velocity Bloodspatter Unravel the Mystery of a Crime: A Homicide Case Study with No Body." Abstract from meeting of the Northwest Association of Forensic Scientists, spring 1998. http://www.nwafs.org/.

Indiana Department of Correction offender data. http://www.in.gov/indcorrection/ and http://www.in.gov/idoc/.

Lacour, Greg. "Police Have New Hope of Solving 1990 Killing." *Charlotte Observer,* August 20, 2008. http://www.charlotteobserver.com/.

Lewis, Cynthia. "Either/Or." Article about the murder of Kim Thomas. *Charlotte* magazine online, June 1, 2008. http://www.charlottemagazine .com/.

Memorandum. United States Court of Appeals, Ninth Circuit. 17F.3d.394 *Howard v. Blodgett.* No. 92-36993. http://openjurist.org/17/f3d/394/ howard-v-blodgett/.

Michigan Domestic Violence Prevention and Treatment Board report. *Michigan Domestic and Sexual Violence Homicides, October 1999–September 2000.* http://www.mi.gov.

"Monument to Jennie Wade." *New York Times,* September 13, 1901. http:// query.nytimes.com/gst/abstract/html.

North Carolina Department of Correction offender public information. http://www.doc.state.nc.us/offenders/.

"Police Charge Husband in Murder after Finding Note." *Michigan Daily* online, September 20, 2000. www.http://michigandaily.com/.

Rule, Ann. *Without Pity.* New York: Pocket Books, 2003.

Turner, Wallace. "Victim's Relatives Opposing Parole." *New York Times,* April 26, 1987.

Unsolved Crimes Network. History and analysis of Kim Thomas murder. http://unsolved.netfirms.com/kim_Thomas.htm/.

Chapter 5

Akron Police Department reports of investigation for Winda Snipes. September 12 and October 9, 1997.

Association for Crime Scene Reconstruction, official Web site. http://www .acsr.org/.

Bevel, Tom, and Ross M. Gardner. *Bloodstain Pattern Analysis: With an Introduction to Crime Scene Reconstruction.* Boca Raton, Fla.: CRC Press, 2001.

Bloodstain Pattern Analysis Tutorial. J. Slemko Forensic Consulting. http:// www.bloodspatter.com/BPATutorial.htm/.

Boston Channel online. Coverage of Dirk Greineder trial. May 24, 2001– June 20, 2001, and January 2006. http://thebostonchannel.com/.

Cleveland Plain Dealer news archive. Series of articles about the Winda Snipes murder. September 17, 1997–May 23, 1998. http://nl.newsbank. com/ and http://Cleveland.com/.

Courtney, Max. "Blood Spatter Evidence and Reconstruction of Events." Forensic Consultant Services. Fort Worth, Texas. http://www.forensic-lab .com/publications/bloodspatter.html/.

"Criminal Lawyer Ohio Represents Hartmann in the Custody of the Mansfield Correctional Institution of Ohio." August 29, 2005. Criminal Defense Lawyer, official Web site. http://www.criminaldefenselawyer.com/regional-content.cfm/.

Daily Iowegian. Articles about Tyler Opperman death and investigation. January 2009. http://www.dailyiowegian.com/.

Daniel, Mac. "Specialist Details Blood on Jacket." *Boston Globe,* June 16, 2001. http://nl.newsbank.com/.

"Dusting Off a Cold Case." *Forensic Examiner,* December 22, 2005. American College of Forensic Examiners newsletter. http://www.acfei.org/.

Holocaust Research Project. Information about Josef Mengele. http://www.HolocaustResearchProject.org/.

"How Prevalent Is Gun Violence in America?" June 16, 2008. National Institute of Justice, U.S. Department of Justice, official Web site. http://www.ojp.usdoj.gov/nij/topics/crime/gun-violence/.

Web site devoted to proving Brett Hartmann is innocent. http://www.enddeathpenaltyforbretthartmann.com/.

Web site devoted to proving certain inmates in Ohio prisons are innocent. http://www.innocentinmates.org/hartmann/phone.html/.

The Supreme Court of Ohio and Ohio Judicial Center official Web site. http://www.sconet.state.oh.us/.

Official Web site of TruTV library of past articles featured on the site. http://www.crimelibrary.com/.

Web site focused on allegedly haunted places in historic Gettysburg. http://hauntedfieldsofglory.com/gallery/gettysburg/jenniewade/history.html/.

International Association of Bloodstain Pattern Analysts, official Web site. Suggested IABPA Terminology List. http://www.iabpa.org/.

Jastrzemski, Joe. "Execution Date Set for Summit County Man." AkronNewsnow.com, December 3, 2008. http://akronnewsnow.com/.

Jenny Wade House, official Web site. http://www.jennie-wade-house.com/.

Josef Mengele biography. http://thebiographychannel.co.uk/biography_story/.

Murphy, Dennis. "Did a Distinguished Doctor Murder His Wife of 31 Years at a Wellesley Park?" MSNBC.com, July 30, 2006. http://www.msnbc.msn.com/.

National Center for Health Statistics, Centers for Disease Control and Prevention, official Web site. Data on self-inflicted injury/suicide. http://www.cdc.gov/nchs/fastats/suicide.htm/.

Ohio Court Opinions. *State v. Hartman* (2001), 93 Ohio St.3d 274. FindLaw. http://caselaw.lp.findlaw.com/.

"Ohio Supreme Court Sets Execution Dates for Two Condemned Killers." *Herald Dispatch,* April 8, 2009. http://www.herald-dispatch.com/news/briefs/.

Ponce, Ana Castelló, and Fernando A. Verdú Pascual. "Critical Revision of Presumptive Tests for Bloodstains." *Forensic Science Communications* 1, no. 2 (July 1999). http://www.fbi.gov/hq/lab/fsc/backissu/july1999/ponce.htm/.

Renner, James. "Deadline." *Cleveland Scene* magazine online, March 25, 2009. http://www.clevescene.com/.

Small, Cindy L. *The Jennie Wade Story*. Gettysburg, Pa.: Thomas Publications, 1991.

State of Ohio, Adult Parole Authority minutes of special meeting in re: Brett Xavier Hartman, OSP #A357-869. Columbus, Ohio, March 6, 2009. http://www.drc.state.oh.us.

State v. Hartman, case no. 00-1475. Summit County Court of Common Pleas.

Trexler, Phil. "Prepared to Say Goodbye, Tearful Hartmann Gets Stay of Execution." *Beacon Journal* online at Ohio.com, April 1, 2009. http://www.ohio.com/.

TruTV (formerly CourtTV) News. Coverage of Dirk Greineder trial. May 23, 2001–January 15, 2002. http://www.trutv.com/.

Weinberg, Samantha. *Pointing from the Grave*. New York: Miramax Books, 2003.

Chapter 6

"Blake Found Not Guilty." MSNBC.com, March 16, 2005. http://www.msnbc.com/.

Bosco, Joseph. "In the Face of Death." *Time* magazine online, June 2, 1997. http://www.time.com/time/magazine/.

Cartwright, Emily. "A Question of Guilt II: She Catches a Star." August 5, 2002. CBSnews.com. http://www.cbsnews.com/.

Coverage of Bob Crane death. http://www.findadeath.com/.

Coverage of the Mikhail Markhasev trial and verdict. *New York Times,* July 8–16, 1998. http://topics.nytimes.com/topics/reference/timestopics/people/m/mikhail-markhasev/index.html.

Coverage of the murder of Alexis Ficks Welsh and the trial of Kevin McKiever. *New York Times,* June 10, 1991–March 15, 1995, and February 20, 2008. http://www.nytimes.com.

Coverage of the murder of Bob Crane and the subsequent investigation. Casa Grande, Arizona, *Dispatch,* July 6, 1978–November 23, 1994.

Coverage of the O. J. Simpson trial. CNN online. http://www.cnn.com/.

"Excerpts of Marcia Clark's Closing Arguments." *New York Times* online, September 27, 1995. http://www.nytimes.com/books/97/06/15/reviews/clark-excerpts.html/.

Jones, Thomas L. "Analysis of the O. J. Simpson Murder Trial" and additional TruTV coverage of Simpson trial. TruTV online. http://www.trutv.com/library/crime/notorious-murders/famous/simpson/index-1.html.

King, Gary C. Series of articles published on TruTV online covering the murder of Bonny Lee Bakley and the trial of Robert Blake. http://www.trutv.com/library/crime/notorious-murders/family/bakley/1.html.

Lange, Tom, and Vannatter, Philip. 1997. *Evidence Dismissed*. New York: Pocket Books.

"List of the Evidence in the O. J. Simpson Double-Murder Trial." October 18, 1996. *USA Today* online. http://www.usatoday.com/.

Silverman, Stephen M. "Blake Loses Lawyer over Diane Sawyer." *People* magazine online, October 29, 2002. http://www.people.com/.

Stonebraker, M. "Dance of Death." *New York* magazine, August 19, 1991.

Sweetingham, Lisa. "Actor Robert Blake Acquitted of His Wife's Murder." CNN online, March 29, 2005. http://www.cnn.com/.

"The Trial of O. J. Simpson: The Incriminating Evidence." University of Missouri–Kansas City School of Law. http://www.law.umkc.edu/.

Chapter 7

Brass, Kevin. "Murder in Rancho Santa Fe: The Ian Spiro Case." *San Diego* magazine online, October 1995. http://www.sandiego-online.com/.

Coverage of Ian Spiro case. *Los Angeles Times* archives, September 5, 1985–October 18, 1995.

Coverage of Nan Toder murder, investigation, and Nan's Law. *Pittsburgh Post-Gazette* online, December 18, 1999–October 4, 2007. http://www.post-gazette.com/.

Golden, G. Jeff. "San Juan County Case Not Affected by Death Penalty Repeal." Farmington, New Mexico, *Daily Times* online, March 22, 2009. http://www.daily-times.com/.

Malefactor's Register. "Nan's Law." March 31, 2006. http://www.markgribben.com/.

New Mexico Coalition to Repeal the Death Penalty, official Web site. "2009 Repeal in the News." February 16, 2009. http://nmrepeal.org/.

"New Mexico Governor Repeals Death Penalty in State." CNN online, March 18, 2009. http://www.cnn.com/.

Radford serial killer database. Robert Fry information researched and summarized by Nicole Martz, Jamie Klempa, and Rachael Langley, Department of Psychology, Radford University. http://dead=silence.org.

Rybarczyk, Tom. "Handyman Pleads Guilty to '96 Slaying." *Chicago Tribune*, January 31, 2006.

Scott, Robert. *Monster Slayer.* New York: Pinnacle Books, 2005.

Streeter, Michael. "Bizarre Case of the CIA Man, the Hostage, and a Desert Suicide." (London) *Independent,* May 13, 1997.

Sullivan, Terry. "A Safe Room." *Chicago Reporter,* November 2003.

Supreme Court of the State of New Mexico. Opinion no. 2006-NMSC-001, docket no. 27,592. Re: Appeal for Robert Fry.

Terrell, Steve. "Legislature 2009: Political Shift Could Spell End to Death Penalty." *Santa Fe New Mexican* online, November 29–30, 2008. http://www.santafenewmexican.com/.

Chapter 8

Abdullaev, Nabi. "Russia Remains a Dangerous Place." Jamestown Foundation online, February 28, 2002. http://www.Jamestown.org/.

The Charley Project: Rolf Neslund. http://www.charleyproject.org/.

City of Bethel, Alaska, official Web site. http://www.cityofbethel.org/.

Dooley, John. "The Dead Zone." *Portland Mercury* online, March 21, 2002. http://www.portlandmercury.com/news/the-dead-zone/Content?oid=26559.

Enge, Marilee. "Defense Tries to Bar Blood Stain Expert's Testimony." *Anchorage Daily News,* March 29, 1990.

Galeotti, Dr. Mark. "New Guns for Russia's Cops—So What?" October 23, 2008. In Moscow's Shadow: Analysis and Assessment of Russian Crime and Security, blog written by a clinical associate professor at New York University Center for Global Affairs. http://www.inmoscowsshadows.wordpress.com/.

Hunter, Don. "Murder Follows Andrew; Judge Revokes Man's Probation." *Anchorage Daily News,* February 18, 1991.

———. "State Seeks to Revoke Man's Probation Despite Acquittal." *Anchorage Daily News,* January 19, 1991.

Information on Togiak, Alaska. U.S. Census Bureau online. http://factfinder.census.gov/.

Justicia y paz: New Colombia Human Rights 1, no. 1 (fall 1996). Online journal created by the Colombia Support Network, Madison, Wisconsin. http://www.colombiasupport.net/1911/jypfall96.html.

"The List: Murder Capitals of the World." *Foreign Policy* online, September 2008. http://www.foreignpolicy.com/.

"Moscow Diary: Welcome to 'Wild East.' " BBC News Channel online, October 26, 2007. http://news.bbc.co.uk/.

"Murder Capitals of the World: Report." *International Business Times* online, October 1, 2008. http://in.ibtimes.com/.

Rule, Ann. *No Regrets and Other True Crime Cases.* New York: Pocket Books, 2006.

"Russia: Law and Order Under the Soviet System." World Association of International Studies, Stanford University. Online report, February 16, 2005. http://cgi.stanford.edu/.

"Ruth Neslund Murders Her Husband, Rolf Neslund, on Lopez Island on August 8, 1980." Washington State Department of Archeology and Historic Preservation online. http:/www.historylink.org/.

Tizon, Tomas Alex. "America's Taxi Capital: Bethel, Alaska." *Los Angeles Times* online, November 30, 2007. http://www.latimes.com/news/nation world/nation/la-na-taxicabs30nov30,1,3238044.story?coll=la-default -underdog.

Chapter 9

Coverage of Mark Sells case. *Dayton Daily News,* 2003.

"Police in Tipp City Arrest a Suspect in the Sharid Gantz Homicide." WHIOTV.com, January 24, 2003. http://www.whiotv.com/news/3669209/ detail.html.

Smith, Terry. "Supreme Court Schedules Johnson Appeal Hearing." *Idaho Mountain Express,* March 7, 2008. http://www.mtexpress.com/index2. php?ID=2005119704.

Stahl, Greg. "Attorneys Spar Before Johnson Sentencing; Public Defender Seeks to Remove Prosecutor from Case." *Idaho Mountain Express,* June 17, 2005. http://www.mtexpress.com/index2.php?ID=2005103611&var _Year=2005&var_Month=06&var_Day=17.

State v. Sells (Ohio 2006). Ohio Supreme Court, Second District Court of Appeals (April 14, 2006). Docket no. 2005-CA-8-2006-Ohio-1859. http:// vlex.com/vid/state-v-sells-21692734/.

TruTV online coverage of the Sarah Johnson trial, including statements from Blaine County Sheriff's Department. http://www.trutv.com/.

Afterword

"The Future of Forensic DNA Testing." National Institute of Justice, U.S. Department of Justice, 2000. http://www.ncjrs.gov.

Harding, Ben. "New Detergent Washes Away Stains of Murder: Study." November 5, 2008. Reuters, http://www.reuters.com/article/ScienceNews/ idUSTRE4A498620081105.

IABPA News, December 2005. International Association of Bloodstain Pattern Analysts.

Moore, Solomon. "Study Calls for Oversight of Forensics in Crime Labs."
New York Times, February 19, 2009.

National Center for Victims of Crime Library. http://www.ncvc.org/ncvc/.
Statistics on cost of crime.

National Victims' Rights Week Resource Guide 2007. Statistics on cost of
crime. http://www.ojp.usdoj.gov/ovc/ncvrw/2007/welcome.html/.

Richmond, Todd. "Bite Mark Database to Tackle Crime." Discovery Channel
online, May 14, 2008. http://dsc.discovery.com/.

Salleh, Anna. "No Such Thing as a 'Voice Print.' " ABC Science Online, through
Discovery Channel online, December 4, 2008. http://dsc.discovery.com/.

Schmid, Randolph E. "New Fingerprint Tech ID's Particles." Discovery
Channel online, August 7, 2008. http://dsc.discovery.com/.

Temple-Raston, Dina. Three-part series on breakthroughs in forensic technology: "FBI's New Technology Revolutionizes DNA Analysis"; "FBI Unrav-
els the Stories Skulls Tell"; "Voice 'Fingerprints' Change Crime-Solving."
NPR (National Public Radio), January 28, 2008. http://www.npr.org/
templates/story/.

Additional Source

Courthouse Steps Mavens message boards. http://s2.excoboard.com/exco/
index.php?boardid=15776/.

Index